The Time to Manage?

department and faculty heads at work

Peter Earley
and
Felicity Fletcher-Campbell

NFER-NELSON

Published by The NFER-NELSON Publishing Company Ltd.,
Darville House, 2 Oxford Road East,
Windsor, Berkshire SL4 1DF, England.

First Published 1989
© 1989, National Foundation for Educational Research

British Library Cataloguing in Publication Data
Earley, Peter
The Time to Manage?: department and faculty heads at work.
1. England. Secondary Schools. Administration. Role of head teachers & senior teachers
I. Title II. Fletcher-Campbell, Felicity
373.12'012'0942

Printed by Billing & Sons Ltd, Worcester

ISBN 0 7005 1233 0
      0 7005 1234 9 Pbk
Code 8329 024
      8328 024 Pbk

Contents

List of Tables and Figures

Abbreviations

Acknowledgements

NFER Information

1   Why a Study of Department and Faculty Heads?   1
    What is school management?   2
    Why a study of department heads?   3
    The changing role of department heads   5
    Research techniques   8
    Overview of the book   15

2   What do Heads of Department and Faculty do?   19
    Department and faculty heads at work   19
    Weekly diaries of department and faculty heads   27
    The role of the head of department   32
    Job descriptions   34
    Perceptions of the role   37
    Summary and discussion   43

3   What Constitutes Effective Practice?   45
    The expectations of LEA advisers   47
    The expectations of senior staff   48
    Team leadership   50
    Personality   50
    Management style   51
    Accessibility and proximity   54
    Communication   56

Consultation   56
Support of new teachers   57
Administration   59
Ethos   60
Summary and discussion   61

4   *What Difficulties are Faced?*   65
     Difficulties and constraints   65
     Perceptions of advisers and senior staff   78
     Critical incidents   79
     Summary and discussion   85

5   *What Support and Training do Heads of Department Receive?*   88
     Preparation for department headship   88
     School-based INSET for heads of department   90
     Externally provided INSET   92
     Course content and the identification of needs   94
     LEA support for heads of department and faculty   96
     In-school support   98
     Summary and discussion   102

6   *How do Middle Managers Promote Staff Development?*   105
     The staff-development role   106
     Delegation   107
     Creating opportunities for development   112
     Decision-making and meetings   114
     Responsibility for inexperienced staff   116
     Appraising performance   117
     Summary and discussion   126

7   *How is the Curriculum Developed and Change Managed?*   129
     Role perceptions   131
     Change as a process   134
     Initiation   134
     Implementation   146
     Three case studies   149
     Summary and discussion   154

8   *How is the Curriculum Evaluated and the Department Reviewed?*   157
     The department head's role in evaluation   158
     Reviewing and evaluating practice   161
     Summary and discussion   181

9   *How are Decisions made in Departments and Schools?*   184
     Leadership styles   185

Attitudes to decision-making   187
The promotion of participative decision-making   190
   within departments
Collegiality and team-building   191
Department heads and school decision-making   197
Summary and discussion   203

10   *How might Departments and Faculties be Improved?*   206
The academic/pastoral divide   206
Departments or faculties?   207
Alternatives to departments   213
Towards better practice   214
Summary and discussion   231

Appendix   Advisory Committee Members   233

References   235

Index   244

List of Tables and Figures

Tables

1.1   Phase one LEAs and schools
1.2   Phase two LEAs, schools and details of individual nominees
3.1   Effective departments and department heads

Figures

1.1   Project outline
2.1   The role of the head of department
2.2   A job description for a head of department
8.1   Curriculum review, with particular reference to curriculum-led INSET needs
9.1   Types of decision-making
10.1 Recommendations for improving departments (and faculties)

Abbreviations

ACAS	Advisory, Conciliation and Arbitration Service
ASE	Association of Science Education
CDT	Craft, Design and Technology
CPVE	Certificate of Pre-vocational Education
DES	Department of Education and Science
DH	Deputy Head
FE	Further Education
GCSE	General Certificate of Secondary Education
GRIDS	Guidelines for Review and Internal Development in Schools
GRIST	Grant-related In-service Training
HE	Higher Education
H.Ec	Home Economics
HMI	Her Majesty's Inspectorate
HoD	Head of Department
HoF	Head of Faculty
HoY	Head of Year
ILEA	Inner London Education Authority
INSET	In-service Education and Training
LAPP	Lower-attaining Pupils Programme
LEA	Local Education Authority

MPG	Main Professional Grade
MSC	Manpower Services Commission
NALGO	National and Local Government Officers' Association
NATE	National Association for the Teaching of English
NDC	National Development Centre for School Management Training
NFER	National Foundation for Educational Research
OCEA	Oxford Certificate of Educational Achievement
OU	Open University
PE	Physical Education
PGCE	Postgraduate Certificate in Education
PSE	Personal and Social Education
RE	Religious Education
SEC	Secondary Examinations Council
SMT	Senior Management Team
ST	Senior Teacher
TiC	Teacher-in-Charge
TRIST	TVEI-related In-service Training
TVEI	Technical and Vocational Education Initiative

Acknowledgements

We should like to thank the many people who kindly gave up some of their valuable time to contribute to the project. First and foremost our thanks go to the heads and all of the staff of the 21 case-study schools and to the advisers whom we interviewed in the ten local education authorities involved in the research – without their cooperation and assistance the project simply would not have been possible. In particular, we wish to record our gratitude to the nominated heads of faculty and department who were kind enough to allow us to observe them at work.

Throughout the duration of the research, considerable support and assistance was received from the project's advisory committee and the project director, Dick Weindling. Other colleagues from the National Foundation for Educational Research contributed their time and expertise and we should especially mention Lawrie Baker and Penelope Weston for reading the manuscript and making helpful suggestions; and Janet May-Bowles and her colleagues for providing excellent library support. Finally, a special word of thanks goes to Hazel Menezes for her exceptional secretarial support and administration of the project.

The National Foundation for Educational Research

The National Foundation for Educational Research in England and Wales was founded in 1946 and is Britain's leading educational research institution. It is an independent body undertaking research and development projects on issues of current interest in all sectors of the public educational system. Its membership includes all the local education authorities in England and Wales, the main teachers'associations, and a large number of other major organizations with educational interests.

Its approach is scientific, apolitical and non-partisan. By means of research projects and extensive field surveys it has provided objective evidence on important educational issues for the use of teachers, administrators, parents and the research community. The expert and experienced staff that has been built up over the years enables the Foundation to make use of a wide range of modern research techniques, and, in addition to its own work, it undertakes a large number of specially sponsored projects at the request of government departments and other agencies.

The major part of the research programme relates to the maintained educational sector – primary, secondary and further education. A further significant element has to do specifically with local education authorities and training institutions. The current programme includes work on the education of pupils with special needs, monitoring of pupil performance, staff development, national evaluation and major curriculum programmes, test development, and information technology in schools. The Foundation is also the national agency for a number of international research and information exchange networks.

The NFER–NELSON Publishing Company are the main publishers of the Foundation's research reports. These reports are now available in the NFER Research Library, a collection which provides the educational community with up-to-date research into a wide variety of subject areas. In addition, the Foundation and NFER-NELSON work closely together to provide a wide range of open and closed educational tests and a test advisory service. NFER-NELSON also publish Educational Research, the termly journal of the Foundation.

1 Why a Study of Department and Faculty Heads?

In recent years there has been an enormous growth of interest in the activity of school management and a growing recognition that educational institutions need to be managed. This state of affairs has been brought about by, among other things, increased pressures on the educational world to be more accountable to its public; a period of contraction (both in terms of pupil numbers and resources); expectations of better 'value for money' and increased effectiveness; and an increasing professional concern for institutional development and self-evaluation.

The growth of interest in management processes has, not surprisingly, been reflected in the plethora of educational publications dealing with the area. It might therefore be legitimate to ask, at the outset, if there is a need for another study of educational management – to which the answer must be in the affirmative. There are two main factors which make this book significantly different from the majority of others currently available. First, its focus is on secondary school middle managers – more precisely department and faculty heads – rather than on heads, deputies and other senior staff; and secondly, it is research-based. The National Foundation for Educational Research (NFER) study, as will be shown, is derived from a body of empirical evidence and not, as is the case with some other commentaries on school management, on individual reflections, exhortations or personal experiences. Also, unlike the few empirically based studies that do exist, it attempts not simply to describe practice and document events, but rather to focus on examples of effective department and faculty practice as identified by others.

This introductory chapter will attempt, briefly, to define the activity of school management and give reasons for the decision to undertake a study of department and faculty heads. It will also offer a brief history of the role of the head of department, describe the research techniques employed in the NFER study and give an outline and overview of the chapters that follow.

What is school management?

All teachers are managers in the sense that they are responsible for the management of pupils and of the learning process. Only some, however, have responsibility for the work of other teachers. A school manager might be defined as any individual who has responsibility for the work of other adults and the supervision of an aspect of the school. Management, whether it be in the educational world or elsewhere, is essentially about getting things done by working with and through other people. It is concerned with the achievement of goals through the collaborative efforts of groups of people. As such, it is 'a highly practical activity concerned with creating effective organizational means to ensure that educational values, goals and intentions are put into practice' (Glatter *et al.*, 1988).

The management task usually involves a combination of planning, organizing, resourcing, leading, controlling and evaluating. For Bell and Maher (1986), management is made up of three distinct but related activities: 'getting things done, or administration; doing new things, or innovation; reacting to crisis, or salvation'. The effective management of any organization, they add, 'comes only through establishing the right balance between those three activities'. Similarly, Latcham and Cuthbert (1979) make reference to three kinds of managerial activity: 'keeping things going'; 'coping with breakdown'; and 'doing new things'. However, they identify a fourth – 'bringing things together' – which refers to the manager's responsibility to coordinate the above activities to ensure there is a right balance between them. 'This kind of co-ordination', they suggest, 'is the quintessence of the manager's role – it can never be delegated.'

Everard and Morris (1985) are also concerned with effective management and they point to three things that any organization will expect of its managers:

1. that they will integrate its resources in the effective pursuit of its goals;
2. that they will be the agents of effective change;

3.   that they will maintain and develop its resources.

The magnitude and significance of school management has been recently noted by the National Development Centre for School Management Training (NDC). This body, which was set up in September 1983 under Circular 3/83 of the Department of Education and Science (DES), has stressed that the importance of school management has never been more apparent. Schools have had to deal with change on an unprecedented scale in recent years and, because of recent legislation, this is likely to continue to be the norm. Furthermore, it was noted that 'at least 130,000 staff have responsibility for school management i.e. for achieving the school's goals by working through and with other professional teachers, which are separate and different from their classroom management roles' (McMahon and Bolam, 1987). Approximately one-third of teachers have formal managerial responsibilities and a very large proportion of these teachers will, of course, be department and faculty heads.

Why a study of department heads?

The significance of leadership qualities and management skills within the education service has become increasingly apparent and has been well documented in recent reports by Her Majesty's Inspectorate (HMI), other official publications and in the findings of educational research. The importance of effective leadership in education has been officially recognized and given continued impetus by the inclusion of management training as a national priority area for In-service Education and Training (INSET) since 1983. However, although attention has been mainly focused on the senior management level and on the formulation of school philosophies, policies, aims and objectives, it is at the departmental level that these are actually implemented. The head of department plays a crucial role in the effective operation of the work of secondary school departments, requiring not only subject knowledge and teaching expertise but also the ability to manage and lead a team.

Her Majesty's Inspectorate in Wales (1984) went as far as to suggest that schools 'rely more for their success on the dynamism and leadership qualities of the head of department than on any other factor' and it was remarked that the role of the department head 'lies at the very heart of the educational process'. Similar sentiments were expressed by a significant proportion of secondary heads involved in a previous NFER project, who remarked that middle managers played a crucial role in encouraging or obstructing curricular and other desired changes (Weindling and Earley, 1987).

Despite the recognition of the key role that heads of department play within schools, there has been little research into how departments are managed or how innovations are successfully introduced. Similarly, little is known about the qualities of successful department heads, the major constraints on the effective performance of their roles and the training they require if they are to become better leaders. There seemed little doubt that an empirical study of the head of department's role was needed.

The NFER project, *Middle Management in Schools: Heads of Department*, which commenced in 1986 and lasted two-and-a-half years, had four broad aims. First, to describe how medium-to-large departments were managed, paying particular attention to the five broad categories identified by HMI in Wales (1984) as being the most common areas of responsibility, namely:

1. routine administration and organization of the department;
2. the planning of pupils' learning experiences;
3. monitoring and evaluating the work of the department;
4. professional development within the department;
5. liaison with other departments, with the pastoral staff, the senior management, and with outside agencies.

Particular attention was to be given to identifying the skills, knowledge and strategies needed to carry out these responsibilities.

The project's second aim was to explore the ways in which the role of the head of department was perceived by advisers, heads, department heads and teachers. Of particular interest was the changing nature of the job, the demands, constraints and pressures currently found and those expected in the future.

Thirdly, the project aimed to focus on the department head's role in two key areas: (a) curriculum management and innovation within the department and (b) policy decision-making within the school as a whole. What part do heads of department play in the formulation of, for example, school aims and objectives? How are teachers in the department involved? How are schemes of work determined and resources made available to meet curriculum ends? How are department heads coming to terms with new forms of assessment, new syllabuses, and demands put on them as curriculum designers, implementers and appraisers, especially with respect to cross-curricular or interdepartmental developments?

Finally, the project hoped to identify those areas where heads of department and others feel there is a need for training and to determine how such needs can be most effectively met.

At the outset it was decided to study 'academic' rather than pastoral middle managers, although there were many obvious areas of overlap between the two and the project's emphasis was on generic management skills. In the original proposal, faculties were not mentioned but it soon became apparent that the research would have to address these and other organizational issues. Although departments 'may be said to exist only where deliberate collaboration takes place' (Ribbins, 1985), the broader questions as to what is meant by 'a department' or 'a subject' were not considered. There have been a number of analyses of subject identities and specialisms, and the argument has been put forward that the conventional curricular division into subject areas is mainly for sociological and historical reasons (see for example Goodson, 1985; Ribbins, 1985). Although the importance of studies in these areas is acknowledged, the NFER research did not attempt to consider in detail definitional issues or the complexities of subject cultures and teacher identities. Rather, it was concerned to look at actual department and faculty units and to examine how they were perceived, by respondents, as operating effectively. The present research thus took as its starting point faculties and departments as they existed in schools in the late 1980s – the limitations of such units and possible alternatives are briefly considered in the final chapter.

The changing role of department heads

The department head has always been a key figure in the life of a school but it must be acknowledged that the nature of the job has changed from earlier times; indeed, as will be discussed later, the role will continue to change. The fact that the first major book on the head of department appeared in the early 1970s (Marland, 1971) is not insignificant, for it was about this time that the role became problematic as many of the assumptions surrounding it began to be questioned. The role of head of subject had largely evolved in the grammar schools and, following the reorganization of secondary schools along comprehensive lines, had to be modified. In the grammar schools, under the tripartite system, the head of department had been accustomed to a relatively homogeneous group of pupils, clear subject definition and an academic orientation. Lacey (1970), in his study of a grammar school, found that departmental meetings were rare. There was little need for them: curriculum and pedagogy were traditional, relatively static and largely unquestioned, and motivation and discipline mainly regarded as external to departments rather than embedded in the curriculum. The head of department was perceived as the senior subject specialist – an acknowledged 'expert' – and it was accepted that, as such, could chiefly engage in sixth form teaching (and sixth forms then were very different, of course, from those of the 1980s – see Dean *et al.*, 1979). The Burnham Report (1954) had made responsibility allowances for heads of department mandatory in schools doing 'O' and 'A' level work and optional in other secondary schools.

When local education authorities (LEAs), in response to directives from central government, began to provide comprehensive secondary education, middle management in schools entered a new era. Those appointed to department headship were suddenly faced with pupils of a much wider ability range and a greater social mix than had previously been encountered in many schools under the tripartite system. Furthermore, both the content and the delivery (pedagogy) of the curriculum had to be extensive enough in order to be appropriate and adequate for all aptitudes, abilities and ages. As well as dealing with increased numbers of pupils, heads of department also found themselves responsible for many more staff, some of whom were not subject specialists, or were only part-time in the department. As a result, record-keeping and administration had to be efficient and communication and other managerial tasks became of considerable importance.

Heads of department in the late 1980s have at least a body of good practice and experience upon which to draw and have, increasingly, spent their own teaching career entirely in comprehensive schools: those in the early 1970s were often entering uncharted waters and they were not helped by the fact that they received little guidance at local or national level as to their responsibilities. Occasional paper A2/11 published by HMI (quoted by Siddle, 1978) noted 'the wide variations in the extent to which department heads are exercising their responsibilities' and commented on the wide differences as regards non-contact time. The new five-point Burnham salary scale introduced in 1971 made no reference to specific department head allowances or responsibilities and an individual's scale largely depended on teacher and subject shortages. Following the recommendations of the Houghton Report in 1974, the five points were reduced to four, scales 3 and 2 being collapsed so that there were some department heads on scale 2.

The situation has in fact changed again as a result of the Teachers' Pay and Conditions Act, which came into effect in October 1987. This legislation abolished the Burnham scale points system and introduced a salary scale of five incentive allowances. Classroom teachers (those on the old scale 1 and many scale 2s) were now referred to as Main Professional Grade (MPG) teachers and incentive allowances were made available to some staff with additional responsibilities. Scale 3, scale 4 and senior teachers were usually allocated responsibility allowances B, C, D or E while, more controversially, only some scale 2 staff were given incentive allowance A. (The number of allowances made available to a school depended on its unit total which was calculated according to the age of pupils and the number on roll.) The research reported here, as it was conducted largely before the introduction of incentive allowances, makes reference to teachers under the previous Burnham system (i.e. scale 1, scale 2 etc.).

The new incentive allowances are payable if at least one of the following criteria is met: responsibilities are undertaken beyond those common to the majority of teachers; outstanding ability as a classroom teacher has been demonstrated; subjects are taught in which there is a shortage of teachers; or the teacher is employed in a post which was difficult to fill. *The School Teachers' Pay and Conditions Document, 1987* (GB.DES, 1987a) states that no incentive allowance shall be payable to a deputy head or to a headteacher and it outlines, in some detail, the professional duties of heads, deputy heads and school teachers. In the light of our earlier comments, it is interesting to note that the professional duties delineated for school teachers (i.e. MPG to allowance E), which they may be required to perform, include coordinating or managing the work of other teachers. The DES document also outlines teachers' conditions of employment and working time. All full-time staff are now required to be available for work for 195 days per annum (five of these days – 'contract days' – are to be for other activities, e.g. INSET) and to perform their duties for 1265 hours in any year. (It is noted, however, that a teacher is required to work such additional hours as may be needed for professional duties – e.g. marking pupils' work, writing reports and preparing lessons – to be discharged effectively.)

As the situation has developed over the years it has become increasingly important for heads of department to have *managerial* rather than merely organizational or administrative skills. This has continued to be the case as the concepts of curriculum and staff development have evolved in the 1970s and 1980s. The technological revolution and the rapid rate of social change that has taken place over the last two decades, in conjunction with unprecedented political pressures at national and local levels, have had implications for the role of the department head. Departments and their heads increasingly need to be sufficiently flexible to accommodate new content, new courses, new pedagogic methods, new forms of assessment and, not least, new types of relationships between teacher and taught. Team-leadership qualities and skills in the management of change thus become key criteria for the effectiveness of departments. Department heads have a central role to play in facilitating and managing educational changes, whether the origins of these be within the school, the LEA or, increasingly, central government. The research project's findings reported here will, it is hoped, contribute to a better understanding of the role and give insights into what makes departments function effectively.

Research techniques

An analysis of the existing literature on the role of the head of department showed that, although wide-ranging and growing, much of it was severely limited in terms of scale and methodology – something also noted by Ribbins (1986). Marland's (1971) classic text was based solely on personal experience while the edited volume by Marland and Hill (1981) was similarly limited and the various contributions were fragmentary. More recently, Edwards (1985) provided excellent documentation of good practice but did not have a research base. A large number of small-scale empirical studies existed in the form of higher degree dissertations but these were both largely inaccessible and of varying quality. Also found were some subject association publications which contained useful material for practitioners – some of it of high quality – but whose generalizability was seldom exploited. (For a review of the middle management literature – both 'academic' and pastoral – see Fletcher-Campbell, 1988.) Also, as Ribbins (1985) stated, 'such accounts too often tend to confuse what ought to happen with what does', and he remarked that 'far too little systematic, empirical or theoretical research has taken place', while there was a virtual absence of ethnographic studies. The NFER research, while wanting to be qualitative in orientation, rejected the ethnographic approach as it was thought that the resulting work, though making interesting reading, would be too limited and thus unable to make helpful generalizations or pursue policy applications. It was decided that the focus of the NFER project would be on effective practice and thus a purely observational methodology – as, for example, employed for the Open University's study of headteachers (Hall et al., 1986) – was seen as too restricting, although it does have the advantage that the situational context is very clear, social meanings become apparent and theoretical statements emerge from the data collected.

It was thought more appropriate to utilize, primarily, a case study approach. The nature of the topic under investigation, allied with the fact that department heads are a very heterogeneous group, suggested that few benefits would be gained by employing conventional quantitative research techniques. It was never the project's intention, for example, to draw up a statistical picture of the 'average' head of department in terms of such variables as age, gender, educational qualifications or levels of support received. Neither was it intended to comment either on what might be termed common perceptions of the head of department's role or on typical, or average, departmental practices. It was decided that a detailed study of a range of schools and departments would best meet the project's aims.

Previous research has used the approach whereby nominated effective practitioners are studied. For example, in the United States, Blumberg and Greenfield (1980) focused on five male and three female elementary and secondary school principals. The researchers asked 'numerous teachers, principals and faculty colleagues to nominate principals whom they knew were leading their schools and making a difference'. The core of the study was a series of informal, open-ended interviews with each of the eight participants. For the second phase of fieldwork, the NFER project adopted an approach similar to that of Blumberg and Greenfield.

During the initial months of the NFER project, a review of the literature was undertaken and preliminary semi-structured interviews were conducted with headteachers, advisers, HMI and people involved with running INSET management courses for heads of department. From these activities, the main issues and problems facing middle managers began to emerge and formed the foundations of the initial interview schedules for phase one of the research.

The first fieldwork phase explored in broad terms a range of issues and problems associated with middle management in secondary schools. Five LEAs were selected and included a London borough, a metropolitan district and three shire counties. In each of these five LEAs, interviews were held with chief and/or senior secondary advisers who were asked for their perceptions of what constituted effective departmental practices, what the training needs of department heads were and what the current LEA provision for middle management was. Two medium-to-large comprehensive schools in each LEA were then selected to be visited by the researchers. It was intended that one of the schools should be selected on the recommendation of the advisers while the other should be chosen randomly. The advisers were asked to nominate schools in their authority that they thought were well managed and

Table 1.1: *Phase-one LEAs and schools*

	School	Location	Age range	No. of pupils	No. of teachers	Split site	Organizational structure	Contact ratio for HoDs/HoFs
LEA 1	A	medium-sized town	11–18	1100	64	no	departments and faculties	0.78
(Shire county)	B	medium-sized town	11–18	1500	90	no	6 faculties	0.73
LEA 2	C	inner city	11–18	1100	72	no	5 faculties	0.68
(London borough)	D	London suburb	11–18	1300	105	yes	departments and curriculum co-ordinaters	0.74
LEA 3	E	small town	11–18	1000	66	no	3 faculties	0.72
(Shire county)	F	small town	11–18	1700	115	yes	5 faculties	0.72
LEA 4	G	suburbia	11–18	1050	68	no	departments and faculties	0.80
(Metropolitan district)	H	suburbia	11–18	1500	90	no	6 faculties	0.62
LEA 5	I	small town (rural)	11–16	1100	60	yes	8 faculties	0.75
(Shire county)	J	medium-sized city	11–18	1150	63	no	7 faculties	0.78

included some effective department and faculty heads. However, after a couple of schools selected randomly had been visited, it was decided to take up two of the advisers' recommendations in each authority as it was thought that more would be learnt and the researchers' time more usefully deployed in those schools. The ten schools having been identified, headteachers were contacted and in all cases were pleased to be involved in the research. Although it was not plar.ned for the researchers to feed back information to the schools concerned, two headteachers specifically requested this and, after all the interviewees involved in the two schools had been so informed, this duly took place.

Two schools were visited by the two researchers together; the other eight were divided between them. About ten research days (generally consecutively) were spent in each of the ten schools and, in total, interviews were conducted with 10 heads, 21 deputies, 27 heads of faculty, 94 heads of department and 78 members of departmental teams. All interviews were, of course, voluntary and held during 'non-contact' time but, despite the fact that the fieldwork took place during a period of industrial action, only a handful of staff were unwilling to participate. Three semi-structured interview schedules had been constructed – for senior staff, heads of department and faculty, and other teachers – and covered a range of issues, including changes introduced in the department, staff development, decision-making, difficulties and constraints, and training needs. On average, about an hour and a half was spent with the headteacher, one hour with deputies and middle managers, and 30 to 45 minutes with other teachers. Extensive field notes were taken during interviews and these were then ordered (where necessary) and put onto tape – usually on the evening of the day they took place, while they were fresh in the researcher's memory – and later typed up.

Phase two of the research took a different orientation and, as earlier noted, focused specifically on effective practice. A second set of five LEAs was selected according to criteria similar to those of phase one (a range of types of authority) but accessibility was an added consideration as the researchers wanted to be able to visit the schools for occasional days – even, indeed, for the odd hour if there happened to be a particularly interesting meeting, for example. The research team did not want to be constrained by having to fit everything into one calendar week as was necessary when considerable travel and overnight accommodation was involved. Thus, although one Welsh authority was involved in this phase of the research, four (a London borough, a metropolitan district and two shire counties) were within relatively easy reach (under two hours' travelling time).

Table 1.2: *Phase-two LEAs, schools and details of individual nominees*

	School and size	Curriculum area	Status	Gender	Years in post
LEA 6 (Metropolitan district)	K (950)	humanities (geog.)	HoF	M	1 1/2
		perf. arts (PE)	HoF	F	2
		science (biology)	HoF	M	3
		H.Ec.	HoD	F	1 1/2
	L (1300)	modern languages	HoD	M	15
	M (1200)	H.Ec.	HoD	F	11/2
		art	HoD	M	10
LEA 7 (Shire county)	N (700)	maths	HoD	M	5
		CDT	HoD	M	13
	O (1000)	Special Needs	HoD	M	5
		science	HoF	M	6
LEA 8 (London borough)	P (1000)	Special Needs	HoD	F	2
	Q (1300)	exp. arts (Eng.)	HoF	M	2 1/2
		creat. arts (H.Ec)	HoF	F	1 1/2
LEA 9 (Shire county)	R (600)	science	HoD	M	2 1/2
		English	HoD	F	2 1/2
		creat. arts (Art)	HoF	F	1
	S (1800) (split site)	PE	HoD	M	2
		English	HoD	F	1
LEA 10 (Shire county)		design	HoF	M	2
	T (1250)	humanities (geog)	HoF	M	2
		PE	HoD	F	1
	U (700) (split site)	creat. arts (PE)	HoF	F	5
		design	HoF	M	3
		maths	HoD	M	12

SM in dept	Internal promotion	Location in school	No in dept/ faculty	Contact ratio	Other (e.g. posts of responsibility)
DH, ST	no	adjacent rooms	9 f/t	0.75	
-	yes	separate rooms	8 f/t; 1 p/t	0.75	
HT, ST	yes	purpose built suite	7 f/t 3 p/t	0.75	
-	yes	purpose built suite	3 f/t 1 p/t	0.75	
-	no	separate block	7 f/t	0.85	i/c profiling
-	no	separate block	4 f/t	0.76	
-	no	separate block	3 f/t 1 p/t	0.68	HoD careers
-	no	adjacent rooms	6 f/t	0.79	teacher
-	no	separate block	4 f/t	0.79	govenor
-	no	suite	7 f/t	0.78	
-	no	suite	7 f/t; 1 p/t	0.78 tutor	prof. dev.
-	yes	adjacent rooms	4 f/t 3 p/t	0.77	Year 5 careers links w prim schs
-	yes	adj. rms mainly	12 f/t	0.75	teacher
-	yes	adjacent rooms/ separate blocks	16 f/t	0.85	governor
DH	no	adjacent labs	5 f/t 1 p/t	0.70	resp. IT/tech
HT DH	no	adjacent rooms	4 f/t 3 p/t	0.80	union rep.
-	no	adj. rms mainly	8 f/t 1 p/t	0.85	
-	yes	separate sites	5 f/t 4 p/t	0.77	
-	no	adj. rms mainly	10 f/t 8 p/t	0.74	
-	yes	separate block	11 f/t	0.75	
-	no	separate block	13 f/t	0.75	
-	yes	separate block	4 f/t	0.85	
-	no	sports centre	8 f/t	0.75	
DH	yes	separate blocks	6 f/t	0.75	
DH	no	adj. rms. mainly	4 f/t 4 p/t	0.75	

(Details of the LEAs and schools involved in the first research phase are given in Table 1.1, while Table 1.2 provides information concerning the phase two recommended practitioners.)

In each authority, the senior adviser(s) and four or five subject advisers were interviewed individually, the latter being selected to ensure that all the main secondary school subject areas (and Special Needs) were represented. At the end of the interview, subject advisers were asked to recommend practitioners whom they thought it would be worthwhile to study (in interview, they had given their criteria for effectiveness). Once all the nominations had been made, the researchers had a shortlist of possible schools and were able to select the case study schools to include: 'young', 'old', 'experienced' and 'new' heads of department; men and women; heads of department who were also heads of faculty; representatives of the main subject areas (maths; science; English; craft, design and technology (CDT); physical education (PE); modern languages; home economics; humanities; art) and Special Needs. As the focus of the research was on the management of medium-to-large departments and faculties, the vast majority of the nominees were responsible for four or more staff. A number of schools had several independent nominations (one, in fact, had four) so the effective deployment of the researchers' time was made possible by studying two or three departments or faculties within one school.

When the schools were initially approached by telephone, the headteachers were asked if they agreed with the advisers' recommendations. In all cases except one they did, although some suggested further candidates whom they considered on a par with, or superior to, the advisers' nominees. (This could be explained by the fact that not all advisers in each authority were interviewed and the headteacher's nominee was very often from one of the subjects not covered in that LEA.) It was important to obtain confirmatory views regarding effective practice lest the research design be criticized for overreliance on advisers' conceptions – conceptions which may, for example, overemphasize involvement in curriculum development and educational innovation. In some instances, slight reservations about the practitioners were expressed by heads during face-to-face interviews at a later stage – but this did not adversely affect the research which was looking for different varieties of effective practice rather than one blueprint or paragon of virtue. Some practitioners, in fact, expressed surprise that they had been recommended as they felt that their departments were far from the state they would wish them to be in! But these cases provided useful data for consideration of the difficulties and constraints that heads of department face.

In the 11 phase two schools, interviews were conducted with the head and deputy head (curriculum); the 25 nominated practitioners (usually on two or three separate occasions); all departmental staff (or a representative sample in the larger units); and heads of department in the faculty where the nominee was also head of faculty. A total of 135 interviews were conducted in phase two: 22 senior staff, 38 department and faculty heads, 69 teachers and 6 ancillary staff. In addition, 13 of the recommended practitioners were 'shadowed' for a day at various stages of the school year to provide observational data; they were all asked to identify and describe two or three 'critical incidents' (incidents or events which they had found difficult to cope with but which they felt they had tackled fairly successfully); and meetings and working parties involving middle managers were observed where possible. Documentation referring to school, faculty and departmental policy and practice (e.g. minutes of meetings, job descriptions) was also collected.

The recommended practitioners were not asked to keep diaries, as had been intended in the original proposal, as it was felt that this would involve a substantial encroachment upon their time – a lot of which they had generously given for interview – and, equally, it was thought that there would be little significant return by way of data that could not be ascertained by interview or in the course of the observation days. However, in order to obtain some data by this research method, experienced heads of department known to the researchers were asked to keep a diary for a week of their choice.

(The two research phases of the project are represented diagrammatically in Figure 1.1.)

Overview of the book

The NFER research project attempted to combine a detailed study of what department and faculty heads actually did with analyses of effective practice as defined by others. The result has meant that a large amount of case study data has been gathered over the course of the project. The intention is not, however, to present the case studies as a series of studies of individual schools, departments or faculties but rather to explore issues and themes that emerged from an analysis of all the case study data. In presenting the data in this manner there is the disadvantage that comments and practices may at times appear contextless, but it was felt that a thematic approach would be of greatest value to the reader.

Figure 1.1: *Project outline*

Phase 1:

The exploration of issues associated with department headship

(June–November 1986)

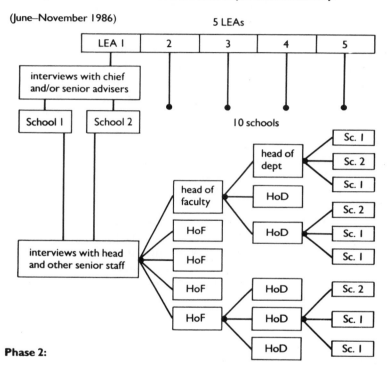

Phase 2:

The successful practice of department headship

(February–October 1987)

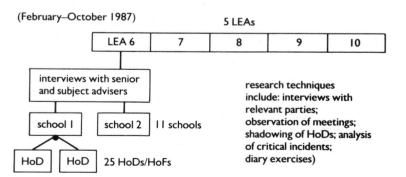

The following chapter draws on the observational data and the completed diaries and attempts to offer insights into what heads of department and faculty actually do. It develops the earlier remarks about the nature of managerial activities and, by analysing the existing literature on middle management, attempts to delineate a model regarding the department head's role. Job descriptions are also analysed, suggestions put forward as to how these might be constructed, and perceptions of the role of the department head documented.

Chapter 3 attempts to answer the question of what constitutes effective department and faculty practices. It does this by drawing on the interviews with advisers, heads and teachers to present a set of expectations that are commonly held. The chapter is largely descriptive but although not wishing to present a blueprint, it does draw up a composite of 'good' department and faculty practices.

Chapter 4 uses both interview data and critical incident analysis to examine the main difficulties and constraints faced by middle managers involved in the research. Chapter 5 investigates the main forms of support available to practitioners and also documents some of the most pressing training and development needs of department heads (and these are further explored in the final chapter).

The following four chapters (6 to 9) all explore key components of the role of the department and faculty head. For the purposes of analysis and data presentation, the areas of staff development, the management of change, departmental review and evaluation, and decision-making processes are treated separately. Chapter 6 examines the crucial, yet seemingly undeveloped, staff development role of department heads in terms of such areas as professional development, delegation and performance review, while Chapter 7 attempts to draw on the relevant literature and case studies to offer insights into curriculum development and the management of change. The following chapter continues the theme of the change process by considering how the curriculum is evaluated and departments are reviewed. Chapter 9 focuses on the processes of decision-making within both departments and schools and gives particular attention to the middle manager's role in whole-school matters.

The final chapter examines different organizational structures, considers the relative merits of departments and faculties and questions whether conventional models of curricular divisions are best suited to the demands currently being made of schools. Also, it attempts to bring together the main findings of the research in order to make a number of recommendations as to how departments and faculties might be improved thereby enhancing the quality of the learning process. As the title of the book implies, there is a need to give greater significance to the management function of the department and faculty head. This needs to be done not only by allocating more time (or using existing time to better effect) to enable key managerial activities to take place, but also (and this is of equal if not greater importance) by encouraging all practitioners to understand and embrace fully what it means to be a *manager*. It is hoped that the study gives insight into the generic management skills required which can complement the subject-specific texts for heads of department published by some of the subject associations.

2   What do Heads of Department and Faculty do?

This chapter will examine the day-to-day life of faculty and department heads, drawing on the observational data collected from the case studies and making reference to the existing literature and to actual job descriptions collected from schools. Perceptions of the role of head of department, gathered from the research interviews, will also be discussed. The chapter is largely descriptive and provides an overview whereas subsequent chapters are more analytical, exploring the main components of the role in far more detail. It begins, however, by documenting a day in the life of a head of faculty and a head of department.

Department and faculty heads at work

A day in the life of a head of faculty

The practitioner was head of the faculty of expressive arts and head of English at an urban comprehensive school with 1300 pupils on roll and had been in post for 18 months. He was responsible for 12 staff (eight English, two music, two drama). In normal circumstances he had 25 per cent non-contact time. The observation took place on a Thursday towards the end of a summer term.

08.30   HoF arrived at school and went to the staff room. Spoke to scale 1 English teacher about the problems that another teacher was having with a Year 3 group and about examination invigilation for the afternoon. Discussed the previous evening's governors' meeting with a senior teacher. Made some coffee and departed for English office on the next floor.

08.50   Collected various documents and then went to photo-

	copy them. Returned to office, unlocking classrooms for pupils on the way.
09.00	Another faculty head came into the office to discuss matters arising from the governors' meeting – the new salary structure and the school's proposed multicultural policy.
09.15	(The HoF had two periods free as Year 5 were doing exams.) Went to the staffroom to check pigeon-hole and then returned to English office to prepare video on GCSE oral assessment for the staff.
09.20	HoF introduced the video to the three members of staff who had arrived to watch it.
09.30	Interruption from pupil about a textbook and from DH3 about the timetable. HoF left teachers watching the video and went to talk to a pupil about 'A' level work.
09.35	HoF stopped the video and started discussion.
09.55	Continued watching video with pauses for discussion until the end of the lesson.
10.35	Went to the staffroom for coffee and checked the cover list. Talked to HoD drama about capitation and that evening's faculty meeting.
10.55	Went to school office for some forms and spoke to DH3 about staffing of the Upper School for the following year.
11.05	Returned to English office and put away the TV and video equipment. Went to school office to get some carbon paper.
11.15	Phone call from the office with a query about which room a group were in: HoF went to check. HoF rang the secretary to make an appointment to see the head and then started working on capitation allocation.
11.30	Pupil entered office with a query about a book. HoF continued with capitation work.
11.55	Pupil came with book forms to be signed.
12.05	Second-in-command entered and HoF discussed capitation, the staffing for the following year (when the HoF would have left), a racial awareness course and the need for a gender working party.
12.20	HoF popped out to local high street to purchase a sandwich.
12.35	HoF went to staffroom and talked to a teacher about the governors' meeting and the multicultural document.
12.50	Pupil asked to see HoF about returning some books. HoF

	arranged to see the head briefly later in the afternoon and then returned to department office to talk to the scale 1 about a job application for which the HoF had given a reference. Spoke to HoD drama about capitation and to another scale 1 about the exam invigilation.
13.05	HoF registered Year 4 GCSE class in room next to office and reprimanded them for the fact that about 50 per cent had been absent the previous day. Taught them for the rest of period.
14.10	HoF returned to office, left books and then went to make sure that the exam was under control.
14.20	Went to see the head about the discussion of multicultural issues at the governors' meeting, forthcoming racial awareness course and staffing for the following year.
14.50	Left head's office and did some photocopying on the way back to the office.
14.55	Did stationery order.
15.05	Scale 2 entered and talked about a pupil. HoF mentioned exam cover arrangements and supply requirements for later in the term (a teacher was leaving mid-term).
15.10	Went to the staffroom and arranged to meet HoD Special Needs the following afternoon.
15.15	Faculty meeting. Lengthy discussion about capitation and then about staffing and the school INSET committee.
15.50	HoF went to senior staff meeting (DHs, HoFs and HoYs) which had already started. Discussion of INSET committee and GRIST proposals; job descriptions; staffing; primary school liaison; homework; racism awareness training; and the governors' meeting.
17.15	Meeting closed. HoF talked to another HoF about capitation and raised a query with the DH3.
17.25	Home.

A day in the life of a head of department

The practitioner was head of PE in a county comprehensive school with 1750 pupils on roll and had been in post for two years. He was responsible for nine members of staff (five full-time and four part-time). In normal circumstances he had 23 per cent non-contact time. The observation took place on a Thursday towards the end of a spring term.

08.00	HoD arrived at school. Spoke to DH2 about staffing for the following term and then rang the garage about the school minibus.
08.15	Discussed with second-in-command the time allocation for PE in the new school curriculum and the problem of 'cover' teachers arriving for lessons late.
08.35	Rang teacher in charge of boys' PE about the minibus and then went to collect the minibus from the garage.
08.55	Arrived back at school. Tried to see the headteacher about a recent PE inspector's report and rang a parent about a pupil's lost trousers.
09.15	Had brief conversations with two members of the department and supervised boys changing. Checked five or six pupils' letters of excuses and allocated some sport-related project work to do.
09.20	Went from upper-school changing rooms to the gym and started Year 3 (mixed) lesson. The lesson was uninterrupted (the department had asked that the office should not put through phone calls when they were teaching).
10.20	At the end of the lesson the HoD returned to the upper school to check the work of the pupils who had not been in the gym.
10.25	Went to departmental office and talked to a scale 1 teacher about Year 2 lessons.
10.30	Went to staffroom for coffee, checked pigeon-hole and talked to non-PE staff. Returned to office and prepared to supervise student (a form had to be completed after each lesson observed).
10.40	Walked over to lower-school gym.
10.45	Periods 3 and 4: observed student.
12.05	Returned to upper-school office and then went to referee lunchtime basketball for Year 4.
12.45	Lunch. Spoke to several staff and the school secretary.
13.00	Went to staffroom. Checked pigeon-hole and had conversation about pupil commitment to after-school activities.
13.20	Refereed a basketball game.
13.45	Returned to office and rang headteacher's secretary to enquire if the head was free. He was, so the HoD went to see him, going in through the secretary's office: meanwhile, another teacher had entered the head's

	office directly and so the HoD could not see the head. HoD returned to departmental office.
14.00	Dealt with pupils who had no kit and set them some work. Rang another school about a match fixture and then rang the local teachers' centre about a proposed leavers' day at the sports centre. Went through folder of items for the weekly departmental meeting. Looked at report on remedial gymnastics prepared by second-in-command and wrote some letters.
14.30	Went to resources centre in the lower school to collect some photocopying and to see DH1 to discuss the new timetable arrangements. DH1 not available so the HoD went to the squash club (on the school site) to talk to the manager about the possibility of the pupils using the weight-training room. Returned to lower school. DH1 had gone off to teach so the HoD went back to the departmental office.
14.50	Made coffee and phoned manager of the sports centre about the booking for the leavers' day.
15.00	Went to see admin officer about capitation for the following year.
15.10	Returned to office and talked to scale 2 teacher about plans for the after-school match.
15.15	Took phone call about staffing for the following year.
15.20	Went over to sixth-form block to collect minibus and drove to the upper-school block to pick up the U16 basketball team.
15.30	Left for a match at another school.
17.35	After the match, dropped pupils off at various villages.
18.50	Returned to school and put minibus in garage.
19.00	Home.

These accounts give something of the flavour of the multifarious activities that occupy a head of department or faculty during a school day. They each represent an actual – rather than a composite – account and are selected from the days when heads of department and heads of faculty among the 25 practitioners studied in phase two were shadowed by an NFER researcher. All the department and faculty heads thus observed stressed that the selected day should be seen in context as no two days were exactly the same and each reflected the varying demands of the academic year. The shadowing days were, in fact, selected when the nominees had most 'free' periods and were therefore more likely to be engaged in managerial activities. They were distributed throughout the school year so that practitioners were observed in the first week of the autumn term right through to public examination time in the summer. Thus, although any one practitioner may have been preoccupied by a particular concern on any one observation day, as a group, the days typified the activities that middle managers engaged in, the interpersonal contacts they made and the 'pattern' (albeit one of fragmentation) of their lives.[1]

One of the things that was striking about the working day of department and faculty heads was its general similarity to that of headteachers. There were differences, of course (middle managers are 'timetable bound' while headteachers are generally 'diary-bound'), but outside the classroom there was the same 'frantic succession of disconnected activities' (Buckley, 1985). Hall et al. (1986) found that their heads' days were characterized by fragmentation and a range of tasks and were 'people-intensive' – just as Mintzberg (1973) found in his studies of managers outside the educational world. These characteristics were true both of the days spent shadowing department and faculty heads and of the diary accounts that were submitted. The jobs that required uninterrupted hours clearly had to be done elsewhere – and most faculty and department heads said that they took administrative work (lists, returns etc.) home with them, together with their normal teaching preparation and marking. The shadowing exercise, together with the completed diaries, revealed the innumerable interpersonal exchanges engaged in when the department and faculty heads were not in the classroom (and they were, in fact, on occasion interrupted in the classroom). Often, half a dozen totally unrelated matters (ranging over the personal, comments about individual pupils, curriculum ideas, external matters etc.) would be referred to in the course of ten minutes or so before school as staff came into the departmental or faculty office or staff room.

Interspersed with exchanges with the staff were interchanges with pupils (outside of lesson times) who either came to the head of department or had to be 'chased up'. Some of these incidents were of an administrative nature – a returned book to be signed in or permission sought; others were disciplinary – these often being time-consuming and, invariably, unplanned. Middle managers spent time waiting their turn to catch senior staff and also talking to technicians, clerical staff and librarians. Heads of department who were also heads of faculty had an extra dimension in that they had to keep their department heads and teachers in charge of subject

---

[1] Further examples of observation days are available on request from the authors

informed about the matters which concerned them – the outcomes of a finance committee meeting for example. Phone calls had to be both taken and made – for example, to parents, feeder and consortium schools, the education office – and these would often take up a lot of time, especially when the department or faculty head had to wait for one of only two outside lines in a busy general office, only to be told that the person being rung was unavailable.

In non-contact periods, when there were fewer people around to interact with, heads of department and faculty were able to do tasks which required longer stretches of uninterrupted time. Heads of some subjects and areas (for example, CDT, home economics) sometimes had to go to buy materials; a head of PE might take the minibus for refuelling ready to take a team off after school; a nearby feeder school might be visited. Occasionally, a department meeting or working party might be held if by happy coincidence (for only in very rare instances were these deliberately timetabled) the relevant teachers were free at the same time. Photocopying had to be done, mail dealt with (and matters arising set in motion), lists checked, equipment collected and returned and so forth. In addition, on account of their involvement with curriculum initiatives – generated both within the school and externally – there were an increasing number of visitors to be attended to. Visitors who were present on the shadowing days, for example, included Technical and Vocational Education Initiative (TVEI) and Oxford Certificate of Educational Achievement (OCEA) representatives, a teacher seconded to the authority to research profiling, some teachers from another authority who wanted to consult the head of faculty about the way in which religious education (RE) was accommodated in the modular humanities course and a teacher from a consortium school wanting to talk about assessment. A head of faculty who had intended to talk to the researcher between morning break and lunchtime, had to cancel the interview on account of some visitors. He said that the same thing had happened every Friday that term (and he had thus regularly been deprived of a considerable amount of 'free' time). When there were students in the department, meetings with college tutors had to be arranged (as well as time spent counselling the student). Middle managers had, like other teachers, to take their turn providing cover and this further eroded non-contact time.

After-school activities included departmental clubs and detentions; departmental and middle management meetings; school-wide committees and working parties; departmental open evenings for parents, and school parents' evenings; attendance at INSET sessions; subject association meetings; and LEA panels. It was not unusual for a middle manager to have a meeting after school most days. (The research was, it must be remembered, undertaken before the '1265 hours' contract came into effect – and teacher action was taking place during much of the first research phase.) Among the effective departments and faculties, evening meetings at the home of the head of department or faculty were by no means infrequent – sometimes happening as often as once a week when a new course was being prepared; and heads of faculty who were also senior teachers were, in a few instances, involved with senior staff meetings at someone's home in the evenings.

These were the visible things which kept department and faculty heads active and 'busy'. There were also the invisible ones – the work that was taken home because of lack of time and opportunity to attend to it in the course of the school day (and some of those interviewed, at all levels, felt very strongly that this was what middle managers 'were being paid extra for'). It is, perhaps, unsurprising that department heads had very little time for activities such as observation or, often, for the solitary reflection and planning which, it is suggested, must be the prelude to, or at least accompany, formal evaluation procedures. Flisher (1986), writing about the use of time by secondary heads and deputies, asks why spaces for thinking time are not scheduled:

> Time must be gained from somewhere for critical reflection following the assessment of situations and for both short and long term planning. If it is not, action will be little more than reaction to situations that have arisen because they were not foreseen.

The middle manager's day was very full and had its own momentum. Many of the phase two nominees arrived at school at about 8.00 a.m. or earlier and did not leave until 5.00 p.m. or later. One of them remarked that there was never a time when he could say that he had done everything and he thought that being a deputy head was, in fact, less stressful than being in charge of a department – this practitioner has since been promoted to deputy headship! (Interestingly, Freeman (1987) suggests that *pastoral* middle managers are, in fact, 'busier' and more stressed than more senior colleagues.) A similar point was made by a senior teacher who had previously been a head of science: he said that it was, for example, a tremendous relief to be able to go home without worrying about whether laboratories and stores had been locked up properly. Another head of department commented that things got progressively busier as the week and the term progressed and so he was never able to clear everything up at the end of the day – there was always something pending. A faculty head remarked that his job was like 'juggling lots of balls in the air at the same time'. Middle managers often listed the things that were waiting to be done.

Although the shadowing days provide useful data and give the reader an insight into the 'gadfly' nature of school management, it was decided not to undertake a detailed task analysis or to quantify the time spent on various activities. Some researchers (e.g. Flisher, 1986; Weightman, 1988) have done this but it was felt that the exercise would be of limited value in that it would not show the quality or effectiveness of the various interactions. One department head may spend several hours per week with a probationer for example, but not be as helpful as another devoting less time yet focusing on the most salient issues. Moreover, such analyses are unable to take account of the differing contexts in which middle managers work. For example, a head of a large department made up predominantly of specialists might need to spend less time on producing materials – as much of this could be delegated – than would his or her counterpart with a staff of part-timers and non-specialists. Task analyses are of some value, however, and can be used for training purposes, especially to enable individuals to see how their time is being used and whether or not this reflects their priorities.

Weekly diaries of department and faculty heads

The shadowing days revealed the pace of the subject head's life and something of its nature, showing that not only did practitioners have most moments occupied but that they had to have 'grasshopper minds' in order to change topics of consideration in quick succession. So that more could be learnt about the breadth of the responsibilities of the department and faculty heads and in order to build on the data collected by the shadowing days, some were asked to complete a diary of a week's activities. It was thought to be too much of an imposition to ask the nominated practitioners studied in phase two to do this exercise as it represented a considerable encroachment on their time, much of which they had already willingly given up for the project team. Thus the diaries were kept by department and faculty heads not participating in phase two of the research but nevertheless regarded by others as effective practitioners. Before an attempt is made to analyse the role of the head of department/faculty, one of the diaries submitted[1] will be presented in an attempt to give a greater understanding of the nature of

---

[1] Further examples of diaries are available from the authors on request.

the role. The diaries differed from the observation days in that they included reflections and comments on the part of the diarists.

A week in the life of a head of biology and head of science faculty

The diarist was head of science in a multi-ethnic, urban comprehensive school with 1150 pupils on roll and had been in post for two years (appointed department head seven years previous to that). She was responsible for 13 members of staff (all full-time) and the faculty was accommodated in a suite of rooms. The diary was kept in the first half of a spring term.

Monday
(Had a very heavy cold and felt awful but it is much easier going in to work than making all the arrangements for people to do things for you and setting work etc.)

08.15	Collected mail from staffroom and saw DH1 about Year 3 options and recommendations made by the science department.
09.00	Non-contact time. Dealt with mail and parcels; finalized Year 3 grades (having chased up some staff for missing grades); sent out notes for Year 4 registers *re* science test; discussed Year 6 practical work for next few weeks with the colleague who teaches it with me; finalized assess-' ment for practical coursework.
10.30	Science department meeting. Gave out grades, went over report writing procedures and reminded staff that they must report homework defaulters. (It is useful for the whole faculty to get together as there are three prep rooms.)
10.50	Talked to PGCE student about lesson preparation and went through his lesson notes from last week. (He is still not making any effort despite chidings last term.)
11.30	Marked Year 2 books. (These were awful. I had not marked for some weeks as I had been on a course.)
12.30	Finished marking and got out apparatus for Year 6 practical lesson. Found mock exam papers and checked through mark scheme.
13.30	Year 6 practical lesson.
15.15	Loaned out books to Year 6 and gave advice about investigations to be reported. Collected videos from Media Resources.

16.00	Home.
Evening	Spent two hours reviewing a new series of videos and accompanying materials. (Never any time to do this at school: far too many teachers show videos without doing any preparation.) Filled in some order forms for free leaflets and posters.

Tuesday

08.15	Collected mail. Spoke to: colleague who had been to Computers across the Curriculum meeting and was going to visit BBC Education Department; member of department about her personal problems; PGCE student in physics dept. re her progress.
09.00	Dealt with mail and sorted out invoices etc. with technician. Chased up caretaker re the fact that gas supplies in two labs still not repaired. (Fault was reported six months ago but no action taken – no one in the LEA seems to want to know. Meanwhile, labs not fully usable.) Ordered film for Young Ornithologists' Club, having phoned to confirm its availability.
09.50	Year 4 group.
10.30	Coffee and social chat. Handed out to staff for evaluation software received for inspection.
10.50	Did filing and cleared desk, directing various material to appropriate members of staff.
11.30	Went over scheme of work for Year 4 course module with two colleagues. (Possible as CPVE pupils out on work experience.)
12.30	HoFs meeting. Discussed my involvement with NFER research and a relevant HMI report. (A working lunch – some useful exchanges of ideas.)
13.30	Year 4 group.
14.35	Checked that biology student had prepared Wednesday's lessons and asked technician to do some costings for equipment. Looked at new computer program. Sorted out late Year 3 grades. Checked in school office how much GCSE money there was left.
15.20	Home.
Evening	Spent two hours writing a review of some wallcharts (received free if reviewed). Reviewed some computer software and read some articles on curriculum development in science.

Wednesday

07.30	Phone call from student to say that he would not be coming in (I suspected a hangover – some students are more trouble than they are worth!)
08.15	Dealt with mail. Talked about some non-exam pupils with HoY5, discussed buying some model aeroplanes and followed up Tuesday's talk *re* scheme of work.
09.00	Update on colleague with problems. Checked up, once again, on Year 3 grades. Read and filed minutes of meetings.
09.30	Checked what student had ordered for his lessons and prepared for these.
10.00	Went to strong room and checked papers for Thursday's test.
10.30	Phone calls to colleague at another school and to suppliers.
10.50	Finalized arrangements for Year 4 test with HoY, caretaker etc. and put notes in Year 4 registers.
11.30	Year 3 group. (I discovered that the student had not marked the books so I had to check them quickly in class.)
12.30	Lunch. Visit from DH *re* minutes of last science faculty meeting. (He had not liked what he had read!)
13.30	Year 5 group. (Had to go over last lesson as the student had not done it properly.)
14.30	Year 4 group.
15.15	Discussed 'Girls and Science' with a colleague who attended an Equal Opportunities working party at lunchtime.

Thursday

08.15	Checked mail and got papers from strong-room. Went to hall and put out 120 candidate numbers. Organized pupils into sets and gave out papers.
09.10	Supervised test.
09.50	Told pupils about next module and GCSE coursework. Despatched pupils to classrooms and then talked to my set about the rest of the course.
10.30	Sorted out test papers and returned them to strong-room. Discussed the student with his tutor from college. Discussed the student with his tutor from college.
10.50	Year 2 group.
11.50	Organized some equipment in prep room. (Tempted

	to go into student's lesson with badly behaved Year 5 group.)
12.45	Further discussion with student's tutor.
13.00	Lunch. Sorted out stationery with technician and another colleague.
13.30	Continued filing newly duplicated worksheets while student taught a very noisy group.
14.15	Year 3 group. Detained them for ten minutes to finish an experiment.
15.25	Tidied up and ordered apparatus for Friday.
15.35	Home.
Evening	Read the TES, documents on equal opportunities, and colleagues' comments re assessment. Looked at two books on AIDS. Drew up agenda for science faculty meeting and a document for circulation re Year 3 and 4 course organization for the following year.

Friday

08.15	Saw head re new technician.
08.30	Collected mail and followed up query from DH re option system.
08.50	Year 4 group.
09.50	Had serious talk with student re poor lesson preparation and said that I expected it done properly by Monday. '
10.30	Head's staff meeting.
10.50	Year 6 group.
12.10	Out for lunch.
13.10	Finished some orders. Checked with HoD chemistry re GCSE textbooks (Year 4 have not all got them and I wonder if there will be enough money) and saw HoD physics re a course he was going on next week.
14.00	Year 2 group.
15.00	Detained pupils to finish work properly.
15.20	Marked some work and collected up more to take home.
16.00	Home.
Evening	Two hours' work on Sunday evening.

Within this head of science's week there was no calm point and the 'busyness' of single days was maintained throughout the week. However much they planned their week, heads of department and faculty said that they were invariably not in control of their time and unexpected events continually occurred. 'Crises', the immediate needs of staff and pupils (giving help, disciplining, for example) and interruptions arising from the essentially dynamic and interactive nature of school life meant that schedules drawn up at the weekend, or whenever, frequently had to be abandoned and activities shelved. The life of middle managers was not unlike that of their senior colleagues and the situation was exacerbated by the fact that they were interacting and negotiating with people whose days were similarly unpredictable. The reality of life as it is actually lived is rarely reflected in the job descriptions of heads of department and faculty, and formal analyses give no indication of the piecemeal fashion in which much management activity is undertaken.

In order to give some coherence to the disparate activities which are clearly evidenced in the diary and shadowing days, some categorization of the specific tasks of department and faculty heads and some theoretical consideration of the role are necessary.

The role of the head of department

A survey of the literature (see Fletcher-Campbell, 1988) shows that various attempts have been made to analyse the role of department and faculty heads.

Drawing on his experience as a department head in several schools, Marland (1971) was the first writer to address seriously the issue of encouraging heads of department to understand their role – something on which, he contended, the very success of the comprehensive school rested. He identified the pivotal nature of the role (an image which is echoed in such phrases as 'boiler house', 'engine room', 'kingpin' and 'hub of the school' frequently used by respondents in the NFER research) and stressed the importance of delegation and communication so that a complementary team might be nurtured in a 'climate of discussion'.

Building on this pioneering work, one of the earliest attempts to construct a theoretical model for the role of the head of department was that of Lambert (1975) whose work was later developed by Brydson (1983). However, the terminology and categorization used by these authors is not particularly helpful: Brydson (1983), for example, considered 'leadership' as a separate function whereas there are good arguments, from empirical evidence, for seeing the middle manager as a leader operating in a number of areas. Such conceptualizations have formed the basis of some of the more helpful categorizations. For example, a handbook produced by an LEA (West Sussex County Council, 1981) for new heads of department stresses that department heads are senior members of staff (and must therefore be aware of the 'context' in which they operate – they should, for example, be conversant with whole-school issues) and have responsibilities for: aims and objectives; staffing; the work of the department; resources; pupils; communication; and records.

Her Majesty's Inspectorate in Wales (1984) – in a document which was partly instrumental in generating both the NFER research and the Welsh Office Project (Edwards and Bennett, 1985) – identified five areas of responsibility for heads of department: routine administration and organization; planning of pupils' learning experiences; monitoring and evaluating the work of the department; professional development within the department; and liaison with other departments, pastoral staff, senior management and outside agencies.

Torrington and Weightman (1985) divided the middle manager's role into three areas – technical (the actual teaching), administrative and managerial – and drew attention to the balance that needs to be kept between them. Too much emphasis on one area can lead to neglect in another: prioritizing needs to be carefully thought out – an issue which formidable lists of duties (as in some job descriptions) tend to ignore. More recently (Weightman, 1988), they have added social and personal areas (to form the acronym STAMP) and have analysed the use of time by department heads and other school managers with respect to the five areas.

Edwards (1985) argued that 'uncertainty as to the role is probably the greatest single obstacle to more effective departmental organization'. He questioned whether the mere lists of duties produced by some schools represented a rank order and an organic whole, or whether they had grown by accretion. The author, in analysing the department head's role, drew up a three-dimensional framework composed of two themes (leadership and communication) which infuse all the department head's activities; and four areas of responsibility (pupils, staff, curriculum and resources) which must be attended to within three contexts (the department, the school and beyond the school). To this framework could be added the extra dimension of routine and developmental activities. This distinction, which operates over all the department head's areas of activity, was referred to by respondents in the NFER research as 'keeping the wheels turning' and 'keeping the wheels moving forward'. The resultant conceptualization, adapted from Edwards (1985), is illustrated in Figure 2.1. (For a further exploration of leadership see Chapter 9.)

Edwards' (1985) model is particularly useful in that it creates a sense of the interaction of tasks and functions which empirical evidence suggests is at the heart of the department head's role. For example, drawing up a scheme of work involves, or could involve,

Figure 2.1: *The role of the head of department*

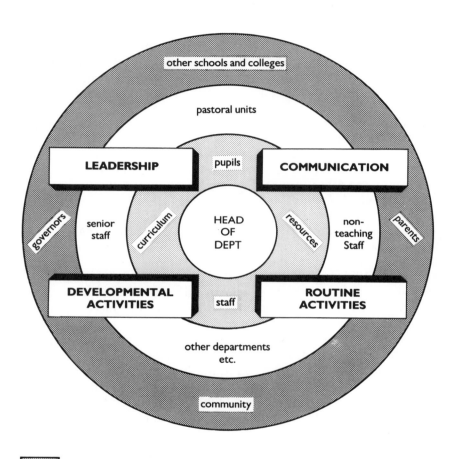

Figure 2.1: *The role of the head of department (continued)*

Two general *themes*:

1 *Leadership*:	a HoD is expected to 'lead by inspiration, showing by attitude and approach that there is a worthwhile job to be done and that its accomplishment is not impossible'.
2 *Communication*:	HoDs are expected to 'promote a sense of the unity of knowledge' and relate the work of their own departments to that of others and to the general purposes of the school.

Four main areas of *responsibility*:

1 *Pupils*:	their organization into teaching groups; their guidance, discipline and welfare; the monitoring and assessment of their progress; provision for pupils with Special Needs; the maintenance of appropriate records.
2 *Staff*:	the deployment, appointment, induction and professional development of the departmental team, including not only its full-time members but occasional teachers, students in training and ancillary staff.
3 *Curriculum*:	planning the whole range of pupils' learning experiences; defining aims and objectives, and translating them into meaningful course content; evaluating success and assessing priorities.
4 *Resources*:	the selection, production, control and utilization of appropriate learning materials; the management of the learning environment.

Three *contexts*:

1 *The department*:	as a distinct unit of school organization: the HoD acts as a leader and guide to staff and pupils, curriculum planner and resource manager.
2 *The school*:	as a whole: the HoD acts as communicator and negotiator with colleagues, and as contributor to the making and implementation of whole-school policies.
3 *Beyond the school*	the HoD acts as investigator, public relations officer and diplomat.

(from Edwards, 1985)

Two *dimensions*:

1 *Routine: activities*	e.g. exam entries, cover arrangements, room allocation, stationery.
2 *Developmental: activities*	e.g. staff development, curriculum evaluation, liaison with other curriculum areas, participation in whole-school working parties.

team leadership, management of resources, capitation considerations and liaison with other departments as well as being a major exercise in professional development. Some models of the role of head of department are deficient in that they create the impression of linear, self-contained units of responsibility. The head of department may be in a pivotal position but increasingly may, furthermore, be the *key pivot* or the one who recognizes, or even establishes, *other* pivots. Department heads are unlikely to be on all working parties in large departments or be the coordinator for all external initiatives, for example. Other teachers may be the 'expert' or specialist to whom the head of department turns for information regarding whole-school policies, such as multiculturalism or equal opportunities, where these are discussed in open working parties rather than being confined to senior or middle management meetings.

The execution of the department head's responsibilities may thus be much more complex than might be assumed from task-centred lists in job descriptions. Those documents which leant towards the 'facilitator' and 'politician' aspects would seem to be much more aware of what is required of the head of department in schools in the late 1980s and 1990s (see, for example, Tyldesley, 1984).

Job descriptions

An LEA paper on job descriptions in secondary schools noted: 'Poor practice would be identified either by a total lack of job descriptions or by descriptions which are calculated to antagonize the reader.' Four reasons were given for schools having job descriptions: to enable teachers to understand the nature of their responsibility; to allow individual teachers to see how their responsibilities fitted into the total management structure of the school; to place on the headteacher the onus of seeing that the management of the school was a shared responsibility; and to give job applicants a clear idea of the school's expectations. (For some pertinent research, see Hall and Thomas, 1978; Fellows and Potter, 1984; and for the relevance of job descriptions to appraisal, McMahon, 1987). The LEA document argued that below senior management level, the job descriptions should carry the acceptance that senior staff had a responsibility to see that there were systems and structures which permitted the teachers to carry out their responsibilities effectively.

Two influential reports concerned with school improvement – Cockcroft (1982) on mathematics teaching, and Hargreaves (1984) on ILEA schools – both saw what the head of department *did* as being central to the quality of what went on in schools. For example, the Hargreaves Report stated: 'Head teachers should issue clear and detailed job specifications so heads of department know what is expected of them and, in their turn, heads of department should make clear what the duties and responsibilities of departmental members are.' The head of department, according to the Report, had an important role to play in school improvement and should, amongst other things weld the department into a team; create high morale; plan coherent courses; generate syllabuses which engage the pupils; coordinate with other subjects in implementing whole-school policies; monitor; provide colleagues with opportunities for displaying their strengths and help to remedy their weaknesses; and be active in the professional development of the team. Rather ironically, the Report concluded: 'In addition to these functions, heads of department often carry substantial teaching loads.'

During the NFER project, job descriptions were collected from schools visited and from other sources: these were found to vary enormously, ranging from a formidable checklist of nearly 70 duties to attempts to categorize tasks in areas and bring out the team-leadership aspect of the role.

All the schools involved in phase two of the research had job descriptions of some sort (albeit in some instances general ones in the staff handbook) for their heads of department and faculty. At one school, the job description was in two parts – one for general, and one for specific, responsibility. Interestingly, some of the items listed under the department head's general responsibility appeared later in the handbook under the specific responsibility of the second-in-charge – evidence of structured delegation. At another school, department heads were generally 'responsible for the nature, quality and development of work in their subject area within the overall framework of the school'. Five areas of consideration were offered: team leadership and staff development; standards of assessment; communication (re courses and syllabus); organization and administration; and policy (attendance at meetings, liaison with other heads of department). Another job description, offering six areas, did not, however, mention team leadership or 'climate'.

Five roles were given in one job description. The head of department had to be a leader, a professional expert, an ambassador, a pragmatist (cultivating the art of the possible!), and an accountant/auditor. The relative simplicity of this was sullied by a random list of 37 'frames of consideration' in which 'readability in your subject' and 'innovation in your subject' were apparently of equal importance. This is not unlike the findings of Edwards (1985) who wrote: It is unusual and refreshing to find a head of department required 'to sleep a minimum of eight hours each night during term'. The bad news is that this sympathetic exhortation appears as number 19 on the list of priorities.

An example of a job description is given in Figure 2.2.[1] It is not the intention here to consider in detail how a job description is best drawn up, except to mention that the most accessible ones attempted to put the job in context, categorize tasks in areas or roles, and brought out the team-leadership aspect of the job. In general, the documentation differs only in the varieties of categorization – the number of categories and the apportioning of tasks within them – and the way of presentation. There is considerable emphasis on *content*, with less focus on objectives and how things are done. Yet it is the *method* (combined, of course, with content) which would seem central to effectiveness – although, of course, department and faculty heads must have a curricular area to be effective in.

Different functions may take priority at various stages of a department's development: the issues concerning the departments in the NFER case study schools which had had a succession of effective leaders were very different from those being addressed in departments trying to come to terms with the basics of organization. This is not the same as individual heads of department prioritizing among the various tasks facing them. For example, a department clearly must have a scheme of work before it can consider common assessment throughout a year group; but a department that has schemes of work may have to consider with which year group to start initiating common assessment techniques. The phase two nominees frequently spoke of the current project and how they were going to build on that to develop the department in the future.

Indeed, it is easy to forget that heads of department often have very few non-teaching periods allocated to carry out their specific responsibilities. The non-contact time of heads of department involved in the NFER research ranged from 15 to 35 per cent with faculty heads having, on average, one or two more 'free' periods than department heads. Like their colleagues, department and faculty heads were also required at times to cover for absent staff. Torrington and Weightman (1982) have pointed out that some middle managers outside of education suffer from 'technical atrophy' as they no longer practise their technical skills or engage in professional activity, being entirely engaged in managing and administrating: clearly, this is not the

---

[1] Examples of different types of job description – both subject-specific and general – are available from the authors on request.

Figure 2.2: *A job description for a head of department*

In defining this role the senior management team recognizes its responsibility to create policies and systems which will enable the head of department to carry out these tasks. Heads of departments should expect to play an important part in the review of such policies.

1 *The educational progress of children*
(a) To examine the purposes of teaching the subject at various age and ability levels and the methods to achieve them, including the organization of teaching groups and the deployment of staff.
(b) To advise colleagues and cooperate with them on teaching programmes, methods, equipment and the choice of materials.
(c) To develop and implement a departmental scheme of assessment and reporting in line with the overall school policy.
(d) To deal with pupils who are presenting behavioural problems in department lessons and examine the appropriateness of the teacher's methods.

2 *The leadership of a team*
(a) To keep the department abreast of developments within the subject.
(b) To organize opportunities for members of the department to see their colleagues teach and the quality of their pupils' exercise books.
(c) To supervise and monitor the work of colleagues, ensuring that lesson content, teaching methods, monitoring and assessing procedures are within departmental and school requirements.
(d) To organize regular departmental meetings with a formal agenda and written minutes.
(e) To ensure that departmental rooms and adjoining circulation areas are maintained in a clean, tidy and attractive condition.
(f) To supervise, where appropriate, the work of non-teaching staff.

3 *Staff development*
(a) To take part in the appointment of staff to the department.
(b) To care for the personal and career development of all staff in the department, particularly for probationers and students.
(c) To encourage in-service training, both school-based and out of school courses.

4 *Resources*
(a) To allocate equipment, books, stationery etc. from within the department's share of capitation.
(b) To organize efficient use of teaching spaces and efficient methods of stock and equipment control.
(c) To use external resources, e.g. universities, colleges, advisers etc.

case with teachers in middle management positions as they continue doing the same work as those staff for whom they have responsibility. Heads of department and faculty are, first and foremost – at least in terms of time allocation – still *teachers* and the actual business of the classroom occupies most of their time. Hence the title of this book – the problem for many middle managers is not only finding sufficient time to undertake the many and varied responsibilities associated with the job but also, as will later be suggested, actually coming to terms with the *management* role that they must now embrace.

Whatever the categorization however, the chief use of the job description lies in the way it can help practitioners to break down the role for evaluation purposes and be aware of its complexity and demands. It can be argued that the effective practitioner is one who understands what is involved in the job (and is then able to translate this into action). A categorization alone does not provide any details but it is probably more helpful than random lists of tasks.

Perceptions of the role

That practitioners involved in the study had job descriptions did not mean to say that they were aware of what was in them nor that they found them particularly useful. Neither did the heads of department cite them when asked in interview what they did and what the role involved. All the various areas of responsibility referred to in the literature and documentation were mentioned by someone at some time but certainly in no systematic way. Respondents had not had an opportunity to prepare replies and so the fact that something was not mentioned in interview was not particularly significant. (In fact, in follow-up sessions or when meeting the researcher on another occasion, interviewees often said: 'Oh, I forgot to say . . .'.) A task was often so much taken for granted that it was not commented upon and the heads of department were not asked to rank tasks. When asked what their most important task was, they often identified what was of immediate concern – a curriculum initiative or a new course (GCSE, for example).

Department heads were often unclear as to what 'officially' they were expected to do and there seemed to be a fair amount of 'muddling through'. The following comments were not untypical:

Perhaps we need training on what our role is. The role is laid out in the handbook but it is really only the nuts and bolts. What we need to know is how to apply it on a day-to-day basis.

I think that the whole of middle management needs to be

defined, especially when you are new to the job; otherwise you spend an awful lot of time doing something only to find that someone else has already done it.

> The school is very good on paper but written statements
> do not reflect what actually goes on. For most staff,
> areas of responsibility are far too vague and full of
> empty phrases.

All these comments refer to the fact that job descriptions have to be translated into practice and related to those of others in the school. Some department heads could have read all the extant literature and still be uncertain what to do in their school. Some headteachers were aware of this. One said:

> My overall aim is to have a library of job descriptions to include
> scale 1s and probationers so that in *toto* these would provide
> an abstract of the work of the school and would ensure that
> Mr Bloggs, scale 3, does the following jobs – e.g. form tutor,
> subject teacher, member of X working party. At the moment, it
> is a hotch-potch.

The fact that individual circumstances vary was borne out by several comments. For example:

> I am interested in how the role of head of department is
> very different according to school size. A member of my
> department complained to the DH that my second-in-command
> was doing my job – giving out the graph paper. He had come
> from a small school where the HoD had to do such
> things.

> I have worked for two heads: the first saw my role as an
> administrator and the second as much more a personnel
> manager.

One phase one head of department revised his job description annually in the light of those of the staff in his department – as different people took on different things each year.

Some heads of department, especially the effective ones, were able to stand back and forget the 'nuts and bolts' and observe that, for example, they were 'head of people, not a subject' and were aware of both the context and the ultimate aim of the department:

> Staff can devise elaborate schemes of work but I try
> to ensure that what is done is for the benefit of
> the pupils.

> I went on a course where a head said the first obligation of the
> HoD is to the school as a whole and not to the department. This
> I thought was the most useful assertion about the role – it put it
> in its right place.

Heads of faculty in phase two of the study were all experienced
department heads. As regards their present function, they were aware
of weightier responsibilities.

> I must appear to be competent, democratic and know the
> lot of life of staff here – this was not so when I was a
> deputy HoF.

> I think that in my previous job I just organized the department.
> I had no real role in the school. Outside the department I
> made no decisions whereas inside it I made them all. . . When
> I became HoF I was much more a manager. I had to deal with
> local government unions, implement county policy, budget, deal
> with auditors etc.

The nominated faculty heads were generally able to take an objective
look at the departments in their care and evaluate them, conscious of
their strengths and weaknesses and aware of the balance that had to
be maintained between them. Previously, they had had to do these
things with people within one department – now, they were considering larger units (the departments: groups of people) and letting the
individual heads of department deal with more detailed matters with
the individuals.

The difficulties encountered by heads of department and faculty in
carrying out their responsibilities will be discussed in Chapter 4 – some
of them are, indeed, implicit in the descriptions of their working lives
(lack of time, inaccessibility of telephones and shortage of ancillary
assistance, for example).

Similarly, training for middle management is explored at a later
stage. However, from an analysis of what heads of department actually
do, it would seem that they need both a general awareness of what
the role involves and a more detailed, school-specific understanding.
The former is necessary in order that practitioners' vision is not
distorted by the particular concerns of the school; the latter, so
that they have a guide to their day-to-day life and some basis
for an evaluation of what they are doing. Data collected in the
study suggest that very often practitioners have not thought clearly
about what the role involves in general; and it would seem that
there is some confusion as to the boundaries of roles
in schools.

Summary and discussion

An attempt has been made to provide an overview of the middle manager's role by analysing the NFER case study data and by referring to the existing literature. The focus has been primarily descriptive although an analytical model of the role was presented. The observational data and the diaries gave insights into the day-to-day lives of department and faculty heads and described some of the many activities undertaken. Their work, like that of their senior management counterparts, tended to be characterized by fragmentation and involved them in a myriad of social interactions with both adults and pupils. Department and faculty heads were 'busy' people and tasks that involved long uninterrupted spells invariably had to be undertaken at home. Although a typical day was very full, little time was found for planning, evaluating, reflecting or observing colleagues; crisis management appeared to be much more the norm. Middle managers spoke of the difficulties and stresses of doing so many different activities at the same time, and of the need to have a 'grasshopper mind'. Reference was also made to the frustrations associated with appearing never to complete the job – there were always matters pending.

Various authors have attempted an analysis of the department head's role, which is generally seen as of great importance, with the incumbent acting as the key link between senior staff and classroom teachers. The role's importance and pivotal nature was reflected in the NFER research by the use of such terms as 'boiler house', 'engine room' and 'hub of the school' and there was agreement that the department head was central to the quality of the learning process and what went on in classrooms. The head of department's areas of responsibility have been categorized in a number of ways but the diagrammatic model presented (Figure 2.1) – which draws heavily on the earlier work of Edwards (1985) – tried to demonstrate the interaction of tasks and functions as reflected in the reality of department headship and as shown by the observational data.

It was noted that the complexity of the role was often not reflected in conventional role analyses or job descriptions. The latter were found to vary in terms of their presentation and the most accessible tried to put the job in context, delineate task groupings and give particular attention to the notion of team leadership. Job descriptions were thought to be useful in that they enabled practitioners to gain an understanding of what their role entailed – a key factor when it was suggested that lack of clarity and uncertainty were perhaps the biggest barriers to more effective departmental functioning. They were also helpful in that they enabled teachers to see their role in the total management structure of the school; the school's expectations were made clear and headteachers were encouraged to see the school's management as a shared responsibility. Job descriptions are likely to be given greater importance as appraisal schemes become more common and, since the time of the research, the 1987 Teachers' Conditions of Service Act has delineated, in detail, the professional duties of heads, deputies and teachers. In effect, these are job descriptions but it is not clear at the time of writing how these will be used by schools.

The magnitude of the head of department's job became clearer when it was realized that, unlike their senior colleagues, middle managers had few non-contact or 'free' periods in which to undertake their allocated duties and responsibilities. The few that they did have were also likely to be reduced by the need to cover for absent colleagues. On the basis of time allocation, middle managers were, therefore, primarily teachers: the extent to which they conceived of themselves in similar terms was clearly central to the effective performance of the *management* role. How department heads 'managed' also depended upon the assumptions they held about what constituted 'management'. The interview data presented seemed to suggest that there was some confusion over boundaries between roles and, as will be later discussed, there was a reluctance on the part of some to accept their responsibilities as managers; indeed, examples were given where senior managers had not encouraged this. As might be expected, heads of faculty were less likely to hold limited conceptions of their managerial functions. However, it was clear that there is a need for training for all parties on the management role of the head of department. More specifically, there is a need for a general and wide-ranging understanding of its nature and for a more detailed, school-specific understanding in order to guide actual performance and encourage critical self-reflection and evaluation.

3 What Constitutes Effective Practice?

This chapter provides a general overview of the various characteristics of effective practice as perceived by those involved in the NFER research. Particular attention is given to the attributes and qualities that were commonly seen as contributing towards 'good' department headship and departmental practice. This chapter, as of necessity, is wide-ranging but it is planned to explore specific areas in greater detail at a later stage.

Any attempt to delineate 'effective' practice, be it lodged in an individual head of department or in a department, is a precarious business: on the one hand, it begs the question as to the criteria for applying the epithet; on the other, it admits the danger of laying down a blueprint. Effectiveness is, clearly, context-related and determined by the situation. Indeed, in order to talk sensibly about 'effective' department heads, it is necessary to go through the logically prior stages of identifying not only what the role of the head of department presently entails, in terms of responsibilities and tasks, but also what the expectations of others are regarding the role, how individual practitioners interpret the role and how organizations allow the role to be implemented. Having a job description is one thing: *how* it is realized is another. Two people may fulfil their obligations in principle, but in vastly different ways, the gap between them having not a little to do with identifying 'effectiveness'. Heads of department are only effective insofar as they enable certain things to come about and certain aims to be realized – desired outcomes often being largely fixed by factors outside the head of department's control and, of course, varying according to individual schools and LEAs. The efficient head of department is not necessarily the same as the effective head of department. An LEA adviser remarked:

Someone can create the idea that the department is good

by getting themselves into a lot of things, being prompt
with administration and reports, and interacting noticeably with
senior staff. But this sort of departmental head can be inflexible
and unwilling to respond to others' ideas; they think that they
know best.

Chapter 1 has briefly outlined the history of the role and the major
change that has come about since the reorganization of schools along
comprehensive lines. It is thus clear that the effective post-holder
of pre-reorganization days would not necessarily be the effective
post-holder in a large comprehensive school today, for different skills
are required and there are new criteria for evaluation. As a broad
definition, it might be assumed that the effective head of department
is someone who is aware of the demands that the role makes and
either has, or is developing, the necessary skills and strategies to meet
these. Effective department heads are not simply nominal leaders with
designated responsibilities for other adults but, rather, leaders with
earned status and authority.

When, in phase two of the research, the heads of department
recommended as being 'good' or effective were being studied, a
variety of practice was found – both by way of the different styles
of those carrying out the role and the various stages of development
that each had reached. Each school, each department has its own
history and, indeed, its own future: were one of the 'good' departments visited today, it might well be that the accolade would have to
be withdrawn.

Effectiveness is a continuous process rather than a pinnacle of
achievement – something which is realized organically by the
'good' departments in their concern, for example, with curriculum
development, review and evaluation (see Chapters 7 and 8). However,
paragons of virtue were not being sought, for it is doubtful whether
such exist! There is a corpus of literature on 'how to do it' but with
a few exceptions, it lacks an empirical base. The NFER research
was essentially concerned with looking at the actual practitioners in
particular schools to see how they reacted in those situations which,
though emerging from a particular history and thus unique, are, nevertheless, relatable to many other cases.

The pivotal position of the head of department as middle manager
has often been referred to (for example, see Marland, 1971). One
of its consequences is that the department head has to meet the
expectations of LEA advisers (some of whom, by virtue of their own
experience and background are still very subject-orientated, although
others, especially those with pastoral responsibility for a whole
school, are aware of the subject department's interaction in the

school), headteachers and the whole range of departmental members – probationers and experienced teachers, full-time and part-time staff and so forth. In addition, there are the expectations of parents, the community and the government. However, it did appear that there was a large degree of consensus amongst the NFER respondents regarding expectations. Before the features of effective department practices are considered thematically, consideration will be given to specific matters raised by senior staff in schools and LEAs.

The expectations of LEA advisers

In each of the selected LEAs, advisers and inspectors were interviewed. How did they recognize the effective department as they visited schools? Many spoke of the quality of relationships between pupils and staff, and the pupils' attitudes to the subject – were they 'happy' and was there a 'buzz' in the atmosphere? Management, said one adviser, was 'the infrastructure that facilitates the quality of the pupil's experience'. The effective department had a sure set of aims and its policy and practice were clearly laid down – the scheme of work was a working document, material for reflecting on, which provided both questions and answers and allowed newcomers to appreciate what the department was trying to do. High standards were demanded of both pupils and staff and there was no complacency. The curriculum was regularly reviewed and sensibly paced. Wall displays and notice boards gave visual clues. Less tangibly, the effective department was open and open to discussion – staff gave voice to tentative ideas and were not afraid of exposing weaknesses in front of colleagues.

The good head of department was a catalyst and inspirer; one who was not necessarily the best at everything – although credibility was lost if there was too great a disparity between the performance of the head of department and that of the staff. The effective department head deployed resources successfully, especially the human ones, developing the right atmosphere for people to grow, wanting others to become effective, and regarding INSET as central.

Putting the department in context, advisers thought that effective departments contributed to school aims and explored cross-curricular issues. Good departments benefited from, but did not depend on, a supportive environment in the school – they could retreat within themselves (though, obviously, this was to the detriment of the school as a whole). It was possible – though not desirable – to have an effective department with a poor department head: for example, in cases where the head of department was incapable of initiating anything but would not block those who did.

The expectations of senior staff

What did heads and deputies look for in their middle managers? What criteria were used to identify a successful department or faculty? Open-ended questions were asked and it was not thought appropriate to draw up a list of desired qualities and skills and ask respondents to comment or place them in rank order. Some people clearly had 'an ideal type' in mind, while others were obviously scanning the relevant people in their schools.

A few senior managers started with the effect of department heads on the pupils and it is, perhaps, not inappropriate to mention these first in order to bring to the fore the very obvious fact that schools exist for the education of pupils and that it is for their benefit that it is deemed important that heads of department have, for example, appropriate management skills.

Senior staff remarked:

> HoDs must structure things to make things easier for the children, which is really what it is all about.

> The most important aspect of all our jobs is doing the best for the pupils – to ensure that they not only enjoy learning but do actually learn.

> I want to know if pupils have developed as a consequence of lessons.

Pupils' enthusiasm for a subject and fourth year option take-up were frequently cited as reliable, if somewhat crude, benchmarks for determining departmental effectiveness or success. Examination results should be 'satisfactory' (gauged by the ability of the pupils and their performance in other areas).

That heads and deputies did not immediately speak of the head of department's classroom skills did not indicate lack of importance attached to this area: rather, it was taken for granted. It was assumed that heads of department had good classroom management and up-to-date knowledge of developments in the subject and senior managers were looking for particular additional skills by way of team leadership and 'helicopter vision'.

Heads of department were seen to have a maintenance function: 'HoDs must keep staff's eyes on classroom performance . . . teachers are easily distracted . . . they may see teaching as incidental to, for example, pastoral care.' One head quoted a statement, borrowed from HMI, which he had included in his head of department job specification: 'The head of department should show by his/her attitude/approach that there is a worthwhile job to be done and that its accomplishment is possible.'

The maintenance function of heads of department, according to senior staff, extended to trouble-shooting and problem-solving as regards the day-to-day running. Indeed, one middle manager remarked (referring to dealing with difficult parents):

> An important aspect of the job is to take the heat off my staff. I am paid to take the flack. I don't mean this in a patronising way. What I mean is that I am there to do that job so that they can get on with their jobs more effectively.

The heads of the case study schools all expected their middle managers to be pro-, rather than reactive: 'can do' rather than 'wait and see' people, as one head put it. Heads of department were expected to have both breadth of vision – seeing their subject and department in the context of whole-school issues – and foresight, so that they were open to, and prepared for, change. 'The effective HoD can spot where there's scope for development, both in terms of course content and in terms of personnel development.' 'Nothing runs well if it stands still.' The maintainer who has 'to keep the wheels turning' must also be the source of propulsion 'to ensure things roll forward'. Senior staff commented that (in some circumstances) they had to be seen to tolerate change which failed so that heads of department did not feel that they had to 'play safe'.

Some headteachers liked the fighting spirit shown by department heads and spoke with warmth of 'the one who comes into my office and bangs his fist on my desk and says what he wants'. A head remarked that he did not appoint 'yes men' (or women) as middle managers – he wanted complementary ideas, and a deputy said that department heads 'must be prepared to talk about their beliefs which may differ from those of the head or deputies'. A second-in-command of one of the recommended departments commented wryly: 'Quite honestly, if the HoD wants something, the head does not stand a chance!'

Senior staff liked being 'pestered' and associated it with the effective head of department, provided that the issue was sufficiently significant and reasonable in the light of the school context. One head of department – most certainly effective within the department and extremely conscientious as regards implementing school policies (e.g. individualized learning, multiculturalism) but, as yet, 'narrow-minded' and in need of intellectual development – was censured by a deputy for forever sending petty little memos. And a head criticized another recommended practitioner, who as yet lacked maturity because: 'He keeps pressurizing me for more capitation. He carries on about "curriculum innovation" but fails to realize that it is dependent on limited available resources.'

Some specific qualities of effective department heads will now be examined by reference to comments made by staff at all levels.

Team leadership

The overriding attribute of effective heads of department, referred to in the ideal post-holder and, invariably, in the particular individuals studied, was team leadership. Headteachers essentially regarded department heads as facilitators. Frequently, heads of department were excused being weak administrators or ill-equipped to teach 'A' level on the grounds that 'what you get out of others is more important than what you do yourself.'

A deputy observed: 'The department itself is very competent although I don't think that it is outstanding, so all credit to the HoD that things operate as well as they do.' Middle managers had to maximize the talents of the staff in the department and a deputy remarked: 'The longer I go on teaching, the more I realize how vast is the gap between the minimum that people can do and the maximum that you can get out of them.' A head was uncompromising: 'If it proves impossible to channel the staff's energies, the HoD has failed.' Such sentiments are, of course, entirely in concordance with recent HMI thinking and the leadership theory which contends that good leaders can transform their followers.

Departmental staff were not slow in picking up this particular characteristic: 'He acts as a catalyst and generates ideas from us.' 'He has incredible energy and dedication and it rubs off on us.' Frequently, there was reference to the necessity of welding together a group of individual teachers into a team and the realization of this is, perhaps, the hallmark of the truly effective department. How it is done, of course, bears further investigation and will be explored in a later chapter.

Personality

Generally, it is true to say that it was more *what* effective heads of department did, than what they themselves *were* in terms of personality, that was the decisive factor. Clearly, the two things cannot be divorced and the insecure isolate is, perhaps, psychologically unable to do the things (hold open discussions, delegate responsibility, share ideas) that seem to be widely practised in the most effective departments. Advisers and senior staff interviewed mentioned personality traits (such as 'rounded personality' or 'sense of humour') but chiefly focused on skills and strategies; whereas departmental staff frequently described the sort of person they held to be the good head of department. Interestingly, the list of all the individual qualities mentioned by those interviewed (see Table 3.1) bears close resemblance to the desired attributes of headteachers found in previous NFER research (Weindling and Earley, 1987). And, indeed, it is suggested that the qualities are those which anyone would choose to see in a colleague. It may be that it is more important that they are evident in the team leader but they are not, it could be argued, in any way peculiar to the role of the department head. Marland (1986) has recently stated that school management 'requires intelligence, imagination, energy, warmth of personality, humility and persistence', adding that 'these and other human qualities can probably not be learned from books, but many aspects of the task can be thought out in advance and the skills prepared for'.

Undue emphasis on personality traits necessary for leadership is, as management theorists have pointed out (Handy, 1981), not particularly useful or constructive, for people largely have them or they do not and, even if they are crucial, then there is relatively little that can be achieved by way of training or professional development. Nevertheless, perhaps it ought to be mentioned that nearly all the recommended practitioners were friendly, accessible people and 'we all get on very well together' was a recurring comment from nearly all the departments researched in phase two. This was, indeed, borne out by the researchers' observations in departments, attendance at meetings, and so forth. It goes without saying that there were some clashes of personality within the nominated departments and these often constituted problems for the head of department but only in one instance was the relationship between the head of department and a 'rival' having a deleterious effect on the operation of the team.

Management style

Specific questions were not asked about 'management style' or style of leadership and there were almost no references to theory in the interviews. Indeed, theoretically, most of the effective heads of department seemed to adopt – unconsciously – a 'best fit' approach. To a certain extent, subject disciplines and their associated organizational constraints dictated style. The head of science, for example, has to ensure that resources and equipment are efficiently utilized; technicians have to know what is required when and where; and there is little leeway when equipment is limited and budgets for chemicals tight. Science teachers are, generally, accustomed to 'taking lessons off the shelf'

Table 3.1: *Effective departments and department heads*

The effective head of department	The effective department
Qualities	*General ethos*
Warm; approachable; enthusiastic; 'rounded'; balanced; tactful and diplomatic; dynamic; strong but not authoritarian; prepared to make decisions; able to inspire, motivate and get people working as a team; ready to praise and show appreciation; able to criticize positively, without giving offence; able to recognize, analyse and come to terms with failure; open to change – has eye for development; clear thinker.	The staff have a sense of group spirit; support each other; are keen to develop and improve; volunteer for extra responsibilities. The pupils enjoy going to lessons and do not want to miss them.
Well informed in subject area; well qualified; first-class practitioner and able to lead by example.	*In the classroom* Clear expectations; good discipline and behaviour; appropriate and up-to-date methods and materials; high quality of work; positive relationships; pupils actively participate; provision for all abilities.
Behaviour Formalizes structures – does not assume that things will happen. Promotes a positive image and the needs of the department within the school. Ensures that good practice is not isolated. Ensures that career avenues do not stagnate. Allocates rooms, groups and resources fairly and efficiently. Establishes a 'house style' for the department. Ensures that communication is good. Cooperates with other departments. Represents the department to senior management – and vice versa. Delegates; gives adequate time for the performance of tasks. Involves all departmental members, including part-timers and non-specialists. Controls meetings effectively.	*Management* Efficient response to administrative requirements; regular meetings to discuss educational issues; effective channel of communication; reciprocal observation; appraisal and self-assessment; identification and satisfaction of INSET needs.

and teaching to a tightly constructed schedule: it is, indeed, in their interests, and in the interests of the department as a whole, that they do so, and it is a contributory factor in their department's effectiveness. Other departments followed coursebooks which set a framework yet allowed for individual inputs, while others had very broad schemes of work within which teachers had considerable flexibility.

It was only very rarely that department heads themselves reflected on their style and then it was very much on the lines of 'If I have a style, I suppose it's . . ... It was recognized that in order to achieve objectives, things had to be done in a certain way. Headteachers would very often compare their middle managers, especially in phase two when they were asked to comment on the strengths of the individuals proposed by the advisers. The researchers never invited any sort of 'ranking' for, as has been stated before, the intention was to collect a variety of examples of good practice; interestingly, however, no head ever attempted to offer a ranking – not, probably, on account of professional scruples (the interviewees were very open and, of course, research confidentiality was assured) but because they were so aware of the *different* strengths of the people being studied. One head, for example, categorized the three recommended heads of department in his school as 'the laid-back bookish waffler', 'the practitioner' and 'the moderate and reasonable'. This same head also mentioned additional effective practitioners from within the school – not recommended as their respective subject advisers had not been interviewed – each of whom had further strengths and was being effective in context.

The research thus confirmed what might have been expected, that there is no one preferred style for all occasions. This accords with research on heads and principals which concludes that at this level of management there is also a great variety of successful styles (Rutter *et al.*, 1979; Manasse, 1985). Indeed, part of effectiveness seemed to be the selection of the appropriate style – of knowing when an issue should be discussed in depth by the whole department; or when it was a matter solely for the head of department. In addition, of course, different individuals have different needs as regards support and direction.

What all the phase two recommended department heads did was to discuss, to involve all departmental members (including part-timers), keep staff informed and give reasons for decisions. Involvement in discussion is a key factor in curriculum and staff development – another hallmark of the successful department – but primarily it was seen as a means of team-building. (See Chapter 9 for a further discussion of many of the points raised in this section.)

Accessibility and proximity

Effective heads of department were 'around'. To a certain extent whether or not the department had a suite of rooms and a departmental office was often out of the control of the head of department. Geographical location matters enormously and research has shown that physical barriers can hinder the formation of groups (Handy, 1981). A deputy head, ex-head of faculty, told the story of how he had removed a large table from the centre of the faculty office. Before he had done this, the teachers sat around in departmental clusters; after, they began to mix and the faculty consciousness began to form. It could be argued that the effective head of department successfully negotiates the right conditions and helps create them. A headteacher admitted that he gave inferior teaching accommodation to one department as he knew that he could not to another as the department head (a phase two nominee) would have none of it. Several heads of department had created departmental rooms, obtained easy chairs, kettles and so forth in order to create a focal point. Many were hardly the lap of luxury and the purpose-built were rare, but they provided somewhere for the department to meet over coffee.

'We meet all the time informally' was another common theme in phase two departments and faculties and such statements were substantiated by the researchers' observations. Interestingly, with one exception, all the departments studied in phase two had offices and were happy, friendly places where the middle manager was very much a key figure. As one teacher remarked:

> The office is very crowded and you can't have disagreements for long because they are just snuffed out. There is never any sourness between two people because the other members of the department just won't let it get to this stage.

Teachers often made the point that though the department got on very well socially, there was always a lot of professional discussion in the department offices. Some teachers were able to contrast this with experiences in other schools:

> There's a big difference in this department compared with that at my old school where there was no interest in the subject itself and all we talked about was gossip or what had happened at the weekend. Here, everyone talks about professional matters. . .
> No, I do not think that it is necessarily the influence of the school – it is the department.

In contrast, the following observation was made by a teacher in one of the phase one schools (split, on three sites):

You can go weeks without seeing a member of the department unless you make a point of seeking them out. The HoD doesn't come into block A at all and only goes into block B at lunchtimes – to have sandwiches, not to discuss anything; otherwise he keeps to block C.

The effective heads of department did their utmost to overcome the problems arising in split-site schools: one made a point of going over in her non-contact time to a portacabin a few minutes' walk away in order to see one of her staff based there 'because otherwise she can feel very isolated'.

Middle managers were aware of the danger of departments becoming isolated from the main staffroom but felt the advantages of gathering together outweighed the disadvantages. In subject areas reliant on ancillary help – for example, science and home economics – there was the added advantage that the technicians could be included if the team met in the department. Without exception, the ancillary staff interviewed in phase two spoke warmly of the way that they had been included in the department and were treated as people with a very real contribution to make: 'The pupils treat us all the same and will go to anyone, including the technician, for advice. . . . we all muck in when there is a crisis.'

One nominated department was an exemplar of how diverse experience and talents could be welded into a team, with the head of department including specialist and non-specialist teachers, welfare assistants and ancillary helpers in all decisions (see Chapter 7).

Some heads of department and faculty made it their business to spend time in the main staffroom to maintain contacts and keep up a profile but, again, school design and tradition were often decisive factors. One school had no central staffroom – teachers went either to departmental or house bases; another had three staffrooms in each of three blocks, each with its residents who hardly recognized colleagues from other sites; other staffrooms were overcrowded at morning break, empty at other times. All this has implications for departmental management: not only for inter-, but also for intradepartmental liaison. At the time of the research there was an increasing emphasis within schools on cross-curricular links and multidisciplinary courses and it was therefore important for departments to have opportunities to meet and get to know others as well as forging their own identities. This would seem to be an area relatively neglected: frequently, too little is known of what goes on elsewhere in the school at anything below deputy level. In those instances when departments had held open days or mounted special exhibitions, teachers remarked that their colleagues had said: 'Oh, I didn't know that you did that sort of thing in your department.'

Communication

It was suggested by senior staff that effective departments were marked by a lot of informal contact. Heads of department were, however, aware of the need for formal meetings where appropriate, especially in situations where there were part-time teachers who might otherwise be left out. One observed that: 'There is a danger that the people constantly chatting in the department office represent the department.' And it was, in fact, a teacher from this department who admitted that: 'I tend to think of the department as being the six of us who are full-time in it and always around.'

Such awareness on the part of the effective heads of department obviously comes under the general matter of 'communication'. Often, 'must be a good communicator' was given in answer to the question 'What are the qualities of a good head of department?' but perceptions were largely limited to interpersonal skills. Effective middle managers were, consciously or unconsciously, aware that communication is a two-way process and that the message must be seen to be received rather than just sent. Teachers spoke of experiences in other schools where middle managers operated on the strength of memos issued from an isolated office. With the effective practitioners, however, not only was the openness of the channels apparent from the researchers' observations (particularly on the 'shadowing' days), but also, departmental staff invariably said that they knew what was going on; heads of department were scrupulous about reporting back from middle management meetings, interviews with senior staff or external visitors and were very aware of their representative function here. As pointed out earlier, the research took place during extended periods of industrial action and some of the case study schools were very hard hit by this. The phase two recommended practitioners chiefly kept their departments going by personal contacts during this time.

Consultation

Being made to feel part of a team was something very much valued by the staff within effective departments; teachers frequently compared their present experiences with previous ones in other schools. Young staff and probationers appreciated their opinions being sought: one commented that she stopped feeling like a student the day her head of department said to her, 'What do you think?' In all the recommended departments, staff felt that they had opportunities to make their feelings known and were not afraid to speak out. They also felt that their department head listened, was 'reasonable' and ready to amend his or her own opinions. This was in marked contrast to the feelings commonly held by teachers about their participation in the decision-making of the school as a whole: in this area, teachers frequently felt that, though usually given a voice, their views were often not taken account of.

In the effective departments, a lot of attention was given to meetings and working parties: it was not unusual for the department to meet at the head of department's house for an evening in a week or during the holidays. Never was this resented, largely because the meetings were well run and staff felt that something positive had been accomplished: the 'good' departments did not have meetings for the sake of them.

Support of new teachers

The effective heads of department gave staff practical and moral support. Again, anecdotes were substantiated by the researchers' observations. A young teacher remarked of her department head: 'I have free access to her resources: her Aladdin's cave is never locked.' The good head of department 'makes it clear that knowledge of the subject area is not assumed and makes the staff feel at ease in ignorance'. This was particularly important with young teachers to whom the head of department needs to be particularly sensitive. In some cases, the probationer, straight from university and initial teacher training, may have knowledge and expertise to give and teach the head of department (and the effective department head utilizes, rather than feels threatened by, this); in other cases, young teachers may find themselves teaching something which they have not studied (a physicist teaching biology in integrated science; a geographer, history in integrated humanities; an English specialist teaching a period of literature not previously read). The head of department clearly has to give the right support and advice here – or ensure that it is given by someone. There was evidence that less experienced teachers conceived of their head of department in 'subject-expert' terms and very much identified with the subject culture.

Probationers and young teachers were particularly concerned with discipline and the majority of those interviewed cited 'helps with discipline' as something they expected of the 'good' head of department. Here, again, the department head was thought of as the 'super-professional'. The phase two nominees were all regarded as supportive in this respect and a large proportion of departments studied dealt with their own discipline problems, rather than passing them to pastoral heads. Senior staff, when asked how they would recognize an effective department, often cited 'absence of referrals' as an indicator. Middle managers often held departmental detentions which, because of the team spirit engendered, were respected by the departmental staff. A teacher, who had recently completed probation, noted:

> We have similar views on discipline. It is not like this in other departments. For example, a friend of mine works in a department where one member of staff will not stay behind for detentions and so the kids know that they can play fast and loose with this teacher and it doesn't matter if he gives them detentions because they won't have to do them.

In contrast to this is the comment:

> If anyone, for example a new member of staff, has a problem, then they always know that there are about three teachers in the office who will immediately come out and back them up . . . kids can't play one teacher off against the other in this department.

Probationers' expectations of the head of department were very much to do with helping them to survive their early months of teaching – providing disciplinary back-up, generating ideas, planning the pace of the syllabus and so forth. Interestingly, they had not often been prepared, in initial teacher training, to expect anything of heads of department and had not considered the role. Supervision of probationers and students was a common feature of job descriptions and the literature overwhelmingly points to the importance of the head of department here (for example, Kerry, 1982). The nominees took their responsibilities seriously, frequently setting aside a regular weekly time – perhaps off-site, in order to get some peace! – to meet with probationers individually. Clearly, some departments had more probationers than others – in more remote parts of the country, probationers were a rare breed and teaching-practice students non-existent. The effective departments in city schools generally had a good supply of students – a further indication of the esteem in which they were held by teacher-training institutions.

Support of the recently trained is part of general staff development, which will be considered in greater depth in Chapter 6, but teachers spoke of previous schools where they were not given support or guidance in their early months in the profession. A teacher in a recommended department spoke of the fact that a probationer had 'failed' and left the profession during a time when the head of department was away on secondment and the second-in-command was acting in his place; the teacher commented that this failure would not have happened if the 'good' head of department had been at school. Similarly a head commended a new young head of department, a phase two nominee, for transforming two teachers previously regarded as 'failures'.

There were two parallel cases of nominated department heads who each supervised a student and a probationer. In both cases, under their guidance the students had been so successful that they had been offered appointments in the department. The probationers had also flourished (they had, for example, been the departmental representative for subject association conferences and exciting authority initiatives and were very grateful for this). Interestingly, both the heads of department had just been seconded to implement authority-wide initiatives and both were planning to return to school to continue their work with the two young teachers.

Administration

Most teachers wanted heads of department to be good organizers. Again, this was something infrequently remarked upon by senior staff who *assumed* that there would be good organization within the department as the management of capitation and administration affected the middle manager's facilitating role which was regarded so highly. Teachers appreciated having ready access to resources and 'banks' of worksheets, etc. It was not the organization *per se* that was important: ineffective departments can be well organized in administrative terms. Rather, it was the fact that the group was working together as a team, sharing ideas, involved with the scheme of work and clear as to objectives that made the pooling and organization of resources obvious and inevitable. There was the recognition that there was mutual benefit in cooperation. Teachers in some of the less developed departments visited in phase one spoke of isolated departmental members preparing their own worksheets and 'reinventing the wheel'. As regards resources, the departments with an office and a suite of rooms were clearly in a privileged position in comparison with those geographically scattered, as materials were much more accessible and teachers could be much more flexible as regards lesson materials.

Staff respected heads of department for sharing teaching across the range of ages and abilities. Occasionally, on split-site campuses, for example, this was not always possible, but certainly all the recommended practitioners took their fair share of the less able and the 'difficult' groups. And though this may seem well-established 'good practice' the researchers were given ample evidence that it is not always the case. Teachers' comments were paralleled by those of advisers, who spoke of schools where 'heads of department hogged all the 'A' level work' or gave prestigious groups to their favoured colleagues (nepotism was not absent!) and where 'you worked your way up from the bottom groups and when you reached the top you squabbled'. The motive of the effective department heads, apart from 'fairness', was to lead by example and share experiences; they frequently spoke of being loath to ask anyone else to do something that they would not do themselves. They had none of the arrogance of a middle manager encountered during phase one of the fieldwork who said: 'I am the HoD. I am the best teacher. Therefore all pupils should have the benefit of me teaching them.' (There were, of course, instances where the head of department was one of the few specialists qualified to do higher level work and thus, of necessity, had a timetable biased towards upper-school teaching. This happened, for example, in some maths departments – see also Straker, 1987.)

Ethos

The effective departments involved in the research gave a sense of security to all those involved in them. It was remarked that in a good department the pupils know what is going on. Similarly, staff in such departments knew what was going on, not only in terms of the 'diary of events', the result of meetings, whole-school issues and so forth, but also professionally, in terms of the boundaries of responsibility within the department and of what the work of the department represented. As regards the latter, all the effective departments had schemes of work or were currently developing them. In itself this was not particularly significant: many ineffective departments have schemes of work; discussion of them is a regular feature on middle management courses and they are frequently demanded by schools. Their significance lay in the fact that they were 'owned' by the department. A head remarked: 'A department's scheme of work should embody all the discussions that have taken place within the department' and this was borne out in the case of the recommended practitioners. 'There's a house style in the department and this reflects a general consensus about what the subject teaching involves.' 'A scheme of work is an instrument for making people think what they're doing.'

Although in no way an accurate indication of general effectiveness, the personal testimony of individuals working under recommended heads of department cannot be ignored. Sometimes, admittedly, middle managers took time to get to know and were superficially off-putting, perhaps because their standards were so high as, for example: 'He's very rigorous in terms of the standards he sets for pupils and staff. He can be very hard to live up to and I sometimes wonder if he allows others to flourish and surface easily.' However, more common were such comments as:

I will miss him dreadfully when he goes.

I've never worked with anyone as supportive, enthusiastic and interested in innovation and getting things right as the present HoD.

The HoD is widely respected by the governors, the senior management team and the rest of the staff. I suppose we bask in her reflected glory.

Summary and discussion

Effectiveness is an elusive concept but it has been used in this chapter in a broad sense to refer to practices that enable certain desired outcomes to be achieved. An effective middle manager was therefore someone who was aware of what the job entailed in its entirety and had, or was developing, the requisite skills and strategies. Effectiveness has, however, to be seen as an on-going process – something that has to be continually worked at by both middle managers and their staff. Reference has been made to effective departments and effective heads of department: there is no guarantee, however, that the two necessarily go together. They are likely to be associated but, as some NFER respondents noted, it was possible, although rare, to have a 'good' department with a relatively ineffective nominal head, if that department consisted of talented individual teachers and a strong second-in-charge. Furthermore, department heads' weaknesses or limitations could be overcome in other ways. For example, not being an 'ideas' person or an initiator did not necessarily matter so long as suggestions emanated from somewhere and the department head was not 'blocking' and preventing initiatives from being implemented. Of course, the overall level of effectiveness was likely to be considerably enhanced and the department's performance improved, if the necessary leadership was demonstrated in all areas.

By drawing on the data derived from interviews with senior staff, advisers and teachers, an attempt has been made to examine the department head's role in terms of the varying expectations held. There appeared to be a considerable degree of consensus, especially from headteachers and advisers, who both pointed to the importance of the curriculum that was offered to the pupils and the quality of relationships between teachers and taught. Essential criteria for effective departments and their leaders included whether or not children were engaged in purposeful activity and if there was a positive attitude to the subject. Effective departments were also identified by means of other 'performance indicators' such as option take-up, the absence of discipline referrals and, perhaps unsurprisingly, examination results. The latter were usually judged in relation to the pupils' ability and their performance in other subjects.

Effective departments had, under the purposeful leadership of their heads, drawn up a set of generally agreed aims and objectives which were consistent with those of the school and which were reflected in carefully thought out and constructed schemes of work. It was taken for granted that department heads would be good class-room practitioners, up to date with recent educational developments and sufficiently good administrators and organizers to ensure that the department functioned smoothly. Higher level skills required included the ability to encourage and motivate staff and to facilitate desired change. Effective department heads and their staffs were never complacent, wanting to improve practice by constantly reviewing what was being offered. Effective departments did not stand still but continued to develop.

It was the ability to create a team that was often perceived as the most significant attribute of a middle manager. What the leader was able to get out of other members of the team was often identified by senior staff as the critical factor. Teachers within effective departments felt secure, freely expressed opinions, constructively criticized each other's practices and were not reluctant to admit possible weaknesses. Effective department heads were able to create the sort of climate or ethos in which people – and the curriculum – could develop. This, and the sense of belonging to a team, was likely to be enhanced if the department was fortunate enough to have a suite of rooms, or possess an office or staffroom. Considerable formal and informal contact with team members was important, thus ensuring all matters of significance were communicated and that all departmental staff – including ancillary staff – were fully consulted and their views sought. The head of department's ability to offer support, to listen and be prepared to change opinions were key factors as far as departmental staff were concerned.

A composite profile of desired attributes and features of depart-ments and department heads has been presented and provides a useful summary of the range of qualities needed. This largely concurs with other research into desired managerial attributes and shows the type of leadership style more favoured. It has been suggested, and this is again supported by research findings, that the most effective managers were those who were flexible and able to match their style to the occasion, the issue faced and the staff involved. There was no one management style for all situations.

In broader terms, effective departments contributed to school aims and explored cross-curricular issues; effective department heads were seen as team leaders and were expected to have a vision that went beyond the confines of a subject area or department. Senior staff considered that this 'helicopter vision' was desirable in department heads but imperative in faculty heads. Many of the characteristics of effective departments and effective practitioners identified in the NFER study are confirmed in HMI's appraisal of secondary schools (GB.DES, 1988b).

Little has been said so far as regards heads of faculty – the focus of the chapter has been very much on effective departments and heads of department. But what of heads of faculty? Do they require different attributes or are they just heads of department writ large? Perhaps it should be mentioned that the reality if not the *raison d'être* of many faculties was administrative rather than curricular and respondents spoke of middle managers being heads of faculty in name only – perhaps an extra scale point had been given 'to persuade a good physicist to stay', for example. Generally, however, faculty heads were 'developed' department heads even if they were not fully aware of what the role of the head of faculty could embrace. Whereas a teacher who seemed to be full of ideas (ripe for development) and have lots of potential, but was inexperienced on the management side, might be appointed to a department headship, heads of faculty were expected to have proved themselves as heads of department and have a good track record of managing people and programmes.

Headteachers often liked having another layer of management so that they could incorporate faculty heads into the senior management team and thus overcome the problem of unwieldy middle-management meetings which included 'one-person' departments alongside larger units such as science and English. Because they were regarded as 'senior' middle managers, faculty heads were expected to have a whole-school perspective and be able to take on board wider educational issues. Although, as noted above, this was considered *desirable* in heads of department and the effective practitioners generally showed such awareness, headteachers were conscious that many department heads were very subject-bound and compartmentalized and this had to be accepted: it could not be accepted for heads of faculty, however. Faculty heads had to balance departmental interests even when they were also heads of department and not 'free-standing' heads of faculty.

The issue of faculty structures is explored in more detail in Chapter 10. This chapter, in attempting to give a broad picture of what was commonly perceived as effective practice has, of necessity, been rather general and wide-ranging. Specific areas of responsibility associated with the role of the department or faculty head are pursued in more detail in subsequent chapters. Before proceeding to consider these key areas, however, it is intended to outline some of the difficulties and constraints under which middle managers operate.

4 *What Difficulties are Faced?*

As was stated in the previous chapter, one of senior management's requirements of middle managers was that they should be able to cope with problems. However accommodating the structures and however efficient the administration, heads of department whatever their degree of effectiveness are bound to encounter constraints and difficulties. The NFER research was interested in what these were perceived to be and, perhaps more importantly, how the department and faculty heads coped with them.

The project was not designed so that respondents were presented with a checklist or asked to remark on specific concerns; rather, open-ended questions asked heads of department and faculty to comment on what they saw as the most difficult aspects of their job and what were the chief constraints on the effective performance of the role. The phase two nominees were also asked to document several 'critical incidents' – particular problematic or difficult situations which they thought they had dealt with reasonably successfully. The following discussion presents these difficulties and constraints. In exploring such matters, it is hoped to be able to delineate strategies that can be related to, and used in, other situations, and also to make recommendations concerning ways in which not only could schools be more supportive but also the training needs of department and faculty heads be met more satisfactorily.

Difficulties and constraints

Time

It will come as no great revelation to report that the vast majority of the department and faculty heads interviewed – in phase one as

well as phase two – spoke of lack of time as a major constraint. All
teachers are, of course, hard pressed: how they spend their time will
be increasingly scrutinized now that the teachers' contract of 1265
hours per year has come into effect. Some heads of department were
sensitive to the pressure on their staff and their reluctance to delegate
was often occasioned by this awareness (see Chapter 6). A phase one
head of department, trying to use her department meetings for staff
development, remarked:

> Yes, I distribute discussion papers in advance but I know that
> the scale-one teachers don't have time to read them; they just
> skim them five minutes before the meeting. It's not that they are
> unwilling – they are just so busy.

Department heads were aware of the need for *all* teachers – not
just those with management responsibility – to have more time for
curriculum development, INSET, evaluation and reflection.

Heads of department had to take a lot of work home – many
spoke of this and there were some indications of domestic strain
and role conflict: 'My kids just think of me as the man who comes
home, has a meal and then retires to his room.' Frequently, in-trays,
'pending' files and piles of unmarked exercise books were referred to.
Heads of department generally accepted this as part of their job and
there was little resentment among those interviewed. However, many
practitioners were concerned about the lack of time while in school,
which precluded doing things which they felt would enhance the
effectiveness of their departments. Administration and marking can
often be done at home: talking to people and observing colleagues
teaching cannot. And, it was suggested, the former has more to
do with efficiency and the latter with effectiveness and school
and departmental improvement. (The value of observation and its
relation to evaluation and appraisal is discussed in greater depth in
Chapter 6.) Some middle managers wanted to do more observation
but were unable to on account of teaching commitments for, as has
been pointed out in an earlier chapter, they are primarily engaged in
teaching and are timetable rather than diary-bound. Heads of department involved in the research taught for between 65 and 85 per cent of
their timetable while the figure for heads of faculty was slightly lower.
What non-contact time they did have in school hours was frequently
encroached upon by visitors (e.g. OCEA and TVEI representatives, staff
from other schools in consortia, and NFER researchers!); by covering
for absent colleagues; by providing – albeit voluntarily – back-up disciplinary support services for the school; by 'shopping' – in the case
of CDT and home economics departments for example; and by innumerable and invaluable interpersonal contacts with pupils and staff.

The 'shadowing' days showed the plethora of activities that devour the (ill-named) 'free' periods on the timetable.

In common with management training generally, middle management courses often include sessions or modules on time management, and some practitioners, feeling their inadequacy over this, identified it as a major training need. However, there was the feeling that, on account of the nature of external factors, it was not, perhaps, a skill that overcame all problems. A head of faculty confessed:

> The LEA showed the John Cleese videos on Time Management and I found them very interesting. I used to sit down on a Sunday evening and prioritize my time but increasingly I'm not master of my own time because of the pressures from without and responses being continually demanded. So I do not do this prioritizing exercise any more. . . . I am forced to be reactive rather than proactive.

The escalating amount of paperwork was something that concerned the effective practitioners – again, not because of the extra stress that it imposed on them personally (although this ought not to be ignored) but because of the activities that it displaced. Heads of department were often given a short time in which to reply to school and LEA documents so they could not plan for these. Senior managers can, of course, be insensitive and unrealistic in demands but more often it seemed to be the combination of their demands, those of the LEA and those of the DES which caused the overload. Department and faculty heads have been accustomed to the chameleon nature of the school year and they were always at pains to point out – when being 'shadowed' – that no day or week was typical or representative: indeed, no one who has weathered a school year can be unaware of this. But, until fairly recently, the year has at least followed a pattern, so 'stock-taking' or 'option-choice time' could be planned for. Now, with increasing demands for such things as GRIST submissions, and participation in centralized initiatives – TVEI, the Lower-attaining Pupils Programme (LAPP), CPVE – often involving liaison with other agencies (e.g. the Training Agency) and new examination bodies, department heads' non-contact time was disappearing before they could apply themselves to strictly departmental concerns – observations, curriculum review etc. – let alone their own professional practice:

> Sometimes I wish that I could just teach – there's so much admin, paperwork and follow-up of discipline to do when you're a HoD. Teaching suffers on account of this. If you prioritize and say that teaching comes first and admin second, you are labelled as inefficient and a poor HoD.

One head of faculty, commenting on paperwork, hinted at the root of the problem:

> My pigeon-hole is always bulging – e.g. a TVEI response wanted by Monday. The DH (curriculum) is responsible for one set of things and sends blurb around about them; and the DH (pastoral) does the same for his concerns. I also get stuff on multicultural, Special Needs etc., and, of course, from the subject adviser. None of the empires works with reference to the others. We've got CPVE, OCEA, TVEI and school working parties (cross-curricular, mixed-ability teaching, accommodation). All are very valid but I now ignore bits of paper and reckon that if something is sufficiently important, someone will come and see me about it.

This would seem not only to be a classic case of information overload but also to indicate blockage in the communication channels in the school as a whole. It could be either that the appropriate channels had not been set up in the first place or that they were not operating satisfactorily. Whatever the case, there were serious implications at middle management level, affecting the operations of the head of department or faculty, which no amount of personal skill could alone counteract.

One of the things expected of department heads is that they should keep abreast of curriculum development and trends in their subject area. In principle, heads of department agreed with this and the recommended practitioners were certainly active in LEA groups and, often, national subject associations (e.g. the National Association for the Teaching of English, and the Association of Science Education). However, time again constrained the amount that middle managers could read. One phase two nominee, recently seconded to be involved with initial teacher training, remarked that when he found himself in a university school of education environment, he was horrified at all the journals and papers that he had not had time to read over the years he had been in post.

Departmental staff with other commitments

A head of faculty commented that he had done some work with a large public company who: 'fell about laughing when I said that I had a DH under me one moment and above me the next'. Schools, unlike businesses and industry, do not have one hierarchical structure into which all staff fit neatly, occupying just one slot. Lines of responsibility for any one individual can vary from hour to hour. Obviously, scale 1 teachers are responsible to both head of department and head of year. Yet the fact that there are a number of groups in any one school, and any one individual can change 'status' according to the present group, can cause difficulties for the head of department. The problem manifests itself for the department head as regards the composition of the departmental team. For those with a second-in-command on scale 3, several scale 2s with points for work in the department and several scale 1s, life is relatively uncomplicated. But most departments are but cells in a matrix structure consisting of the academic and the pastoral.

Where headteachers and deputies were members of the department there were particular problems relating to the fact that they were prone to being called out frequently and lessons were often late starting. It was, indeed, because of this that some headteachers elected not to teach regularly but to be available for cover. Where senior staff were in a department there were constraints in that they were often unavailable for cover, for departmental working parties on curriculum development or for the preparation of materials, and delegated tasks had to be apportioned to fewer people. If there were other middle managers in the department – such as heads of year or house, TVEI or CPVE coordinators – then the difficulties were compounded, for, although these people were not unwilling, their priorities were likely to lie elsewhere and prior commitments precluded full involvement in the department. In those departments that were 'all chiefs and no Indians', heads of department had to take on far more, in extreme cases shouldering all the responsibility and unable to delegate anything.

There were cases of excellent seconds-in-command in a department being 'rewarded' with pastoral responsibility in order either to keep them at the school or to compensate them for having narrowly missed being internally appointed to departmental headship. Such arrangements can cause deterioration in the department as the number two is no longer able to work in tandem with the head of department as effectively as before.

Heads of department also found difficulty accommodating staff who only taught for a couple of periods in their department, the rest of their time being spent in other areas; and part-time staff with whom it was often difficult to communicate and involve in departmental discussion. These problems arose particularly in shortage subject areas – for example, maths, science, CDT and business studies. Educational conditions have changed: falling rolls, financial restraint and redeployment, for example, have decreased the likelihood of departments consisting of a collection of single-subject specialists. In some departments it may be that the head of department is the only subject specialist and the departmental team is made up of staff teaching their second or even third subject. Similarly, there may be teachers appointed to the department on a temporary or part-time basis.

Although an individual head of department might have all the skills, strategies and qualities to be effective, the department might be underachieving through pressure of circumstances. One of the phase two recommended departments was working well, but, until the term it was visited, had been staffed entirely by part-time teachers and teachers who all had considerable responsibility elsewhere (including the head of department who was also in charge of careers). The headteacher commented that he had deliberately appointed to that department a new member of staff who had no commitment other than to the subject area so that she could focus her thoughts and energies there.

Role overload

A number of heads of department themselves had other commitments; for example, many were also form tutors, while a much smaller number were year or house heads, or had school-wide responsibilities (e.g. for staff development). They spoke of the problems arising from these extra commitments. In schools where the tutor did not move up with the tutor group, department heads (being the more experienced teachers) tended to be allocated forms higher up in the school which meant, of course, that they were involved in option choices, exam monitoring and sixth form counselling – all very time-consuming and important tasks. Heads of department expressed concern that on the one hand they were performing their pastoral role unsatisfactorily, while on the other, the smooth running of the department was disrupted as they were, for example, with their form group at the beginning of the day when there were such things to attend to as cover arrangements. Where heads of department were teaching the first period of the morning, there was the likelihood of ten minutes or so of time with that class being eroded by their having to deal with administrative matters when they returned to the office after registration. On the same count, it was sometimes impossible to go to year group meetings if these were held in the mornings. Helpful room siting was a key issue and those heads of department who had their tutor group base in their teaching rooms or, at least, in the subject suite, found life much easier; where this was not the case, communication problems could arise. One dual-role middle manager had a head of year office in one block and a departmental office in another.

Heads of department who were also heads of year were the

exception rather than the rule in the study and, mostly, those with responsibility for the role had the energy and will to take up the challenge. Often, additional responsibilities had been given by senior staff in order to widen the teachers' experience as they were seen as individuals who were candidates for promotion. For the teacher concerned, it was, perhaps, not worth the risk turning down the offer. One head of department commented: 'It's frustrating because it's not in my best interests, career-wise, to run the department: I must broaden my horizons if I'm to achieve promotion.'

Senior staff would seem to have a responsibility to look at the structure of the department in order to reduce some of the inevitable strain on those expected to fulfil dual roles. In one school, the individual concerned had been given no extra non-contact time for pastoral work so the time allowed for departmental business was relinquished for pastoral crisis management and the department lost out. In another school, however, the head had created another scale 2 post to relieve the head of department of some administration when he was appointed head of year.

There were few problems where the department head or, more commonly, the head of faculty, was created senior teacher as, in the main, the individual was an extremely experienced and respected middle manager of some years' standing who was well able to take on the extra responsibility. Indeed, as Blackburn (1986) pointed out, at a time of lack of mobility in the profession and when 'teachers increasingly have to find their renewal within existing roles', such internal promotion was seen as a means of relieving personal boredom in the job – even if this had not manifested itself in any deterioration in departmental effectiveness. However, the practice can have adverse effects as HMI in Wales (1984) noted:

> Some schools have . . . promoted good heads of department
> to senior teacher status, with responsibility for giving a positive
> lead to heads of department as a group; regrettably, and contrary
> to the original intention in their creation, these posts have
> frequently been allocated for responsibility not directly linked
> with pupils' learning experiences.

Staff discipline and interpersonal relations

As regards personnel, heads of department sometimes encountered interpersonal difficulties where their predecessors remained as members of the team and exerted negative power:

> The ex-HoD is still in the department – he was made to
> move sideways – and he makes life difficult for me by

quiet harassment: he spends ages doing anything I ask
him to do.

The deputy head, ex-HoD, is in the department and was rather
aggressive when I came – he was obviously anxious that I would
not be able to cope.

One headteacher commented that he would have to make it clear to a
department head promoted to head of faculty and senior teacher that
he had left subject management behind and must not interfere with
his successor though he was to continue to teach in the department.

Heads of department felt very reluctant to reprimand unsatisfactory
teachers, or 'develop' underperforming ones, especially when these
were older than themselves. They felt quite happy dealing with
students, probationers and young teachers but felt uncomfortable
in the case of other colleagues (see Chapter 6). Obviously, they
needed to be helped to ameliorate the situation, for it frequently
had an adverse effect on the efficacy of the departmental team:
'I have an idle number two and this has knock-on effects: others see him doing nothing and wonder why they should put
themselves out.'

Doubtless the rigid autocrat who demands unquestioning
compliance exists somewhere – but such individuals were not
found in the research schools. There, when identifying problems
and difficulties, the responses of heads of department were often
in the nature of: 'getting people to do things that they do not
want to do but which are necessary for the school' and 'keeping on asking people to do something if they repeatedly fail to
deliver the goods'. Heads of department also felt loath to reprimand staff for unpunctuality, for example, when the same teachers
had willingly given up an evening for a meeting or a Saturday for a
sports fixture.

As will be discussed in relation to staff development (see Chapter 6), the problem lies in the fact that heads of department are
middle managers, having delegated responsibility from senior staff
and required to take on certain roles with respect to this and yet
very aware of – and, indeed, keen to foster – informal collegiality
within the team where many of them wanted to be *primus inter
pares*. Generally, students and probationers expect, and are expected
to be, subject to observation and evaluation; but once past these
stages, teachers neither expect, nor are expected, to be commented
upon. Those schools and departments which have come to terms
with this – and the 'effective' departments have frequently been
in the forefront – have either done it by structured appraisal

schemes or by creating such an environment that it had become commonplace.

The definition of responsibilities

Lack of clarity regarding role has been shown to be a cause of stress for teachers (Dunham, 1978, 1984). Most of the 'effective' heads of department were quite clear as to their responsibilities, although their awareness stemmed more from their experience and courses that they had attended, for example, than from well-constructed job descriptions. Many of the schools expected a high level of performance from them, though again, in some schools, requirements were more implicit than explicit. The recommended department and faculty heads were largely in schools that could also be designated 'effective'; it is clearly not insignificant that in each of the selected phase two LEAs, there were three, and in one instance four, independently recommended departments in any one school (see Chapter 1). All the phase two schools provided job descriptions for department heads but there were some feelings of unease. In one school a head of department remarked:

> I'd like requirements in our job description – other than what I was told at interview. It's very difficult getting accurate feedback on how I'm performing. I ask the department from time to time but they are a bit hesitant. I'd like to talk to someone about my role.

Lack of clarity reduces effectiveness. A phase one head of department spoke of uncertainty resulting in her doing things only to find that they had been done by someone else who claimed responsibility, while at the same time she was being reprimanded for failing to do things which were regarded as her province.

Inadequate preparation

Heads of department spoke of difficulties which they had overcome by trial and error; of being 'thrown in at the deep end'; and of the assumptions that were made when they took up their post. All were symptoms of a lack of preparation. Although the difficulties cited were often small and the heads of department had overcome them on their own initiative, such a state of affairs was not conducive to maximum effectiveness. As one department head observed: 'I've made management mistakes and in a small world one little mistake can have very big consequences.' No one spoke of being 'nursed' through the initial weeks in post though apparently 'help was there if you needed it'. (The issue of preparation and support for middle managers is discussed in the following chapter.) But it was obviously not an easy time for heads of department: 'It's very different being responsible for all the ordering as opposed to some of it, and having to carry the can', and, 'People came to you for advice about things that you couldn't help them with.' One deputy head commented that: 'A lot of young heads of department have the ideas but lack diplomacy and are bulls in china shops.' Again, the right sort of support from the right quarter can mitigate the adverse effects of this tactlessness to maximize effectiveness.

Ancillary help

Resource-based constraints came to the fore in practical subjects – science, CDT, home economics – dependent on technical assistance. Dealing with technicians and integrating them into a team is an added dimension of the role of head of department in some subject areas. The recommended practitioners rose to the challenge and, generally, the problem was not in directing or liaising with the technicians. Rather, it was in the limited amount of time available to some departments. A well-resourced department was often so on account of history rather than any policy or planning. Some departments were struggling against great odds because of lack of ancillary help. As well as giving rise to some quite intense bitterness towards 'higher status' colleagues (in schools which favoured science over CDT, for example), there were obviously constraints both on the curriculum and on the quality of work being produced. A head of home economics said that she would love to do experiments but did not have the time to set them up; and a head of CDT, having to service all the workshop tools himself, said that it was good going if the lathes got sharpened once a month although, as a craftsman, he knew that they ought to be attended to after every use.

Although technical and ancillary help has traditionally been allocated to the practical subject areas with laboratories and workshops, the NFER research supports the suggestion that it is going to be increasingly advantageous (if not necessary in large departments) to have it allocated to other areas (maths, humanities, English) in order to relieve the growing pressure on teaching staff, especially with regard to the amount of continuous assessment required by GCSE courses. One teacher remembered the boon of having a maths secretary in a previous school. Quantitative data regarding the amount of time spent by teachers over photocopying and duplicating, setting up video recorders and so forth were not available. However, the NFER research supports the observation that departments are increasingly producing their own materials, individualized learning schemes, course booklets and so forth, and that the reproduction of these is taking up a lot of teachers' time that might be more effectively spent elsewhere. One head of department made the point that pupils are now accustomed to a high standard of printed material and what would pass with motivated pupils in the grammar school would not do for low-ability pupils, for example.

Management of physical resources

Heads of department responsible for equipment that required maintenance and repairs (science, CDT, home economics) were often very vocal regarding the frustrations of not having control over this. For example, a head of science referred to the complicated bureaucratic process that had to be gone through in order to get something repaired. The form-filling was time-consuming but this was not resented as much as the delay which meant that the pupils were unable to do certain experiments. In tight examination syllabuses there simply was not time to go back to the work several months later when the repair had been carried out. Once again, the discontent was not on account of the personal frustration at lack of control, but from the fact that the effectiveness of the department was diminished and the pupils were losing out.

A phase two head of home economics was distressed by the fact that she could not have control of a cheque book for a departmental account. She felt a certain amount of personal affront in that she was trusted with many thousands of pounds' worth of equipment in a purpose-built suite, with the safety aspect of lighting ovens and so forth, yet was not trusted with a relatively small amount of money. Over and above this was, once again, the frustration that the work of the department was constrained. With curriculum developments which now meant pupils increasingly made individual decisions regarding the article to be produced and took responsibility for their own problem-solving and design, staff needed to be flexible in the purchase of materials: school administrative structures do not always accommodate this satisfactorily. It may well be that the advent of Local Management of Schools, whereby schools are given greater financial autonomy than hitherto, will alleviate some of the externally imposed problems encountered by heads of department in the management of resources although, equally, other restrictions may intervene.

The timetable

Timetable constraints were often referred to, albeit with an awareness that these were brought about by the needs and demands of others in the organization and that often a compromise had to be arrived at for the general wellbeing of the school. Discontent was found in those departments which felt that senior staff regarded them as low status and put them into the timetable last:

> There would be complaints if science occurred every Thursday and Friday afternoons and PE every Monday morning – this says something about the subject.

> My department is a dumping ground alongside X as far as the curriculum is concerned.

One head of department remarked that TVEI took priority, the small groups occupying a lot of rooms and ousting the department from accommodation previously available. A head of PE observed that his department was put onto the timetable last which was all right so long as the weather was fine but, if they could not work outside, there were problems as all the rooms had been taken and videos allocated.

Timetabling affected possible pupil groupings lower in the school and, obviously, option choices for the fourth year. (The position, regarding this is bound, of course, to be affected by the demands of a national curriculum.) Some heads of department resented the fact that their department tended to get a high proportion of low-ability pupils and yet they were apparently judged on their examination results alongside those departments which had a more promising intake. They felt that they were in a vicious circle and that it was difficult to raise the status of the department. The attitudes of other staff counselling pupils not to take certain subjects – often of a practical orientation – were resented.

On a split site it was often very difficult for staff to commute and so they were liable to encounter a more limited age range of pupils than they would have desired. The conventional school day was seen as restricting what could be done by way of fieldwork, for example, but an ostensibly more flexible structure offering modular courses also posed problems for departmental operation. For example, one head of faculty had been in discussion with a head of careers regarding work experience: if pupils were out for two or three weeks from a traditional two-year course, then there were few problems; but if the time was taken from a ten-week module, then there were serious implications.

Those teachers who were (in normal circumstances) commonly occupied with pupils at lunchtimes – particularly in music and PE – spoke of the fact that afternoon lessons suffered as they had neither time to recharge batteries nor time to reflect on their afternoon's teaching. Industrial action and withdrawal of lunch-hour activities had brought this home to many.

Conflict of styles

Middle managers involved in the research usually compared their present school favourably with previous ones and found the environment supportive and the climate invigorating. There could, however, be initial problems when management styles at two schools were very different. For example, one department head remarked that having previously worked in schools with no consultative meetings, he felt threatened when people questioned him in meetings at his present school – he did not realize that they were trying to be constructive. A similar situation happened within a faculty. A new head of faculty remarked that his predecessor had been autocratic and though staff were keen to get involved, getting them used to thinking for themselves had been a long process.

Amalgamation also caused problems, especially as regards departmental organization and the middle management level. As noted:

With amalgamation, various posts were made and people applied for scales rather than for jobs. Staff ended up with responsibilities but it didn't necessarily mean that they did them.

Amalgamation brought together staff with different approaches and that can create problems for the HoD.

Parental pressure

At some schools, parental pressures made the life of the head of department more difficult: 'At this school you feel accountable to the parents rather than just to the pupils. At my previous schools, parents were very grateful for what you did for their children rather than being critical of you as here.' Another department head said: 'Parents have definite expectations that their children will do 'O' levels in certain subjects. They do not see the Design department as being for them.' A senior adviser commented:

It worries me that we are now becoming commercial concerns and not educational establishments. Parents are requiring certain standards of literacy, they like school uniform and look for successful exam results . . . In this climate curriculum development and change is most difficult. And headteachers simply cannot afford to be radical and adopt curriculum initiatives. For example, some are reluctant to introduce PSE [Personal and Social Education].

This was borne out by the words of a deputy head:

This HoD wanted to move towards a practical, problem-solving approach. My query is, although it leads to very interesting work, does it enable pupils to pass exams? A school is judged very much by its exam successes so we can't ignore this.

The situation is clearly going to be complicated by the 1988 Education Reform Act introducing the open enrolment of schools, a national curriculum and providing the opportunity for schools to opt out of LEA control and achieve 'grant-maintained status.'

Accommodation

Heads of department cited storage problems. One said that he had to store the 16+ coursework in the girls' loo, while another complained: 'We have resources in five different places (four at the back of class-rooms) and two stores are 50 yards from where most staff teach.' But they saw these as difficulties – things which just added to the incon-veniences of life – rather than constraints. The loss of the gym to the PE department throughout the examination period was, however, a constraint on the curriculum. Lack of specialist rooms meant that displays could not be put up and overuse of rooms meant that the head of department, or other staff, could not get to the room at any time during the week to put up, or change, displays. One head of music, for example, had the principal teaching room used for community education immediately school ended – her mornings were involved with a tutor group and lunchtimes with extra-curricular activities.

Perceptions of advisers and senior staff

Before examining in more detail some specific 'critical incidents' described by the phase two practitioners, it is worth while looking at what LEA advisers felt were the things that department heads found most difficult. Individuals may sometimes not be in the best position to identify their own problem areas and the objective stance of LEA officers, with their wider experience, can offer a new perspective. Although many areas overlapped, there were some fresh insights. It should be remembered that the advisers were speaking of all the heads of department in their authority or area rather than merely the good practitioners, which explains, for example, such comments as: 'They find it very hard to conceive of themselves as managers rather than senior subject teachers' and 'They do not see themselves as leading a team.' It would, perhaps, be true to say that ineffective heads of department were not the opposite of effective ones in that they did the same things but *badly*. Rather, they had a *different* conception of the role – a conception that was limited and inadequate and did not include things such as staff development, departmental review and evaluation.

Advisers felt that department heads often found it very difficult: dealing with headteachers and deputies (but here the problems could well be caused by the senior staff rather than the middle managers); 'playing the power game' (being aware of the micropolitics of the school); and establishing relations with others in the school (addressing such issues as, for example, 'Who is responsible for study skills programmes?'). They acknowledged the constraints imposed by lack of ancillary help, problems arising from maintenance of plant, and difficulties with capitation (but here again, the senior staff could be to blame if the head of department was 'making bids in the dark'). It was remarked that department heads are often intuitive and do not see the need for positive planning, and become preoccupied with trivia and overwhelmed by department issues. Advisers believed that all heads of department found it difficult to motivate staff in a static work situation (and, of course, the research took place either during, or shortly after, a period of extensive industrial action) and in many cases, the problem was that the department head 'did no honest talking'. Curriculum development (see Chapter 7) and new methods of assessment and recording (for GCSE and records of achievement) were unfamiliar, and thus perceived as difficult areas for all heads of department. But overriding all this was, perhaps unsurprisingly, the whole matter of the management of change. And time and time again came the assertion that department heads found it difficult to develop staff.

Senior staff often mentioned the specific difficulties of individual department heads within their school but, commenting on generic problems, referred to many of the things that the advisers identified. They spoke of some middle managers' inability to think in broad educational terms, to develop staff and to manage a team.

Critical incidents

All the phase two nominated heads of department and faculty were asked to identify two or three 'critical incidents' – particular problems, situations or incidents which had caused them difficulty since being in post – to describe these, to outline what action had been taken and to say what the result was. Some of the critical incidents were relevant to issues explored in subsequent chapters and are more appropriately discussed elsewhere but a sample, highlighting various groups of issues, will now be given. It is not suggested that the middle managers concerned necessarily dealt with the incident in the 'best' way. Neither is it pretended that the descriptions (usually written rather than given in interview) gave anything like a full picture of the complexity of the network of relationships relevant to the incident or trace the incident's history. However, the critical incidents can serve as a basis for discussion and, more importantly, they do provide evidence as to the kinds of issues that were perceived as of major concern.

Problems with staff

Problems with staff were the focus of a large number of critical incidents. It was a mark of effectiveness that heads of department were aware of problems in this area – they knew what was going on in the department. Poor middle managers can help to *create* unsatisfactory teachers by failing to give them adequate guidance and support. As regards the cases dealt with by the phase two practitioners, there were some success stories, some compromises and some stalemates. In them all, the heads of department stressed the importance of talking things through sympathetically with the person concerned; very often, the fact that the heads of department were able to move in at all said much about the sort of atmosphere that had been created in the department and the relationships they enjoyed with members of staff.

Incident 1

A teacher was performing unsatisfactorily on account of domestic problems and a delegation of pupils eventually went to the HoD to complain and demand action. The HoD talked both to the teacher – and persuaded him that he had to present an 'efficient, acceptable aspect' to the pupils – and to the pupils to help build up goodwill. The result was that the teacher started preparing work and marking books regularly and there was a much improved atmosphere in the classroom. The HoD wrote: 'I was able to broach the sensitive issue on account of the "real friendship and warmth" that had built up between us.'

Incident 2

The same department head had to deal with a newly appointed teacher who was seen as generally incompetent, inefficient, lazy and apparently careless. Things came to a head during a residential week after which the HoD reviewed the teacher's work since joining the department, starting with the teacher's strengths and positive contributions to the department before going on to perceived weaknesses and a detailed critique of the teacher's attitude and performance during the residential. The criticism was accepted by the teacher who subsequently made an effort to improve performance. The HoD commented: 'I felt that I had presented a case which was quite unanswerable but had not done it too soon so that by the time I had to complain, I had shown the teacher that I was prepared to work for him, defend his interests and work hard where he was not working hard.'

Incident 3

A newly appointed HoD had complaints from pupils, parents and governors about a teacher in the department who was 'letting classes get away with doing no work'. The HoD was unwilling to reprimand her on the ground that this would lose goodwill and, anyway, she felt that the teacher was *unable* to perform better and needed INSET. For 18 months she supported her and helped provide INSET until she persuaded her that, reputations in a school being hard to shed, she had better take up a post at another school.

That 'bad' departments can be self-perpetuating unless action is taken is illustrated by the above critical incident, which was, in fact, described by a phase two practitioner who had inherited an ineffective department which was in a chaotic state both as regards records and staff; there were a number of supply teachers and there was a feeling of relief 'if someone turned up in front of a class'. The problem teacher had done her teaching practice in the department and subsequently been offered a post there and served her probation. During this crucial time, she had been given no support or guidance from the previous head of department – and thus floundered, probably needlessly. The present head of department admitted that she had been unaware of the situation until the complaints came in as there had been so many other things in the department to sort out which initially took priority over observation and monitoring.

Incident 4

Not all critical incidents had successful resolutions. A 'frustrated' teacher, perceiving career stagnation, asked for 'A' level work and was given one-third of this. At course meetings, the teacher claimed that things were going well but after about six months, two able and responsible pupils came to the HoD saying that they did not want to be disloyal but they were being inadequately prepared by the teacher. The HoD talked to the teacher concerned and had 'a difficult, tense meeting' during which the teacher denied there was any problem. The HoD was told that the accusations were a travesty of the truth. The situation was partly reconciled by the HoD and a colleague giving extra tuition to the group after school.

The HoD admitted that there were few mechanisms to keep in touch with what was happening in the classroom. He did not reveal in what detail work was discussed in meetings, whether staff were expected to produce records of work or whether there were any monitoring procedures which should have prevented such a situation arising. It could well be that the teacher needed INSET before taking on the new work.

Incident 5
A rather different incident involving staffing was identified by a head of PE.

The day before term began, a new member of staff was told that she would have to go into hospital for six weeks, so the HoD was left with 16 periods a week with no specialist teacher on the supply list. Rather than have a non-specialist supply, the HoD said that she would prefer to double up on numbers and take the large group herself. However, after two days of telephoning, she had got six supplies to cover the timetable. The HoD remarked: 'I felt that the situation was greatly eased by the fact that I was active in the subject association in the authority and so I knew all the other departmental heads and it was a matter of "ringing up friends" all of whom were anxious to help.'
(This was another case of the right supportive relationships having been established before the crisis.)

Problems with pupils

Several critical incidents involved the head of department having to deal with disruptive pupils on behalf of a member of their staff.

Incident 1
A 'wild' fourth-year pupil refused to go into a particular class, maintaining that the teacher always 'picked' on him. The HoD removed the pupil and spoke to him at length, being careful not to side with him against the teacher and yet not to ignore his grievance. The HoD had the pupil working on his own in a separate room for a week, after which time the pupil, the teacher and the HoD met together and a contract regarding

the pupil's behaviour was signed by them all. The HoD said: 'It is very important to demonstrate support for my own staff and be firm but reasonable with the pupil. There is a need to make something happen in the eyes of both pupil and teacher.'

Incident 2

A first-year pupil was being bullied by other pupils on account of a physical handicap and consequently became very aggressive. After a relatively insignificant altercation with a teacher, his aggression burst out and he hurled abuse at the teacher. The HoD removed the pupil and reprimanded him 'feeling that it was important that he knew that his behaviour was unacceptable'. After a while, the pupil calmed down and the HoD was able to talk to him about the bullying which had been the cause of the outburst. The HoD wrote: 'It is very important for pupils to know that staff stick together – otherwise they play one off against the other.'

Incident 3

Another incident raised important questions about 'blurred policy' and lack of clarity about decisions between levels of management.

A fourth-year pupil had been put in after-school detention, in accordance with departmental policy, for having incorrect PE kit on two occasions. When the parent complained, the head of year and a senior teacher were not prepared to support the teacher concerned. The HoD pointed out to them that the kit policy was in the departmental handbook which had been accepted by the headteacher, the governors and the inspectors. The matter was referred to the headteacher who suggested a compromise (whereby the pupil was detained at lunchtime) but made no reference to the departmental procedure. The HoD commented: 'I do feel that adherence to agreed and approved procedures should be supported and staff backed up.'

Problems of a professional nature

A further group of incidents was concerned with a variety of professional matters by way of curriculum development, management of resources, interaction with senior staff and team leadership. Some examples follow:

Incident 1

A department was unanimously in favour of a new syllabus
but anxious about the demands by way of teacher assessment at
the end of the course – time allowance was needed. The HoD
had to convince the headteacher of the benefits of the syllabus
and showed him examples of pupils' work before outlining the
time requirements per candidate. The head was supportive and
arrangements were made to provide the necessary cover. The
HoD wrote: 'The presentation of the case was vital. One needed
to be prepared with theory and evidence, to be calm but
persuasive. It was necessary to take the initiative and make
demands: this was a case where "fighting for the department"
was justified.'

Incident 2

A faculty had previously been run by an autocrat/dictator; the
new HoF wanted to create a team style of management with
shared responsibility. He spent a long time getting to know the
staff and the heads and deputies before beginning to unfold his
ideas, noting the responses and reactions. Gradually, the team
evolved and a faculty identity was formed. The HoF said: 'It
is important to have convivial personal relationships but also
to be professional – listening, responding and sharing concerns
with colleagues. I always try to encourage initiatives and provide
support for them.'

Anticipating problems

There was an interesting example of a proactive head of department
who *anticipated* a critical incident and 'managed' so that the problem
never materialized.

The HoD had been internally promoted above other more
experienced and established staff. One senior member of the
department was away on an exchange when the new HoD took
over and the latter anticipated that there might be problems
when this teacher returned regarding his accepting him as HoD
and feeling motivated to work under him. The teacher would
find a lot changed as the new HoD was trying to pull the
department into shape. On the teacher's return, the HoD had
a 'full and frank discussion' with him, examining his role, his
future and his areas of responsibility and they jointly decided
that it was time for him to look at changing certain aspects. The
HoD delegated to the teacher a number of important duties

and responsibilities. The teacher 'responded immediately to the situation. He accepted the role and appeared to thrive on the extra responsibility.'

Summary and discussion

By using a combination of interview data and critical incident analysis, this chapter has attempted to document both the main difficulties of the middle manager's job and the chief constraints militating against effective performance. Lack of time was often mentioned as a factor preventing departments and faculty heads from carrying out some of their management responsibilities (e.g. classroom observation, evaluation and review). It must be remembered that most middle managers were free of classes for only 15 to 35 per cent of the weekly timetable; but it was not clear whether an increase in non-contact time would actually have led to a greater tendency on their part to undertake 'managerial work'. There was some evidence (see also Chapter 6) of a general reluctance to embrace fully what the role entailed and many department heads did not perceive themselves as managers in the broadest sense. This view was endorsed by many of the advisers involved in the research.

Departmental activity was often made more difficult by the fact that departments increasingly were staffed by part-time teachers or those with major commitments outside the department. This made delegation and the allocation of departmental activities difficult and the head of department had to undertake many activities which, in another department or in different circumstances, would most likely have been carried out by the team. Heads of department too may have other commitments (e.g. form tutor or head of year) which can cause problems, yet taking on wider responsibilities within the school was seen, both by senior staff and those in middle management positions, as necessary in order to increase the chances of promotion.

Problems relating to personnel management were also found. There appeared to be a reluctance on the part of many department heads to deal with ineffective and underperforming teachers other than students, probationers or young staff. Often there was a perceived conflict between the leadership and management functions of the department head and the desire to engender feelings of collegiality within the team. By taking on the role of a manager with responsibility for other adults and their performance, it was thought that relationships with colleagues might suffer.

Lack of role clarity and inadequate preparation for the role were also cited as constraining factors and these are explored further in later chapters. Similarly, the importance of sufficient ancillary help and of greater control over physical resources were also seen as significantly affecting levels of departmental effectiveness. As a result of the proposed Local Management of Schools initiatives, schools may well decide to spend a greater proportion of their budgets on non-teaching staff and middle managers might welcome the greater freedom which would enable equipment and facilities to be maintained and repaired more quickly and stock to be acquired more flexibly.

Constraints associated with timetabling and accommodation were mentioned as was the pressure from contrasting management styles. Regarding the question of style – which is pursued in more depth in Chapter 9 – there were occasional problems of adjustment for department heads but, as earlier noted, the case study schools were, in the main, consultative and examples of autocratic leadership styles were not common. Pressures from parents were also noted and these are likely to increase as the move towards wider parental choice, greater accountability and the use of performance indicators gathers momentum. The increased powers of governing bodies and the national curriculum, with its associated programme of testing, are likely to result in middle managers experiencing more pressure from outside the school than hitherto.

The chapter has also presented information on what LEA advisers and senior staff perceived as the particular difficulties and constraints facing heads of department and faculty. Many of the above areas were identified and, as previously mentioned, ineffective department headship was often seen in terms of the incumbent having an inadequate conception of what the role entailed and how it could be enacted. In addition, advisers made reference to the difficulties that department heads had in dealing with senior management, becoming au fait with micropolitical processes and establishing relations with staff outside departments. Concern was also expressed about middle managers' preoccupation with the day-to-day to the detriment of more important activities such as planning, and the difficulty of motivating staff in the prevailing educational climate. Developing the curriculum and coming to terms with the new forms of assessment were mentioned but these tended to be subsumed under the more global concerns of managing change and developing staff – the subject of later chapters.

Examples of the critical incidents documented by the phase two practitioners were given in the latter part of the chapter. The particular problems, incidents and situations identified provided some evidence of those matters that had caused concern and they have been categorized under the headings of problems with staff and pupils, professional problems and the anticipation of problems.

5 What Support and Training do Heads of Department Receive?

It has been argued that two important functions of the head of department concern the development and support of departmental staff. As the next chapter shows, the effective practitioners tried to give these matters considerable attention. However, the developer must be developed and the supporter supported. The issues which will now be addressed are those of how teachers are prepared for department headship and how, once in the role, they are supported both by senior staff in the school and in the LEA.

Preparation for department headship

Had all new heads of department served under department heads who delegated responsibilities and involved them in all aspects of departmental life, then the immediate training needs of the 'new' head of department might not have been as great as the NFER research suggests that they are. Many of the recommended practitioners in phase two of the NFER research were, indeed, preparing younger teachers and their reputation as trainers was, in many cases, one of the reasons that they were nominated. However, the study showed that they would seem to be in the minority among middle managers currently in post and had not themselves always enjoyed similar preparation. Many new heads of department seemed to be ill–prepared for the role and interviewees spoke of being 'thrown in at the deep end' and 'not being confident in terms of my past experience'. One said: 'I just had a letter from the LEA saying that I was acting HoD; I had absolutely no preparation.' An effective phase two head of faculty commented: 'To my mind, it's more of an accident if you're a good HoD.' From both interviews and INSET sessions which the NFER researchers have conducted, it was apparent that a considerable number of department heads did not have a clear conception of what their role involved and, indeed, had not been encouraged to acquire such a conception. Those heads of department who had been able to observe, and work alongside, good models of department headship were therefore at a distinct advantage; the anti-model, although of some value, was not so effective, for observers only saw crises, mistakes and the obvious gaps – they did not see the whole gamut of good practice.

Local education authorities differed in their attitudes towards courses for aspiring heads of department. Arguably, this off-the-job preparation was especially helpful to those teachers working in 'poor' departments, broadening their horizons, giving access to good practice and compensating for the lack of professional development within the department. Several members of 'good' departments said that they only realized how fortunate they were when they went on courses and heard about weaker departments elsewhere. Some advisers tried to provide courses for aspiring heads of department and felt that they were a priority; it was suggested that, amongst other things, the pre-promotion course could serve a useful 'screening' function and 'enable people to work out their own level of incompetence' as it was awful 'not being able to back out having been promoted'. However, others felt that in the present climate of contraction and restricted mobility, such preparatory courses only led to frustration as there were always many more aspirants than posts available. Another adviser thought that there was too often a mismatch between entry characteristics of course participants and the content of the course: 'If the course is pitched at too high a level, it is too threatening and people will withdraw if they feel that they fall too short of expectation.' This adviser felt that coherent packages of courses in stages were required. It was often thought that experience of the job was needed before a course was attended so that issues discussed could be immediately related to the individual's situation.

Senior staff interviewed pointed out that teachers were frequently promoted on account of teaching rather than management skills. One head of department observed: 'I'd always thought that if you were a good organizer you'd be a good HoD but I now know that that's not the case. The best teacher in the world may be a lousy manager.' The view was put forward that the transference from being 'a manager of children' to being 'a manager of adults' was unproblematic. However, although the skills may be similar, managing adults needs new approaches and entails consideration of additional concepts. In one case study school, operating a lower school and upper school on different sites, a senior member of staff contended that 'The HoDs are trained in the lower school and learn how to manage people on a small scale before they have a go in the upper school' but admitted that it was good luck rather than good management or senior management team (SMT) policy if this happened.

It is perhaps worth commenting that new faculty heads generally felt much more confident than new department heads. Although, clearly, both faculty and department heads were taking up new posts with additional responsibilities, the former had at least had experience of 'managing', of organizing a subject area, of leading a team and so forth, whereas the latter rarely had. Furthermore, as faculties are a relatively recent innovation for many schools, those promoted to faculty headship tend to be people who have been successful at department headship and have shown themselves able to develop staff and consider whole-school issues, for it was on these criteria that they were frequently selected. There were, of course, examples of less effective and mediocre heads of faculty in the schools participating in the project and there were, according to headteachers, some ill-judged appointments; however, these tended largely to be on account of circumstances or historical accident – having to make an internal promotion, for example. Generally, it seemed that heads of faculty were only selected when they had 'shown their colours', whereas this was not always the case with heads of department. Faculty headship is largely an extension of department headship, although perspectives have to be broader and the team is larger. Furthermore, the faculty head has to 'manage other managers' (i.e. heads of department) – although, generally, heads of faculty did not hold regular meetings with their team of department heads.

There is a case to be made for there being the post of deputy head of faculty, especially in very large schools, in order to provide training for heads of smaller departments who would like to prepare for promotion. There was often too large a responsibility gap between scale 2 heads of department and their scale 4 head of faculty, with the result that department heads felt insecure when making an application for a faculty headship.

School-based INSET for heads of department

Once in post, what structured opportunities for in-service training do heads of department receive and what are the sources of provision? As the effective heads of department can use departmental meetings for staff development, so can senior staff use main school meetings.

One phase two head of faculty commented that faculty meetings at her school were an excellent form of INSET. Yet all too often middle management meetings seemed to be for information-giving only. 'At HoDs meetings we spend a lot of time on practical matters – the minutiae of everyday administration – rather than talking about how to run a department – in its broad, management sense.'

Heads of department had a tendency to keep with the social unit of the department and did not interact with other department heads, share their concerns or discuss common issues. A commonly identified benefit of external INSET at all levels is that participants are able to meet and discuss with colleagues sharing the same problems as themselves. A deputy head said: 'HoDs need to have time with each other. Time and commitment are needed to disseminate good practice and ideas on site.' The desire for the sharing of experience underlies the frequently stated need for middle management courses, wherever they be, to incorporate workshop sessions – although some underpinning theory was also deemed necessary. 'You need to come up with your own answers but courses can help to make you think.'

The case study schools which had run their own residential weekend, day conference, or after-school course for their heads of department were rare. Where these had taken place, they were considered (by senior staff and course participants) to be of great benefit although, at the time of the research, industrial action had checked much of the momentum generated. With the new INSET funding arrangements, whereby schools are increasingly being given responsibility for their own INSET budget, it may well be that many more schools will be thinking in terms of providing their own INSET for, amongst others, their middle managers as a group. The advantages of this whole-school approach – or 'close-to-the-job' training – as has been rehearsed elsewhere (Ruddock, 1981), are that policies cohere, and change and development is seen as an organic process rather than a 'bolt-on extra'. An ex-headteacher, who was interviewed as part of the NFER research, stressed the importance of the consultancy mode (see, for example, Richardson, 1975), with heads of department getting together on a school-based programme with an external enabler. It was not possible to monitor the immediate or long-term effects of the school-based middle management training encountered in the NFER study, but there is clearly a need for research in this area. Indeed, Bolam (1987) draws attention to the paucity of research which gives data about the outcomes of INSET courses in general in terms of teacher performance and school improvement.

Externally provided INSET

Although only a small number of LEAs were involved in the research, there were found to be considerable differences as regards the amount of training that they offered their heads of department. Externally provided courses were considered to be particularly beneficial to those heads of department whose schools were in an early stage of management development and who thus needed stimulation and advice from other sources. There were various types of courses provided, for example, by the LEA, private organizations and the DES (e.g. 30-day courses in national priority areas such as maths, science and CDT).

In general, attendance on courses was voluntary, although the level of expectation that practitioners would go varied, as did the proportion of current post-holders who had received INSET. One adviser in a small authority with a stable group of heads of department said that all the middle managers in his subject area had been on appropriate courses, but this was logistically impossible elsewhere where the pool was so large as to render most provision inadequate. The provision of LEA-based courses was, too often, largely dependent on individual advisers and both the quality and quantity of courses over the range of subject areas varied considerably within, as well as between, authorities. Size of authority, the structure of the advisory service (which subjects had their own advisers, for example), and the priorities of the individual advisers, all played a part in the provision of INSET for middle managers. Nationally, a few authorities had a coherent rolling programme of management training and development: believing that there was little point in training one level without others to support it, they planned training for headteachers, deputies and middle managers either simultaneously or sequentially.

A major constraint on attendance on external courses was, unsurprisingly, found to be arrangements for cover (Earley, 1986). Many department heads interviewed felt that it was unfair on pupils if they were continually having to bring in supply teachers. The curriculum was disrupted and, furthermore, the teachers going on the course had to prepare the lesson and do any marking that arose from it, and this merely increased their workloads which had probably been added to anyway in the form of preparation for the course. Courses involving once-a-week attendance at the local institute of higher education had to be 'very good value' in order to entice heads of department. There were incidents of practitioners opting out of such courses when they felt that the benefits accruing from them did not balance the ill effects suffered by the school (and particularly the pupils). Headteachers were increasingly reluctant to release staff during the school day. Lack of cover also precluded teachers visiting other schools and departments – something that was generally felt to be very useful for the exchange of ideas but which was rarely possible.

Several authorities participating in the study were finding it both less expensive financially and less disruptive to organize weekend residential courses and were providing for middle managers in this way – and follow-up sessions at a teachers' centre were usually run. Evening meetings following a meal at a hotel were becoming popular and, again, were less expensive and disruptive than arranging for lessons to be covered. Course participants found it of benefit to get to know their colleagues in the area and also to have time with advisers. Common problems and disparate experiences were brought together. Other authorities 'bought in' to courses provided by local colleges: following the general trend in this area, such courses were increasingly of the 'one day a week' variety, occasionally one term's secondment; the year's secondment for middle managers was becoming rare.

Most of the features of 'effective' INSET identified in the literature (e.g. Ruddock, 1981; Bolam, 1987; Wallace, 1988) were articulated by practitioners participating in the NFER research, and advisers and senior staff were suspicious of 'off the shelf' packages which did not lead to institutional change and were not internalized. One adviser spoke of training a few key heads of departments in any one school so that they could lead others, while another had planned to train one or two who would then 'cascade' – but he admitted that this had been unsuccessful in this particular case (doubtless for reasons such as the inability to 'develop' colleagues or 'teach' other adults). Some authorities favoured certain privately run courses to which they sent several practitioners each year, usually during the holidays, thus building up a caucus of people in key positions who were all 'talking the same language'.

In some LEAs, there were generic courses, either for all middle managers (pastoral and academic) or just for heads of department regardless of subject area; in others, the subject advisers were responsible for the management provision. One adviser felt that it was, in fact, easier to get people to go on courses if they thought that the bias was towards their subject area. 'You can ask them what their problems are and then say, "Oh, they are the same as everyone else's!"' This adviser did, in fact, use management training material produced by industry. Often, however, subject-based courses seemed to be devoted mainly to curriculum development rather than to management issues despite the fact that it is debatable if the former can occur without an awareness of the latter. There is research evidence (Fullan, 1982, 1985;

Pocklington, 1987) that strategies for the management of change must be established and are, in fact, the backcloth for the transfer of INSET to classroom practice. (Chapter 7 explores, in depth, the issue of the management of change.)

The problem of transfer to classroom practice was noted by an adviser who remarked that he was, in fact, dubious as to the value of the courses and conferences that he organized. He felt that it was very difficult working with a 'mixed ability audience': the good heads of department knew it all already, the mediocre ones picked up some new ideas but the really weak ones were deaf to the messages and either could not be made aware that their practice could be made more effective or 'just did not want to know'.

Course content and the identification of needs

Course providers felt that they were well aware of the needs of middle managers from talking to them and observing departments at work; none, interestingly, mentioned talking to headteachers and senior staff about their perceptions of the needs of middle managers. With a few exceptions, INSET needs were identified unsystematically; schools and, more particularly, middle managers, seemed ill equipped to determine them although a few courses were beginning to consider this issue. Training would seem to need to alert them to the needs-identification instruments currently available (see, for example, Capell *et al.*, 1987; Weindling, 1987; Oldroyd and Hall, 1988). Those schools involved in a review exercise such as that set out by the *Guidelines for Review and Internal Development in Schools* (GRIDS; McMahon *et al.*, 1984; Birchenough *et al.*, 1989) were often in a stronger position as regards planning INSET as needs had become more obvious as an outcome of the review. Externally imposed innovations (e.g. GCSE) create INSET needs more obviously.

The senior staff involved in the NFER research generally identified personnel management and awareness of broad educational issues as key areas in which heads of department and faculty needed training. Middle managers themselves were frequently anxious for 'survival strategies' by way of time and personnel management ('dealing with the awkward teacher'; 'persuading someone to do something that they do not want to do'; 'ingratiating yourself with the powers that be!'). They then often identified an area of particular concern at their school or in their department at the time and there was little consensus as to what were regarded as the most pressing needs, individual situations being so different. There was certainly no shortage of items to go on the agenda of middle management courses and the problem generally was striking the right balance and establishing priorities at various stages.

A certain amount of training was 'situation training' – guidance that had to be given, for example, to the new head of department who wanted help with the 'nuts and bolts' rather as the probationer or new teacher needs to know everyday details which are taken for granted once a year has been experienced. Matters of concern in this category included resource management, requisitioning and timetabling.

Many courses raised consciousness of generic management issues and the topics were very similar to those found on senior management courses or, indeed, industrial courses. Because this was often unfamiliar territory, department heads were sometimes unsure of what it was exactly that they needed although they were aware that there were a number of 'management skills'; they were, thus, dependent on their needs being recognized and met by the course providers. Issues in this category covered such topics as running meetings, decision-making, team-building, assertiveness, counselling, and the management of change, conflict and stress. One of the phase one authorities sent participants on its secondary management course on 'outward bound' type exercises – which seemed to be thoroughly enjoyed!

Recognizing that many department and faculty heads were going to be both seeking promotion themselves and advising senior staff as to whom to shortlist when a vacancy in the department or faculty arose, some courses had sessions on writing applications, selection procedures and interviewing techniques.

There were then the 'educational' concerns of the middle managers as they considered their academic and pastoral responsibilities. Needs here were in two groups: those that arose from national policies and DES and LEA initiatives; and those that resulted from the particular concerns of individual schools. The former, at the time of the NFER research, centred, unsurprisingly, on GCSE. It had been expected that this would have been the dominating concern of heads of department but, in fact, it was found that many of the effective practitioners had been working along GCSE lines for some time and the innovation was not seen to be particularly revolutionary in principle – although anxiety was expressed about the planning time involved. (It ought, however, to be pointed out that interviews were conducted in the early months of GCSE before problems of assessment, coursework marking and so forth had arisen.) There were instances of LEAs advising heads of department how to 'cascade' as they recognized that teachers often had no experience of teaching their peers, however adept they were at teaching children, and the skills were different. At the time of writing, it is envisaged that the forthcoming national curriculum and the associated assessment procedures will be a focus of courses in the future and middle managers may well be required to 'cascade' to their departmental colleagues.

The role of the middle manager in appraisal was beginning to appear on the agenda for courses – again, largely as a result of reactions to external pressures – and profiling, records of achievement, and departmental evaluation and review were increasingly common topics.

Many curricular issues were broad and generic. Some concerned whole-school policies: anti-racism, multiculturalism, language, equal opportunities, computers, and industrial links for example; others were of a pedagogic nature: active learning, problem-solving and investigation work, for example. The establishing of cross-curricular links and development of interdisciplinary work was a subject for discussion as were subject-specific matters such as integrated humanities, developments in CDT and new approaches in maths. The very nature of the curriculum was also an issue: a modular curriculum, for example, has consequences for departmental organization and management.

As to how this content was delivered, most courses made use of experiential learning and some were multimedia. They employed diverse techniques such as individual, pair and small-group work; discussion; role play; 'in-tray' exercises; formal presentations; and school-based projects. On some courses, participants brought along examples of pupils' work for comment and evaluation by colleagues.

LEA support for heads of department and faculty

To a large extent, many of the activities that advisers organized – certainly termly meetings and annual conferences – were indistinguishable from what would be regarded as support for heads of department on the job and all these activities would come under the umbrella of professional development. However, there was evidence that some advisers supported department and faculty heads on a more individual basis. For example, in several authorities studied, advisers undertook departmental and faculty reviews (see Chapter 8): sometimes for the governors; at others, for the department or the faculty itself. Generally, this was found to be a very useful exercise and its format was often such that it could form the basis of a regular self-evaluation undertaken by the department itself. One (small) LEA had, alongside an out-of-school programme, used TVEI-related In-service Training (TRIST) funds to help underfunctioning departments: three support teachers in particular curricular areas were employed to work in schools and were concerned with the modification of teaching approaches in the classroom.

Where relationships were supportive, department heads welcomed advisers into schools and young practitioners especially appreciated their 'popping in' unannounced 'just to see how things were going'. In such circumstances, advisers could often help heads of department by liaising with the headteacher over some sensitive issue for example, or by giving department heads moral support when the latter felt that senior staff at the school were being unreasonable and undervaluing their subject area. Such advisers got to know the heads of department personally and were thus in a position to guide their professional development. One head of faculty spoke with appreciation of his adviser who had given him a lot of opportunities by way of membership of various curriculum study groups (for example, TVEI Humanities). Where such support was not given, it was commented upon and poor relations (whatever their cause) were a cause of stress:

> My adviser has been the cause of my despair. My morale has
> been rock bottom and he has caused me upset after upset. . . .
> People look to HoDs for support: that is good but I need
> support as well!

In one authority, a head remarked that heads of department in his school preferred not to have advisers around and said: 'That is quite a damning comment really.' Advisory teachers often had more classroom credibility. The situation was easier in smaller authorities for in the larger, dispersed ones, where the education offices were sometimes located at County Hall rather than being area-based, it might take an adviser as much as an hour and a half to travel to a remote school and thus visits were rare and teachers there could feel rather isolated.

Various advisers produced termly newsletters for their heads of department and this was regarded as a source of support to complement the meetings they organized. Interestingly, several advisers had been requested to stop holding monthly meetings for staff in the authority as headteachers complained that teachers were too often unavailable for school meetings. Meetings and newsletters helped to create a sense of unity among the heads of department and faculty. Indeed, one adviser said that he regarded his subject heads 'just like a large department'.

In-school support

School-based INSET has already been commented upon and, as with LEA provision, was often difficult to separate from general support. However, there were ways in which senior staff could help middle managers, who said that they wanted a sympathetic figure who would be prepared to listen to them and someone to talk to – many of the sentiments were similar to those expressed in the NFER study of new headteachers (Weindling and Earley, 1987) for whom establishing the right 'distance' was important. In some schools, heads of department and faculty were assigned to a deputy head or a senior teacher (often outside their own subject specialism) for pastoral and curricular oversight and this worked well for some, badly for others, largely depending on the personalities and the interpersonal skills of the senior staff concerned:

> All departments here have a DH responsible for them but mine is just not interested. When I went for an interview the only thing in her mind was GCSE and she just dismissed all the things I wanted to talk about.

Department heads liked the head to be accessible and not so involved with LEA matters that he or she was out of school a lot. One head, concerned among other things about the possible closure of the school on account of falling rolls, was described as 'always being out on his bike going down to County Hall'. Middle managers favoured heads having 'open-door' policies and being able to clear up problems as and when they occurred. Obviously, open-door policies were not necessarily the best in terms of efficiency and optimal use of time – teachers' access being hampered by long queues of pupils, for example (Weindling and Earley, 1987) – but senior managers clearly had to communicate this to their staff so that they understood about accessibility and could make adequate provision.

Another deciding factor as regards middle managers' perception of support received seemed to be the degree to which the SMT were working together and had a positive policy as regards the middle managers in the school. In one case study school, where the SMT were clearly not working together and where there were a number of personnel and communication problems, a faculty head commented that the SMT could not support middle managers adequately until they had 'put their own house in order'. The situation here contrasted with that in another school where there were a considerable number of favourable references to the support received from senior staff. Heads of department spoke of the fact that the head was very acute and aware of problems before they occurred:

His vision is a means of support – he scans the horizon so that
we are all in advance of what will have to come some time. This
gives us time to prepare ourselves before we have to prepare our
departments.

One of the deputies in this school said: 'HoDs need a listening ear and
I try not to take over when they come to me with problems', while
another remarked:

The deputies have got to get it over to HoDs that they are
not expected to do everything perfectly straightaway. . . There
should be few surprises in the annual formal report – everything
that is going on should be known to SMT. . . I always try to give
as many facts as possible before introducing an innovation – this
helps to overcome insecurity.

This deputy admitted, however, that extra administrative pressures
on senior staff made it harder for them to go out and help
middle managers or observe the departments at work. Senior
staff's involvement in departmental review and staff appraisal was
a considerable source of support and spoken of positively in those
schools in which it occurred. (This issue is explored in depth in
Chapters 6 and 8.)

Teachers in departments can flounder or flourish according to the
support meted out by the department head: the same is true of heads
of department and faculty in the light of help from senior staff. A
deputy head in a school which had introduced departmental review
and appraisal said: 'I can think of some middle management appointments who were not particularly impressive but who with help have
become good heads of department.'

As well as giving individual advice and providing models of good
management skills (chairing meetings, communication etc.) senior
staff can also make the middle manager's task easier by virtue of
structural arrangements and everyday organization. For example, a
deputy head said:

I think it is a function of senior management to enable informal
and regular meetings to happen – for example, to put a faculty in
a block and give them a free period together. The timetable is a
signal that you give to colleagues.

Another said: 'The timetable should be "good" – not merely an
administrative convenience. For example, can you do double physics
after double French?'

Heads of department cited meeting unrealistic deadlines as a
problem which they encountered (see Chapter 4): again, some senior
staff were aware of this: 'I try to give HoDs time to do things – for
example, I ask them for information by break this time next week

rather than today.'

Some heads of department or faculty interviewed in the NFER study spoke positively of the SMT for having thanked them or given them 'a pat on the back' (and the nominated phase two practitioners were often cited by their staff as doing this). However, there were also frequent references to senior staff being 'quick to anger and slow to praise' and clearly this is an area where the SMT could give much more moral and psychological support.

> At this school HoDs have to blow their own trumpets or go disregarded: there is no mechanism for recognition.

> SMT is all criticism and highlighting of problems. Their attitude is 'that's one mountain over, now here's the next one' without any praise for having got over the first mountain.

Individual examples of headteachers' lack of interest were given. At one school, senior staff were said to be 'invisible' and in another, several teachers made the comment that there ought to be a picture of the head in the corridors as otherwise pupils would not know what he looked like, so seldom did he come out of his office. Several heads of home economics wryly remarked that heads only visited the department when they wanted 'cakes for the governors' tea' and departments situated away from the main school buildings – especially those with workshops – rarely got a visit from senior staff. Heads of department felt, rightly or wrongly, that such behaviour made their lives just that much harder as they had no one giving them a boost in the way that they were expected to 'lift' their departmental staff.

Middle managers also felt aggrieved if they were bypassed: for example, a head of department was not told that a member of his staff was going off on a course related to another area of school life (although this probably said as much about poor communication between this head of department and his staff as it did about the relationship between the headteacher and the head of department).

On the positive side, headteachers who went out of their way to give personal support were much appreciated. One phase two head of home economics, for example, spoke of how her head sent HMI documents to her 'with bits underlined' – showing that he had read them and was thinking about their application to the school. Another practitioner in the same school remarked that her department had a tremendous boost when the SMT made the statement that her subject 'was central to the curriculum at this school'. A head of Special Needs at another school commented that the head had been very supportive when integration was being introduced: he had put pressure on reluctant departments in a way that the head of Special Needs would have been unable to do himself. Senior staff were respected when they made themselves available for cover, even if they did not teach regularly, or took the most difficult classes.

That heads of faculty and department must be aware of whole-school policies and implement these in subject areas has been discussed earlier. However, senior staff have to give the lead to middle management and ensure that school aims and objectives are quite clear: 'People here would feel more positive if there were some statements from senior staff about what the school wanted to do. There is no firmly expressed policy or aims and objectives.' Some statement needs to be made rather than merely assuming that all departments are moving in similar directions.

One of the phase two heads of department, who had had a considerable amount of school-management experience outside her present department, remarked that middle managers at the school were given little direction and things were always done at the last minute by senior staff – agendas for middle management meetings, for example, were not published in advance, so no preparation could be done. Things muddled along and were not planned for and the fact that standards at the school were, generally, high was on account of the fact that the staff (because of the favourable location of the school) were particularly able and motivated. At another school, however, faculties had to produce statements relating their work to the school's aims and objectives which were clearly articulated and this was felt to sharpen practice – and was itself a valuable staff-development exercise for departments to undertake. But where this sort of demand was not made, the work of departments was liable to become very isolated. An adviser commented that expectations tended to be low in schools where the headteacher did not demand things of middle managers and, certainly, a number of the nominated practitioners studied in phase two spoke of their awareness that they were expected 'to deliver the goods' and the goods had to be of a high quality.

Clearly, there can be effective departments and faculties regardless of the strength of the support offered by senior staff in much the same way as it is possible for there to be good departmental practice despite a weak head of department. However, as departmental members cannot maximize their potential, either individually or collectively, without effective leadership from the head of department so it is probably true to say that middle managers cannot really flourish unless they have the right environment created and maintained by senior staff in the school and advisory staff in the LEA.

It is not, however, only senior staff who were a source of support for middle managers: seconds-in-command were often valuable as 'sounding boards' for heads of department. Several seconds-in-command interviewed remarked that their department heads discussed everything with them (and they, of course, appreciated the experience that this gave them). There was an instance of an able young probationer being used as a confidant when there was no second-in-command following reallocation of points. Seconds-in-command could often provide support by complementing the department head's skills and compensating for deficiencies. There were several examples of effective practitioners who tended to be disorganized; they remarked that they depended on their deputies to find documents for them.

Technicians were another valuable source of support. The fact that they were allocated to a department often indicated the headteacher's support of that department. Where they were considered as a part of the departmental team they would, in the words of one technician, 'all muck in in an emergency'. Indeed, it was clear that heads of department and faculty derived much support from the team in those cases in which the complementary nature of teachers and ancillary staff was recognized and valued.

Summary and discussion

How well individuals were prepared for taking on the responsibility of leading a department seemed to depend very much on the department heads with whom they had worked and the degree to which the latter were prepared to delegate responsibility and involve staff in departmental activities. Preparation was generally thought to be inadequate and reference was made to a lack of confidence and a feeling of being 'thrown in at the deep end'. Promotion was often related to success as a classroom teacher rather than to the acquisition of the skills of departmental management and administration. Effective preparation for the next stage seemed to be more a matter of good fortune than of deliberate school or LEA policy, although it could be argued that the situation has improved recently on account of the national attention given to school management training and development – albeit primarily focusing on heads and deputies. Suggestions as to how preparation for department headship could be improved were made and these, and others, are developed further in the final chapter.

Once middle managers were in post, the in-service opportunities available to them – whether from within the school or externally provided – varied considerably. School-based INSET specifically for department and faculty heads did not appear to be very common.

However, residential weekends, after-school courses, and day conferences – involving whole staffs or identified groups within schools –
may become more frequent as schools are given greater responsibility
for diagnosing and meeting their own INSET needs. The five annual
'contract' days – some of which will be used for in-service purposes -
and greater control by schools over their INSET budget, are also likely
to lead to significant changes. Participation in training opportunities is
thus less likely to be the voluntary activity it has largely been in the past,
although the amount of INSET undertaken will continue to depend
on the opportunities made available and the individual practitioners'
level of interest.

Because of the problem of covering for colleagues, in-service
training was increasingly being offered out of school hours as
there was found to be a need to ensure that the many benefits
derived from participation in courses and meeting colleagues from
other schools were not outweighed by the 'pupil-disruption' factor.
Diagnosing INSET needs at both school and LEA level was generally
found to be done unsystematically although this is likely to change
as advisers and INSET coordinators make greater use of the various
needs-identification instruments currently available.

Although senior staff identified 'managing people' and an understanding of current educational issues as areas in which middle
managers needed training and developing, the practitioners themselves often made reference to 'survival strategies' (usually associated
with time or personnel management) and whatever happened to be
of concern to them at that particular moment (e.g. GCSE, records of
achievement). Courses for heads of department had to cover some
areas relating to the 'nuts and bolts' of running a department, while
also giving attention to more generic management issues as commonly found on courses for heads and deputies. These included, for
example, effective decision-making, managing change, team-building,
running meetings, interpersonal relations and dealing with stress.
Some middle management courses gave emphasis to preparing for
the next stage and issues such as appraisal, evaluation and review were
increasingly considered.

Support from advisers and inspectors, not unlike the provision of
LEA courses, was again found to vary. Some organized termly meetings
for their middle managers and ran annual conferences; others participated in departmental and faculty reviews. These, and other forms of
support, were generally welcomed but there was a recognition that
advisers were busy people with a number of schools to service and
that advisory teachers were useful change agents.

Heads, deputies and other senior staff were also important sources of support. Examples were given of schools where senior staff were linked to particular departments and faculties, had pastoral and curricular oversight and could act as sympathetic but not uncritical 'curriculum friends' (see Chapter 8 for a discussion of the role of senior staff in departmental evaluation and review). Giving praise, showing interest, being accessible and making the time to deal with department heads' concerns were seen as important qualities in heads and deputies. Also important was the degree to which the SMT was perceived to be working as a team and giving leadership and direction to the school. Different schools seemed to have different expectations of their middle managers.

As well as offering support and advice, senior staff could also provide positive role models (e.g. chairing meetings effectively) and ensure that the school's timetable and organizational arrangements enabled middle managers to discharge their responsibilities with minimal hindrance. Seconds-in-command and ancillary staff were mentioned as important sources of support. It was also noted that although some departments could operate effectively with little or no support from senior staff and/or the education authority, the chances of departments and their staffs developing to their full potential were slim.

6 How do Middle Managers Promote Staff Development?

As has been seen, responsibility for staff development or professional development is often identified as a key area in the job descriptions of heads of department and faculty. The NFER research was interested in examining the actual practice of department and faculty heads in this area, especially the ways in which effective practitioners realized this particular responsibility. Marland (1971) was one of the first commentators to draw attention to the fact that department heads were responsible not only for children but also for other adults and their development. Professional development has been defined as 'the process by which teachers acquire the knowledge and skills essential to good professional practice at each stage of a teaching career' (Hoyle, 1980). In current usage, the terms 'staff development' and 'professional development' seem to be almost synonymous. However, they are distinct: 'staff development' considers the needs of teachers in fulfilling a role and meeting the demands of an institution and/or its organizational subsections; 'professional development' is concerned with the needs of teachers as individuals with particular interests and career aspirations. Despite the sometimes imprecise usage of the terms, there is considerable agreement about the purpose of the activity – namely, to improve the pupils' school experience – though much less agreement about the best means of bringing it about.

This chapter will examine the particular responsibilities of department and faculty heads as regards their staff's professional development, focusing particularly on the key areas of delegation, INSET opportunities and appraisal, and will describe ways in which effective practitioners acted as staff developers.

The staff development role

As far as senior staff were concerned, 'desire for staff development' was seen as one of the hallmarks of a successful department, but the NFER research found a widespread lack of confidence in this area. Heads and deputies commented that many department heads did not see it as part of their role (and it was seldom identified as such by many phase one interviewees) while departmental staff often felt neglected. Advisers, too, remarked that there was generally a limited understanding of the staff development role. Heads of department themselves, when they were aware of their responsibilities in this area, felt that they needed specific training. It was not unusual, for example, for them to have had little experience of working with other adults. A senior adviser observed that:

> Things done in departments are really all staff development issues but they are sadly neglected because of time, other demands of the job, concern with everyday trivia, and the reluctance of heads of department to take on the role of staff developer.

It could be argued that it is of increasing importance that department and faculty heads attend to this area. On the one hand, it is imperative for successful curriculum innovation. Fullan (1982) writes that 'it is essential to recognize the relationship between professional development and the implementation of change'. On the other hand, it is also necessary to maintain staff's involvement and interest in a period of falling rolls and restricted mobility in the profession. Ironically, some heads of department found this militated against their efforts to develop staff. Unable to give financial reward, they could, in addition, no longer say 'it will be good for your career' because there were far too many aspiring department heads for the posts available. One adviser said that courses for aspiring heads of department did, in fact, merely raise false expectations.

One of the phase two nominees noted that 'the key to the whole business of staff development is engaging teachers' interest and attention'; and, most importantly, there was thought to be spin-off in the classroom if this engagement was achieved. A headteacher remarked that: 'You need to let staff know you think well of them and that they are going to help themselves become better.' This is something that the effective middle managers tended to do, engendering a very positive, supportive atmosphere out of which staff development arose. A scale 1 teacher commented that her head of department had helped her professional development by 'helping me to believe in myself', while a member of a recommended Special Needs department remarked:

'For ten years before I came here I was just a glorified baby-sitter; it is great to be part of a developing department now.'

What then is the role of department and faculty heads in staff development and what specifically can be done to promote the right climate? Although preparation for promotion is only one of the functions of staff development, Wallace (1985) stresses the need for it to be achieved through the process of management development lest individuals pursue their own careers in isolation with the result that the school suffers. 'Individual career needs are reconciled with the educational aims of a school through a collaborative process of mutual support.' The department head, as a *manager*, must bear this in mind.

Delegation

Central to the middle manager's role would seem to be the matter of delegation. As laid out in one case study school's handbook:

Delegation is essential not only in practical terms but as an expression of teamwork and partnership and as a process of staff development and training. . . Delegation makes the management process more human.

Pragmatically, it is impossible for heads of department and faculty (unless they have vastly more non-contact time than is presently the norm – as previously stated, this ranged from 15 to 35 per cent) to do all the jobs for which they are technically responsible, so some delegation must be assumed. Delegation is crucial, not only because it allows people to develop, to live up to their responsibilities and to gain a sense of importance, but also because it removes some of the burden from the head of department's shoulders, thus creating time for the performance of other aspects of the role. Delegation is necessary so that time can be found, for example, for reflection, forward planning, support, discussion and observation of colleagues' teaching.

A case study head thought that 'every member of a department should have a responsibility . . . it gives them a feeling of "this is my department and my absence will be noted". Heads of department involved in the project were generally of the opinion that delegation depended on the person being delegated to rather than the issue itself and was related to individuals' strengths and weaknesses rather than to policy; however, the introduction of incentive allowances in the academic year 1987–1988 has complicated the picture and has implications for the issue of delegation.

Rotation of responsibilities

One practitioner made the point that the strict rotation of tasks within a department or faculty did not take account of the individuals' needs, the stage that they were at, or what they were or were not ready to cope with. Another head of department felt that job rotation was commendable in management terms but in practice, when staff had heavy teaching loads, it was more sensible to let teachers be thoroughly familiar with a particular area so that they could do whatever they had to in the shortest possible time. This sentiment was echoed by a head who said: 'There is a danger of creating systems that move people away from what they do best: the curriculum must always come first.' Job rotation was also impractical in departments which had a high turnover of staff.

Where job rotation did exist within a department, it was generally appreciated. Because everyone had experience of doing all tasks, in the words of a scale 1 teacher:

> Everyone knows what you are on about: you are not banging your head against a brick wall. Also, it gives a sense of realism – it's easy to drift into your own world with your own little area of responsibility. And it's good to be reminded of the unattractive things that need to be done.

A probationer in the same department observed that departmental staff did not always have to go running to the head of department for help. An area of responsibility new to any individual would be familiar ground to colleagues – the scale 1 teacher might help the scale 3. And, of course, the fact that one had to train the other was in itself a useful form of staff development. Rotation also prevented staleness and the sort of frustration voiced by one teacher who said: 'I'm in charge of third-year physics and I shall be for the next 25 years.'

Constraints on delegation

Some department and faculty heads – in both phases of the research – were reluctant to delegate for various reasons. Some were loath to delegate anything until they had done the task themselves, knew what it entailed and were in a position to advise others how to do it; others felt that they could not add to the already heavy workload of their colleagues. Heads of department in the study also remarked that if they delegated a job and it was not done well, then this reflected badly on them. In some instances, delegation was not possible on account of the constitution of the department or reluctance within it. There were problems with delegation where the department included a number of staff with considerable commitments elsewhere (for example, head, deputy head, senior teacher, pastoral head) or in such cases as the department which had a lot of part-timers and teachers with little commitment and few ambitions to achieve promotion. Exton (1986) notes that delegation to part-time teachers as regards departmental matters is possible, provided that unreasonable demands are not made and he suggests that as well as being encouraged to attend meetings, they should be given 'a concrete task relating to the particular classes which they teach, and which can be accomplished over a period of time'.

There was a limit, heads of department thought, to the pressure that they could exert on staff: 'One can't invade people's privacy and make them do things'; and 'One can make some progress with disinterested staff but by the time they've moved on a bit the others are streets ahead and there's been further change anyway.' One practitioner said: 'My number three is in a rut and says, "I'm happy: leave me alone." It's difficult to get staff to develop if they do not want to.' The fact that middle managers had to create the right foundations for delegation was illustrated by the comment of one practitioner who said: 'Sharing responsibility in this department is not really possible because people in the department guard their territories.'

Anachronistic structures could also inhibit attempts to delegate sensibly: 'There is a scale 2 but his authority was defined by the head without consultation with me – he's in charge of exchanges and this prevents other staff from volunteering.' Other heads of department thought that job descriptions should be negotiated and were, in fact, all about staff development and developing departments as teams and working towards a common purpose.

In addition, both senior and middle managers spoke of the fact that some scale 1 teachers were reluctant to take on tasks without reward. Indeed, some heads of department were unwilling to delegate if they could not offer financial reward and felt that scale 1 teachers were paid to teach and nothing else. It will be interesting to know to what extent this view changes in the light of the recently introduced incentive allowances and the delineated professional duties for all teachers (GB.DES, 1987b).

Teachers' attitudes to delegation

Teachers' views on delegation may be determined by the environment in which they are working (a senior teacher remarked that 'teachers will take on extra responsibilities if they think that they're working for a good HoD') or by personal motivation ('My HoD will only delegate to people with scale points: I would gladly take on jobs for experience without being paid'). A scale 1 teacher stated: 'You live up to responsibilities given you and this is good for self-esteem.' Teachers often spoke with appreciation of having tasks delegated to them – provided that they were not merely handed out the 'chores' or felt that they were being 'used' (as one teacher said: 'Our HoD only asks what we aspire to when he's stuck to fill the timetable'). Many department heads had been prepared for the role by having worked with a 'good' practitioner themselves: 'The old HoD was excellent: at the time you thought he was trying to get out of doing the job himself but in retrospect you appreciated it.' In those departments in which a team spirit had been engendered, departmental members spoke of wanting to do more in order to relieve the head of department of some pressure; in some instances, teachers saw a need (for cataloguing worksheets, for example) and got on with it on their own initiative.

It is, perhaps, worth while quoting at length a scale 2 teacher in one of the phase one departments:

> We share out the workload a lot and we all feel that we're contributing to the department. There's no sense of competition. The HoD sets a very good example and encourages you if you've got ideas. If you like and respect someone then you will work hard for them. . . It's important to praise people. . . Our HoD will always make time for you: others are in too much of a rush. . . Delegation is a tricky business. My HoD is very good – she decides what is needed and then puts all the things on the newsletter and asks you to say what you would like to do. She gives you time before contacting you and this gives breathing space so that you do not feel that you are rushed into something.

It is only when latent expertise is uncovered that heads of department can get the best out of their department – an ability frequently cited as a necessary quality in the effective department or faculty head. For some interviewees, it was, indeed, more important than what the heads of department or faculty could actually do themselves. Yet, as Marland (1971) observed, it is 'not just a matter of reinforcing what people are good at'; new skills must be developed in staff so that they can achieve promotion if they so desire.

Areas delegated and the means of delegation

Some department heads thought in terms of dividing the whole curriculum area they were responsible for (if curriculum is interpreted as all departmental activity) rather than allocating specific, self-contained tasks, so that all were involved in everything and the team spirit was enhanced. Some subjects seemed to lend themselves to this more readily than others although, in the long run, it was probably more to do with the style and inclination of the head of department. 'In the English department all have to contribute to reading lists, publication of pupils' work and so forth – you can't divide up things like these.' Another head of English said: 'A further form of professional development is to take a book and work together as a department looking at ways of approaching it.'

One practitioner commented: 'I have a certain way of looking at things and it's important to involve others so that everything doesn't just get my stamp.' This head of department was sufficiently aware to acknowledge that he was not the sole source of good practice or interesting ideas. Others were less sure about this. For example, a phase one practitioner said: 'I'm the best person to prepare materials; I'm the HoD after all. I do not think that it is the department's job to produce materials and I do not think that things are best done in discussion with others.'

Caution on the part of department heads was not uncommon. A scale 1 teacher observed of her head of department: 'He keeps close control of some things and thus gives the impression that he does not really trust you', while a head of department confessed: 'I'm not reluctant to delegate anything but I'd be reluctant to relinquish power.' A head of faculty said that he had difficulty persuading his heads of department that a junior member of their staff was capable of taking on responsibility as 'jobs represent power and they don't like to relinquish them'. These attitudes contrast strikingly with a middle manager who thought that good heads of department might have to work to their weaknesses when, for the benefit of their staff, they delegated all the things they enjoyed doing and were good at and were left with the things that they personally were poor at.

As well as relieving the load on department heads, preparing staff for promotion, maintaining teachers' interest and giving them a sense of worth, delegation also has an important part to play in their process of curriculum change. Research into the change process (e.g. Fullan, 1982) has shown that if those involved feel a sense of 'ownership', they are far more likely to take the initiative into their practice within the classroom rather than just paying it lipservice (see Chapter 7). Increasingly, effective heads of department were using departmental working parties to develop new courses: 'A few years ago we rewrote our syllabus and this was a major INSET activity . . . It was a good forum and, although very time-consuming, was the only way that I could get commitment from the staff.'

Handy (1981) draws attention to the fact that how something is delegated is as important as what is delegated. 'True delegation, effective delegation, is delegation with trust and with only the necessary minimum of controls.' The trust must be reciprocal and 'it is no good the superior trusting his [sic] subordinates if they do not trust him'. In the case study schools, this trust was generated by the effective practitioners by way of the support, be it moral or practical, that they gave their staff. In contrast, teachers who had served under less effective department heads spoke of being given a task to do with no advice or guidance and, not liking to ask for this, making mistakes which they were then blamed for. Bell and Maher (1986) stress that training should be concomitant with and, indeed, a precursor of, delegation which 'has more to do with the assignment of responsibility and authority than with the transfer of a task from one person to another'.

Creating opportunities for development

Delegation in all its forms is, of course, an important form of staff development – arguably the most important source as it is within the department that the teacher has to 'perform' and the outcomes of training are realized. However, there are other more obvious 'providers' of staff development and in-service training – institutes of higher education, teachers' centres, private organizations, subject associations, local authorities and so forth. Indeed, one of the things that heads of department and faculty must do is to ensure that information about courses external to the school is made known to all teachers and opportunities created for those who wish to participate. Departmentally based INSET is usually directed towards the specific needs of the curriculum as delivered in that department (although within this, individual weaknesses may be supported and problems overcome). However, Taylor (1980) enunciates the danger of defining staff development too rigidly and of looking for 'direct payoff for specific tasks'. It is, he contends, more a matter of developing the teachers' own responsibility for learning and encouraging their self-educative efforts. Above all, there must be opportunity to reflect – a necessity also stressed by Winrow (1985): 'Experience alone will not provide a satisfactory basis for professional advancement. Teachers and schools need to reflect on and evaluate their experiences. Teachers need to become partners in, and ultimately responsible for, their own learning.' These sentiments do, of course, have significance for the middle manager's role in encouraging self-evaluation, departmental review and participation in appraisal – issues that will be addressed later.

The effective department and faculty heads did not merely make information about courses and meetings available to their staff – they also ensured that the right people were encouraged to go on them.

Some spoke of tactful ways of going about this: 'I say "The department is in need of developing: will you go on this course to help it?"' Probationers and young teachers working with effective heads of department spoke with enthusiasm of being the department's representative at various LEA or subject association meetings, and of being encouraged to think more widely. There was evidence of the sharing, within departments, of both INSET opportunities and the provision of cover to which they gave rise. Such departments tended to be those in which there was good dissemination of what had been gained from INSET attendance.

Aware that the benefits of courses are limited unless there is some sort of feedback and follow-up, effective department heads ensured that the teachers either wrote a report to be circulated among the department (or relevant people in the school) or gave a presentation at a department or faculty meeting. One head of department said that she felt that it was her responsibility to advise less experienced teachers on how to go about such reporting if she felt that they were at all unsure. There were instances of several teachers from the same department going on a course (for example, on active learning) so that they would all have first-hand experience of the topic and would thus be in a better position to relate it to their department practice. Heads of department were aware of the value of staff extending their horizons: 'Many have limited experience because they have only worked at this school; they must be made aware of what is going on in the county.'

Some departments and faculties organized their own INSET activities and, as was noted in Chapter 5, this is likely to become increasingly common as a result of the recently introduced five 'contract' days and as more schools are allocated their own budgets under the new in-service funding arrangements. Department and faculty heads will need to be able to diagnose INSET needs and liaise with the school INSET coordinator. In the departments involved in the research, sometimes a visiting speaker came; in others, members of the department with particular expertise, or colleagues from elsewhere in the school (for example, computing or Special Needs) would take the lead. One PE department, wishing to introduce dance into the curriculum, met together before school every day for a week for dance workshops to prepare themselves. An English teacher spoke of a previous school where all the members of the English department went away together for a weekend to talk about their work. One teacher spoke of the fact that her head of department was always giving her articles to read – and discussing them with her afterwards so she had to read them! She admitted that it was an extra pressure at the time but she much appreciated it as a means of her own professional development.

All good intentions and ideas about INSET were, of course, undermined by the problem of cover and supply (Earley, 1986). Again, as noted in the previous chapter, teachers were reluctant to abandon their classes and often considered that the business of setting suitable work and then marking it was more trouble than it was worth. Where smaller scale INSET occurred within a department, senior staff in some schools were invaluable in agreeing to cover in order to release the head of department and/or another member of staff for INSET. A phase two faculty head voiced his concern over the way that fifth year release time was spent in the summer term – he thought that at present it was often wasted time and could be used much more effectively. He had planned a programme for his staff but would have welcomed greater direction from senior management here.

What was the effect of these INSET activities? The departments where they were going on were noticeable for their openness, for the way in which the curriculum was subject to critical review and for the way in which they wanted to improve their teaching skills. The NFER research cannot, of course, make any empirically based statements about effects in the classroom except to say that senior staff commented on the noticeable 'rise in status' (judged by exam results, option take-up etc.) of departments where such things were going on.

Decision-making and meetings

Almost all the senior staff interviewed spoke of the need for heads of department to 'show leadership', 'create a team' and 'get the department working together'. One of the most effective ways of doing this, while at the same time acknowledging responsibility towards staff development, is by involving staff in departmental decision-making. As very few scale 1 and 2 teachers interviewed felt that they had a major part in decision-making affecting the whole school, it is obviously important that they are involved at the departmental level (see Chapter 9). Indeed, there is some evidence (for example, Dembo and Gibson, 1985) that teachers' sense of efficacy may be related to their participation in decision-making and it is important for school managers, at all levels, to encourage shared goals and responsibilities for decision-making. An adviser felt that professional development involved sharing information, resources and decision-making; she commented on the fact that she and her colleagues were often struck by the 'nobody tells me anything' syndrome in some departments.

Most department heads agreed in principle to involving their staff and most teachers felt that they were listened to. Informal chats of a professional nature on a day-to-day basis are, of course, vital and represent 'on-going staff development' as well as maintaining an open atmosphere which is conducive to review and self-appraisal. However, many subject heads seem to underuse, or misuse, the department or faculty meeting which can play a crucial part in staff development and curriculum reform (Maden, 1974). The formal meeting is also important for team-building as – provided that all are able to attend – it includes both part-time teachers and those full-time teachers who may work chiefly in another department and thus not be around very much for informal chats. As earlier noted it is important that part-timers be encouraged to attend departmental meetings. Often, departmental meetings seem to be used merely for information-giving or for routine matters of administration. Of course, it is vital that staff are kept informed and that organizational matters are made clear but effective practitioners tended to try to keep all this to a minimum so that educational and professional issues could be addressed in meetings. There were many examples of good practice, especially amongst the phase two department and faculty heads, but many more would seem to need to be made aware of the value of circulating discussion papers in advance, asking members of staff to give a brief presentation, rotating the role of chairperson and so forth. Teachers were adamant that they did not want meetings 'just for the sake of them' – recognizing, presumably, that they got nothing from them. Some middle managers, too, resented being told by the head when to hold meetings, preferring, rather, to call them 'as the need arose'. (The recently introduced 'directed time' of 1265 hours has meant heads have had to specify when departmental and other meetings are to be held.) It was noteworthy that those teachers who had been involved in intra- or interdepartmental groups spoke of the collegiality that they engendered. One head of department spoke of using departmental seminars 'as a way of helping staff who were reluctant to confess their weaknesses'. In some of the effective departments staff met together regularly in the evenings or in the holidays at someone's house. Teachers did not object to this, giving the reason as 'because so much gets done' (albeit frequently over a bottle of wine!).

The middle manager clearly needs to acquire the skills of running meetings. Those heads of department and faculty in the study who had a good model in the form, for example, of effectively run middle management meetings, were fortunate but many spoke of the poor quality of such meetings and of the fact, for example, that the agenda was inappropriate for the number of people involved and that senior staff lacked the necessary skills for controlling meetings – such skills as described, for example, by the Association for Science Education/British Gas, (1984); Bell and Maher, (1986); Bulman (1986) and Waters (1987).

Responsibility for inexperienced staff

There was widespread agreement that middle managers were directly responsible for new and inexperienced staff, although in some of the case study schools in the remoter locations, students and probationers were few and far between. Generally, phase two nominees were spoken of very highly with regard to the help that they had given to young teachers, both by these teachers themselves and by senior staff in the schools. Some effective practitioners seemed to have a high turnover of staff (partly because staff went on to achieve promotion elsewhere on account of the experience and training that they had had in the department – although there were, of course, many other factors affecting teacher movement). One long-standing head of faculty said that about half the other heads of department in her subject area in the authority (a small one) had passed through her department at one time or another. This faculty head said that the resultant departments were not all similar as the schools and individual situations were all so different – but she had provided 'a framework of consideration'. A teacher in this same faculty thought that she would 'never have made it' as a probationer had it not been for the constant support and advice of the faculty head.

The effective heads of department and faculty often set aside a time each week for discussing work and lesson material with students and probationers and involved them in the activities of the department. While being sensitive to the fact that new teachers were under a considerable amount of strain from just preparing material, effective department heads nevertheless tried to help them broaden their perspectives. A phase two nominee remarked that there was tremendous frustration in those departments in which the head of department was not 'trying to bring the probationer on'. Probationers in 'strong' departments were particularly grateful for help received, remarking that, elsewhere, new teachers were often left to get on with things alone.

A teacher in a phase two department spoke of the fact that when the head of department had been on a year's secondment and there had been an acting head of department, a probationer had 'failed' and left the profession. In the eyes of the teacher, this would never have happened had the regular head of department been there. A phase two nominee spoke of the situation which he had inherited when he arrived at the school: among other things, a teacher was 'failing badly' and this was attributable to the fact that this teacher had been a student and a probationer under the previous ('weak') head of department and things had gone from bad to worse without any action being taken. It was, in fact, widely believed by those interviewed that department heads could 'make or mar' careers in that often a teacher flourished or floundered according to the amount of support received. Indeed, several phase two practitioners were nominated by advisers on the grounds that their advent at a school had transformed various underperforming teachers. The effective practitioners tended to be those who were aware of what was going on, generated discussion and 'opened up' the department and then helped alleviate the problems thus exposed.

The more established heads of department had often learnt the skills of developing students and probationers from experience; 'newer' ones were sometimes uneasy about the role in that they had been given little guidance as to how best to go about it. The department head's responsibility was assisted in those schools where there was a senior member of staff responsible for new teachers and where there was an induction programme either in the school (where numbers made this possible) or within the authority.

Heads of department in the study had no hesitation about going into the lessons of students and probationers and passing comment on what they saw. This was not the case, however, as regards other colleagues and the whole area of appraisal and review often generated unease.

Appraising performance

Once a department is sharing tasks, planning and decision-making, and is working together as a team, departmental review and appraisal – other forms of staff development – can occur without threat and from within. Indeed, a system of appraisal – both formal and informal – can evolve from departmental review and evaluation. As King (1986) notes:

> We need to involve all teachers in the broader aspects of school organization and curriculum development. Evaluation should be integral to this. Appraising performance should also be part of this but it should be in terms of sharing experience and seeking self-knowledge.

The last few years has seen an enormous growth in the literature on teacher appraisal (e.g. Bunnell, 1987; Dadds, 1987; Dixon, 1987;

Wragg, 1987; Fidler and Cooper, 1988; Hewton, 1988; Turner and Clift, 1988). However, in their various ways all the writers stress the fact that the centre of the issue is teachers' self-education. Target-setting, at the heart of appraisal, is, for example, an 'opportunity to participate in departmental decision-making. The system allows teachers not only to suggest targets for themselves but to influence the planning of the school and the department' (Trethowan, 1987).

The majority of teachers interviewed for the NFER project were prepared to accept an appraisal scheme if it was non-threatening – educative rather than condemnatory – and carried out by someone whom they trusted and respected. Torrington *et al.* (1987) found empirical evidence that 'individual members of staff in schools, like people at work everywhere, hunger for the sort of appraisal that will provide them with constructive feedback on their performance' and Dadds (1987) gives similar evidence from primary and middle school teachers. The word itself is, unfortunately, frequently associated with accountability and often thought of in terms of 'weeding out' the inefficient and dismissing incompetent teachers. Kyriacou (1987) comments on the conflicting purposes of the three chief models: appraisal as management task, as public accountability and as in-service development; and Bell (1987) notes: 'If staff appraisal is to be instrumental in improving the teaching and learning in our schools, then the meanings which are attached to it in practice will need to place considerable emphasis on the staff development aspects of the process.' It is here that heads of department and faculty are directly involved and where they can take the initiative for, as Everard (1986) notes, 'the key agent in the organization for helping people to do a better job is their immediate manager'. Similarity, Trethowan (1987) writes: 'Both target-setting and appraisal are only possible in the context of individual situations and by those in close touch with standards, performances and needs. In a large organization the system has to be operated through the middle management of the school.' If heads of department and faculty have a role as appraisers, their responsibilities are clarified and they are obliged to face their management function.

For some commentators, an appraisal scheme was just part of staff development. The relationship between the two is articulated in *Better Schools* (GB.DES, 1985): 'Regular and formal appraisal of the performance of all teachers is necessary if LEAs are to have the reliable, comprehensive and up-to-date information necessary to facilitate effective professional support and development.' The more recent Advisory, Conciliation and Arbitration Service (ACAS) Report (1986) states: 'The Working Group understands appraisal not as a series of perfunctory periodic events, but as a continuous and systematic process intended to help individual teachers with their professional development and career planning and to help ensure that the in-service training and deployment of teachers matches the complementary needs of the individual teachers and the schools.'

Appraisal involves, inevitably, the identification not only of good practice and effectiveness – which can then be celebrated – but also of weakness and underperformance – which can then be remedied. It is the responsibility of the head of department and faculty to support and help the teacher to overcome his or her problems. An adviser involved in the NFER research considered that there was no real difference in appraising teachers and appraising pupils – both exercises should lead to improvement; and both, stressed a deputy head, should be linked to aims and objectives. King (1986) writes: 'We must see appraisal as just an aspect of school improvement through the encouragement of individual and group evaluation. This requires schools, and in larger schools departments, agreeing goals, developing a common sense of purpose and collaborating to achieve their aims.'

Support for underperforming teachers

Advisers and senior staff, when identifying effective practitioners, frequently cited the fact that weak teachers had overcome their problems and failing teachers had begun to succeed under the guidance of one of the recommended department heads. The new head of department had very often done an informal appraisal, identifying the problems and then setting about remedying them. Effective heads of department often generated the sharing of ideas within departments so that staff benefited from the general environment in a number of ways. Bridges (1986) found that failing teachers frequently had difficulties in a number of areas; they would thus be helped by being in an 'open' department where failures and successes were discussed equally. Less successful heads of department were either unaware of the problem (because there was no monitoring of performance) or ignored it so that the situation deteriorated. In some cases, teachers had left the profession on account of poor leadership and comments were made that this would not have happened had the effective department head been in post at the time.

Criticism and reprimand were, however, things that department and faculty heads were loath to engage in: senior staff spoke of this reluctance and practitioners themselves identified it as a problem area. They felt that they had to rub shoulders with departmental staff on a day-to-day basis and were fearful of ruining relationships, especially where older and more established staff were involved. (They were

usually happy to adopt a more supervisory role in relation to probationers and newly appointed teachers.) Diffey (1987) also noted that
appraisers considered interviews with staff who were 'going through
the motions' – older, established, stable staff – to be the most difficult. A faculty head, however, asked: 'Can people be really happy all
the time they know that they are not providing a good service in
the classroom?' Similarly, Wragg (1987) observes: 'Bad teachers themselves cannot always be too happy, unless their defences are so well
oiled that they have rationalized the problem out of sight, and either
believe it does not exist or that it is the fault of others.' Respondents
in the NFER research commented that weak teachers do not like to
admit their problems, so bringing them out into the open via a formal
appraisal interview can, in fact, give assistance – provided, of course,
that the department and faculty head gives the necessary help and
support. An adviser identified the inability of teachers to expose their
own weaknesses as 'the biggest barrier to staff development'.

Formal appraisal schemes

Clearly, a considerable amount of very worthwhile informal review
takes place within departments and faculties on a day-to-day basis.
However, this often happens largely by good luck and a formal appraisal scheme is a valuable complement to the *ad hoc* activity, helping to
ensure that particular issues (for example, those not of immediate
concern) and various members of staff (part-timers, for example, or
those with heavy pastoral responsibilities, who are not around the
department so often for informal exchanges) are not neglected.

Formal appraisal schemes had been introduced in only three of
the 21 NFER case study schools. In one, the scheme had come from
the initiative of the headteacher; in another, it was recommended by
a working party on staff development which had itself arisen as a result
of a school review exercise. In both schools staff involvement was
voluntary (about two-thirds participated) and teachers could choose
their appraiser. All the teachers interviewed in the two schools gave
very positive feedback, thought that the appraisal interview had been
very beneficial for their own development and said that they looked
forward to the next cycle. In another case study school, a scheme
had been started – middle managers had been allocated to a senior
member of staff and some interviews had taken place – but had
not flourished on account of lack of time, inadequate preparation
by the appraisers and industrial action by the teachers. In none
of the schools was the formal appraisal scheme specifically linked
with promotion.

Individual departments can, with the support and agreement of the senior staff, institute their own forms of appraisal. A few of the case study departments did this; they were, notably, those which had been identified as effective. The head of one of these departments stressed that appraisal is not a 'one-interview-a-year matter: you have to refer to things throughout the term. We have an open-door policy and we often put two groups together.' Another recommended head of faculty saw all staff for an undisturbed double period each term 'to talk about where they are and where they're going', while a teacher remarked: 'The HoD will say, "Come and have a cup of coffee" but you know that you're going to do business rather than have a social chat.'

It was the climate out of which the appraisal arose which seemed to be the significant factor – the departments were open, discussed things together all the time, knew what colleagues were doing and engaged in team-teaching. Dixon (1987) stresses the importance of such a climate for the successful introduction of appraisal and points to the necessity of the most appropriate management style: 'Schemes operating in a highly authoritarian regime may function well mechanically. They are, however, unlikely to achieve the desired aim of motivating and encouraging good classroom practice.' The climate in the case study schools operating appraisal schemes was right for the literal and meta-phorical 'opening up' of classrooms which is, perhaps, much of what staff appraisal is all about. In such a climate, no longer do teachers consider autonomy within classrooms an automatic professional right to be jealously protected. Appraisal, said an adviser, 'develops a sense of shared task'.

Classroom observation

The mutual visiting of classrooms was often mentioned as a prerequisite for staff development and did not necessarily have to be linked with appraisal. The benefits of this were frequently referred to:

Another teacher and I set an example by keeping our doors open and other people have picked up ideas from us. Now, all members of the department are happy to have people in and out of their lessons. This policy has helped the weak teacher immensely – and I've learnt a lot from him too.

We go in and out. The probationer finds this very rewarding and the part-timer has got very excited about computers having seen comparable work in someone else's lessons.

Teachers in open-plan blocks, laboratories and workshops, and involved in PE – as well as those in the situations above – tended to be the least wary of observation and visits. Others, however, had negative perceptions and there was clearly a big gap between different practices. Some were aware of the limitations of the traditional concept of teachers' autonomy: 'Once we shut the classroom door, the only evidence of what we do is exam results.' A phase one head of faculty admitted that he did not know what went on in the faculty – 'people just get reputations'. In another department a teacher said: 'Observation is not encouraged – the majority would be rather reluctant . . . I went into the HoD's room once and later received a note saying that I was not to do this when he was teaching.' At least one authority involved in the DES teacher appraisal pilot schemes used the term 'looking at learning' to reduce the threat engendered by the term 'classroom observation'.

These are, of course, all instances of informal observation or 'glimpses' of classroom activity. Formal observation – over a whole lesson, for example – occurred very infrequently within the schools and departments participating in the NFER research – not least because of insufficient time and the logistical problems. Where the timetable was blocked, department heads were often teaching at the same time as their staff. Elsewhere, if non-contact periods were used, the head of department would always see a teacher with the same group. Even where the logistical problems had been overcome (e.g. by senior staff offering to provide cover) there was then the question as to whether the faculty or department head could afford the time to observe. One head of faculty confessed: 'I said that I'd see all 18 of my staff teach. Over a 38-week year, I must see one every fortnight. This observation must be followed by discussion. I haven't achieved my aims – I simply have insufficient time.'

In a survey of 103 heads of mathematics, Straker (1984) found that most (75 per cent) 'felt that their performance was unsatisfactory when it came to observing lessons' and only one respondent claimed to observe lessons regularly. It was also noted that while lack of time was often given as a reason for this, 'only 14 per cent of heads of mathematics would see this as a first priority given a greater allowance of non-contact time'. Straker concludes by questioning the extent to which department heads see themselves as managers having responsibility for improving teacher performance.

In the NFER project it was in schools where senior staff provided support and offered cover that observation became a reality and a general expectation. Those senior staff who felt that mutual observation was important, sometimes used subtle means to effect it. A senior teacher said: 'I can arrange to go into a scale 1's lesson to evaluate her teaching and then say to the HoD, "I can't make it so will you do it?" It's devious but it gets the HoD in!' A deputy head said: 'I would tell HoDs that it was expected that they observed. I would say, for example, "I will cover for you in period two."'

The earlier reference to feedback is important for it represents the educative part of the exercise. A number of the effective practitioners introduced the idea of observation by inviting their staff into their lessons and then asking them for their critical comments. This accords with peer, or 'bottom-up', appraisal, often advocated (for example, Badley, 1986; Diffey, 1986; Wragg, 1987) for gaining acceptance and credibility. A phase two head of faculty said: 'Before we can discuss their [the department's staff] practice, I want them to discuss mine.' One head of PE, having been introduced to the uses of video at a DES course, returned to school and had his lessons videoed and then assessed by his staff. He then went on to record lessons given by members of his department and these were discussed similarly. The natural outcome of the exercise was that staff started going into each other's lessons to observe at first hand – 'They could not wait for the videos to be shown!'

The attitude to observation in this PE department was very much one of 'let's see what works and help each other to avoid what doesn't': there was no concept of someone putting ticks, crosses or grades on a checklist of skills.

Many middle managers, contemplating the external imposition of an appraisal scheme, stated that they needed training in what to look for in a lesson – with a set of criteria such as would be employed by a PGCE student's tutor, for example (for an introduction, see Wragg, 1987) – and how to conduct an interview or review (see Diffey, 1987). Similarly, the preparation of appraisees was vital. Those being appraised should know how to prepare for an appraisal interview, the form of the interview itself, and the sort of outcomes that could be expected.

Although observation 'checklists' are considered valuable, they were not used in the departments which were visiting each other's lessons. Here observation was part and parcel of the total delivery of the curriculum with which all the teachers in the department were involved, rather than being a totally independent assessment of an individual's skills. 'It's much easier to move in alongside and team-teach. I'd like to see us engaged in classroom research alongside each other. This is much sounder than saying, "I'm coming to see you teach." ' This accords with Kyriacou's (1987) contention that:

> the appraiser's task may need to be closer to that of the LEA
> subject adviser's task, which attempts to foster and support
> developments in teaching and the curriculum through stimulat-
> ing and supporting teachers rather than through evaluation or

prescription, than current discussion of teacher appraisal has so far acknowledged.

Within the NFER case study schools there were many references to the beneficial effects of having to plan and moderate GCSE coursework – an exercise which, though certainly quite revolutionary for some departments, seemed merely to reinforce what the effective ones had been doing for some time.

An example of an appraisal scheme

The appraisal scheme at a phase one case study school had arisen out of a discussion about staff development which had itself been stimulated by the school's involvement in a whole-school review exercise. The deputy head responsible for the review thought that the evolution of appraisal from the school's participation in GRIDS (McMahon et al., 1984) was significant. Although the SMT had initiated the idea of using GRIDS, they had spent a lot of time creating the right climate among the staff and so the actual introduction of the scheme was not really, in their view, a top-down decision. In the opinion of the deputy head, GRIDS had built up, between middle managers and the SMT, the mutual confidence that was a prerequisite for the appraisal scheme: it had also sensitized staff to the importance of evaluation and change.

The deputy head held an after-school session for department and faculty heads to discuss appraisal techniques and watch a training video on appraisal in industry. The appraisal scheme was introduced gradually. Stage one was open to scale 3 teachers and above and there was an 80 per cent take-up from eligible staff; in stage two, the following year, the scheme was open to all teachers and at the end of this stage nearly three-quarters of all the teaching staff had voluntarily participated. The scheme was based on a self-appraisal form and an interview.

The head commented that staff had been very honest and critical of their own performance. The self-appraisal reports went to the appraiser and were entirely confidential (they were not even typed in the school office). The head, deputies and middle managers acted as appraisers and staff were offered a free choice. Targets were set and appraisees were asked what they wanted from senior staff in order to facilitate what they wanted to achieve.

In stage three it was planned to introduce a classroom element in the form of observation which was, in fact, already operating in three departments at the school. The idea had arisen in the original appraisal interview of one head of department who was concerned about getting her staff to coalesce, share ideas and change – they had been teaching the same thing for ten years or more. The deputy head and the head of department decided that mutual observation was one way in which the problem could be solved (the other being to send four members of the department off on the same INSET course) and the deputy head offered to provide cover – although he was concerned about what would happen if mutual observation 'took off in a big way' as he wondered how he would be able to cope with the many requests for cover.

The head of department concerned said that she had originally been introduced to the idea of observation on an INSET course on the role of the head of department. In her previous school there had been an office at the back of her classroom and so she had been accustomed to being observed herself. When she became head of department at her present school she took a 'softly softly' approach with the older, more traditional staff and initially asked them to watch her teach. They had been receptive to this and now they could all visit whomever they liked and morale within the department was much higher. Members of the department had covered for each other although some staff had agreed to observe in their non-contact time. The head of department remarked that her colleagues had found the classroom observation and formal appraisal interviews very constructive. Regarding the former, members of the department made the following observations:

> Being observed does not necessarily mean that you have weaknesses . . . It helps if you team teach and wander in and out of classrooms. It does not feel as if you are being examined. You're just visited. It's nothing new now; we almost expect it. In the past, teachers had been very insular. The idea came up under INSET: Action meant that we could not go on any courses and and so we wanted to do mutual observation. We discussed this at departmental meetings. This year we were asked who we would like to see and we are doing it on a one-to-one basis.

> We discussed observation at departmental meetings; we feel we are learning new ideas and methods. It's amazing how little observation you do in your training and your career . . . Other staff have expressed an interest in observation but we do not have a lot of contact with staff outside the department.

Regarding the whole exercise the head of department noted: 'I suppose it's a mutual admiration process really!' (This accords with Montgomery's (1985) belief that appraisal was really about 'prizing' and 'valuing' what was seen, and Marland's (1987) statement that 'all appraisal produces more praise than anything else'.)

Summary and discussion

Despite the significance attached to the head of department's responsibility regarding staff development, there was a general lack of confidence in this area – at least as perceived by many of the advisers and staff interviewed. Some middle managers did not see it as a central part of their role and it was not undertaken because of the constraints of time, other more pressing issues and a concern with the 'day-to-day' tasks. Others were simply reluctant to embrace fully this aspect of the job. Also, there was a reticence about developing staff if department heads thought that there was little chance of these teachers achieving promotion. Where there was an awareness of their responsibilities in this area, middle managers said that training would be most welcome.

Some of the central aspects of the staff development role have been outlined and attention focused on delegation, the provision of in-service opportunities, meetings, responsibility for new staff, performance review and classroom observation. It was suggested that, given existing class-contact ratios, delegation was crucial not only to enable staff to develop but also to free the department head and thus enable time to be devoted to other aspects of the role. The issue of delegation was, however, found to be a difficult one, often depending on the attitude of the individual teacher concerned. Some middle managers were reluctant to ask staff to take on further responsibilities without extra reward although some teachers would have welcomed the opportunity to gain new experiences.

Since the research was undertaken, the situation has been complicated by the abolition of the Burnham salary structure and the introduction of the new conditions of employment. The *School Teachers' Pay and Conditions Document*, 1987 (GB.DES, 1987b) makes reference to five incentive allowances (see Chapter 1) and lays down in detail the conditions of employment and professional duties of heads, deputies and school teachers. A stipulation for the award of an incentive allowance is that a teacher 'undertakes responsibilities beyond those common to the majority of teachers'. In the transfer from the old system to the new, a significant number of scale 2 teachers were not allocated an incentive allowance 'A' and this has meant, in the short term at least, that there has been some reluctance to take on delegated responsibilities without recognition, financial or otherwise. However, as the research has shown, so much depends – and, it is probably true to say, will continue to depend – on individuals' attitudes to the sharing out of departmental tasks and the extent to which they see themselves as prospective department heads and so wish to develop themselves and acquire new skills. A lot will also depend, it is suggested, on the extent to which the department perceives itself as a team. The problematic position regarding delegation may be partly alleviated in the future as recent recommendations to increase the number (and financial value) of 'A' allowances are implemented (Chilver, 1988) and the professional duties of MPG teachers become clearer.

Delegation has always been problematic and some of the associated difficulties and restraints – for example, major commitments outside the department, few full-time staff – have been documented. Effective delegation requires many skills and it was found essential to attempt a reasonable match between routine tasks and the more creative and developmental activities, in order to ensure that departmental staff do not see themselves as being 'put on' or abused. Delegation involves the development of trust on behalf of all parties and this, like developing a department or faculty identity, takes time to bring about.

Ensuring that opportunities for INSET were made known to staff and that the right people participated in them has been an accepted part of the staff development role of the middle manager. It could be argued that it is of even greater importance in the light of the change in national funding arrangements for INSET and the introduction of the five teacher 'contract' days. The diagnosis of the in-service needs of the department and its staff now falls on the department head who will need to liaise closely with the school's staff development/INSET coordinator. The problem of cover associated with course attendance in school time was also noted and it is the department head's responsibility to ensure that the disruption to pupils' learning is minimized. (Further suggestions as to how improvements could be made in these areas are noted in Chapter 10.)

The importance of good communication, effective and regular meetings, and participative modes of decision-making as forms of staff development were also discussed, as was responsibility for new staff. The areas of performance review or staff appraisal were considered and it was suggested that whereas regular reviews, observation and classroom visiting were an accepted part of the department head's role in relation to new staff and probationers, they were seen as much more problematic in relation to other departmental staff. Where performance review did take place – and it should be stressed that only three of the 21 case study schools had introduced formal appraisal schemes – it was looked upon favourably and staff commented on the benefits that had accrued both to themselves and to their departments. These were more likely if the scheme introduced was non-threatening, the product of a good climate, voluntary (at least initially), carried out by someone whom staff respected and trusted, and couched in terms of staff development rather than accountability.

Teachers, like employees in other spheres, require some form of constructive feedback on their performance: after all, the virtues of giving this to pupils are often voiced. For some schools, it made sense to move towards a scheme of appraisal or performance review as there was an awareness that, before long, a national scheme would be introduced, based on the experiences of the DES-funded pilot schemes (McMahon, 1987) and there was an obligation to participate in any scheme written into the new conditions of service document (GB.DES, 1987b).

Whatever scheme is introduced, department and faculty heads are going to have a key role to play and, it is suggested, their participation is likely to help to clarify and underline the fact that they are middle *managers* with staff development responsibilities for other adults. It is generally recognized that both appraisers and appraisees will require training in order to increase the chances of any scheme being successful. It is important to recognize that appraisal is a two-way process and that peer-group or 'bottom-up' appraisal encourages comments and reflections to be made on the performance of those in management positions.

Reciprocal classroom observation, whether or not linked to a formal appraisal scheme, was also seen as an important element of staff development. Some teachers were more used to visitors than others and reference was made to the limitations of the traditional concept of teachers' classroom autonomy and the recent usage of such terms as 'looking at learning' – an attempt to minimize any threat associated with classroom observation. As with appraisal schemes, few of the NFER case study schools had introduced reciprocal observation or visiting within their departments and faculties, usually because of the logistic problems and insufficient time. However, other research suggests that even if time were made available to enable classroom observation to take place, few department heads would take advantage of it as it was given a low priority (Straker, 1984). This reflects the reluctance of many middle managers to embrace fully their staff development responsibilities, including that of improving teacher performance. For departments and schools to improve their practices, individual and group evaluation needs to be encouraged. One of the tasks of all school managers is to facilitate such activities.

7 How is the Curriculum Developed and Change Managed?

An analysis of job descriptions for faculty and department heads shows that one responsibility, among many others, is responsibility for curriculum innovation and development. An LEA document, for example, states quite clearly that, as a manager, a head of department is expected to:

> continually assess the success of courses and take action if they are inadequate. You must keep informed of developments and decide on ways in which the department should progress. You must consult the head before initiating any curriculum development or changes, taking account of all its implications. When setting up machinery for any such development, you must also build in means of assessing its success.

A job description from a case study school made reference to:

> devising and revising the department's programme, its scheme of work, syllabus and method, being aware of the realities of the situation and of the theories and practicalities of curriculum development.

There was a clear expectation that department heads should maintain an awareness of current educational thought and developments. One job description even noted that it was important that 'the established scholastic reputation of the school be preserved and that innovation is not seen as being in any way synonymous with a decline in standards'.

Similarly, and as was outlined in Chapter 3, there is an expectation on the part of senior staff that middle managers will be 'forward looking and have lots of ideas in the curriculum area' and, most importantly, have the ability to introduce these ideas into the department or faculty. There was a need for department heads to be able to motivate staff, generate ideas and put these into practice. A case study head succinctly remarked: 'I'd look for movement forward: failure is okay but staleness is not', while another noted: 'The HoD has two important roles: the maintenance role – to keep the wheels turning and make sure that things work; and the innovatory role – ensuring things are rolling forward.' A deputy commented: 'I'd expect changes to emerge mainly from HoDs, either from themselves or their staff. I would expect the impetus for change to come from that middle management level as they're in a position to see matters from both ways.'

Before proceeding, it is worth noting that the term 'curriculum' is used so frequently in education that it does not always have a precise meaning. In general terms it is usually used to refer, as above, to the subject content, courses or programmes offered to pupils and, indeed, it has been suggested that many department heads similarly hold such narrow definitions. It is perhaps more helpful to think of the curriculum, in departmental terms, as not just what is taught but the delivery of the subject, the assessment policy, the teaching and learning strategies used and all the other aspects of the department's work, including the physical conditions of the rooms, the corridors etc. This wider definition would incorporate the hidden curriculum and thus include virtually everything that happens within a department or faculty. The primary focus of this chapter, however, is on how curriculum programmes are developed and the change process managed.

A 'good' department or faculty was, among other things, one that was constantly examining what it was doing and one in which innovations were considered and, if necessary, implemented. It was also one where the process of change was effectively managed and the innovations introduced were real in that 'they took place at the classroom/workshop level and not merely on administrators' desks' (Lawley, 1985). The head of department or faculty was seen as the curriculum leader and largely responsible, with support from senior staff, for managing change. Whether all middle managers concurred with such views and embraced this aspect of their role was much more problematic, however, and it will be recalled that one of the reasons for setting up a research project into the role of department heads was that earlier NFER research into newly appointed headteachers had pointed to the crucial role middle managers played in encouraging or obstructing curricular and other desired changes (Weindling and Earley, 1987).

Interestingly, recent research into the Further Education (FE) sector has noted that 'as with all organizations, the greatest defenders of the *status quo* tend to be at middle management level, that is, the heads of department' (Miller *et al.*, 1986). They were often 'seen as the villain of the piece – thwarting and obstructing innovation in order to preserve the *status quo* and their own peace of mind, or the trendy whizz-kid who never stands still long enough to be answerable for his or her actions' (Blezard, 1985). Heads of department can therefore be influential change agents and, as Blezard (1985) notes, their role in the change process is whatever they choose to make of it: provided they have the support of senior staff and departmental colleagues, their 'attitude and commitment to change is arguably the single most important ingredient in whether a particular project succeeds'.

Are department and faculty heads in schools clearly aware of their duties and responsibilities or is much of the impetus for change derived, as in FE, from other sources? Do perceptions of practitioners vary concerning their role in facilitating change and, if so, what can be done to ensure that a greater number see themselves as 'curriculum leaders' and that the necessary skills are acquired to enable effective change to take place? To begin, how did the department and faculty heads involved in the NFER research conceive of their role in relation to curriculum development and the change process?

Role perceptions

It will be recalled from an earlier chapter which attempted to clarify and delineate the head of department's role, that all the middle managers involved in the research were asked what they perceived as the most important aspect of their job. The responses to this open-ended question were often lengthy and wide-ranging. It would be fair to say that the majority of respondents saw themselves as having a general responsibility for the department or faculty and what it offered in terms of curriculum programmes. As might be expected from nominated 'good practitioners', the heads of department and faculty in phase two made more frequent reference than phase one respondents to their role as curriculum leaders and change facilitators. The following remarks were not unusual:

> The most important aspect is probably curriculum development but also INSET for the department and facilitating the work of teachers. It's important to keep up to date with curriculum initiatives, changes and ideas and disseminating such information is an important part of my job.

> I think it is important to be a 'can do' person rather than a 'wait and see person' . . . you must start with the 'can do' philosophy although on occasions you may have to explain to staff why they can't implement an initiative or do something they want to do. It may be on account of restrictions in the school, lack of resources etc.

And, finally, a phase one head of English who was due to take up a deputy headship in another LEA said:

> I'm not sure if there's one particular aspect – perhaps the curriculum. What sort of diet are the pupils getting? Am I coordinating what they get and how does it fit in with the rest of the school's curriculum? I suppose my role is really about curriculum – that's the crucial part of my job. The curriculum needs constant reappraisal.

Heads and deputies remarked upon how departments (and schools) varied in the degree to which they and their leaders placed emphasis on curriculum development. Some, it was argued, still conceived of their role primarily in administrative terms ('management with minimum disturbance') and there was a need for such individuals to embrace a more active role involving academic and curricular leadership ('management with the likelihood of change' – Oxtoby, 1979). Most senior staff concurred with the view that department heads 'must see themselves as front-line participants in a process of curricular change which sees the curriculum as more than the sum of its parts; which recognizes that subjects interact with each other and seeks to organize and profit from these interactions' (Holt, 1981).

Perceptions of their role in facilitating change and the provision of curriculum leadership varied among faculty and department heads. As has been mentioned, the phase two nominees certainly acknowledged their responsibilities in these areas but the project's research methodology, with its qualitative focus, did not enable a statistical or 'average' picture of the department head's role in facilitating change to be constructed. Although those involved in the NFER research spoke of the variety of practice found, there has been little empirical research conducted in this country that has specifically focused on department heads' perceptions of their role as change facilitators and their level of involvement in introducing change. That which does exist (for example Hull and Adams, 1981) is, like the current research, based on a small number of case studies. Siddle's (1978) survey of a sample of heads of science, undertaken in the early 1970s, showed that over three-quarters had initiated new courses in the previous two years which, he suggests, gives some indication of the rate of self-initiated change taking place. It could be argued, however, that these were abnormal circumstances as it was the time when Nuffield Science was being introduced.

Recent work in the United States by Hord and her colleagues (Hord and Murphy, 1985; Hord and Diaz-Ortiz, 1986) has, similarly, pointed to the crucial role that department heads play as change facilitators. They argue that role perceptions vary from the 'paper pusher' at one extreme to the 'commander-in-chief' at the other. Not unlike their British counterparts, most North American high schools are organized on a departmental basis and teachers tend to identify with the department rather than with the school overall, and therefore department heads are 'a leverage point for change' and have responsibility for 'making things go right'. The researchers' initial discussions with heads of department suggested that they did not 'see their role as carrying any power or authority that would support their activity as an agent for change in their departments'. Hord and Murphy's (1985) study did not confirm any one prevailing view; rather, they state: 'The most appropriate characterization of the department head's role is its inconsistency in the way it is operationalized across department heads within a school, within a district, and across all the districts we have studied.' The researchers found great variability in the 30 high schools studied and they developed a typology of heads of department, such as the 'program improver', the 'coordinator manager' and the 'teacher improver'. Drawing on their more recent, questionnaire-based research, which involved a sample of department heads from eight states, they argued that though some did supply the necessary leadership for change efforts, the great majority did not. The essential goal, they state, 'is to understand how the role can become a more effective one in contributing to the improvement of schools and the educational experiences of teachers and students' (Hord and Diaz-Ortiz, 1986).

As far as the United Kingdom is concerned, there is still little research into the relative success of particular strategies adopted by department heads for managing the implementation of change. It is hoped that by focusing in some depth on how the phase two nominees successfully introduced change in their faculties and departments this shortage of information may be partly remedied. However, in order for this task to be undertaken, it is necessary to give further attention to the change process itself.

Change as a process

Planned educational change should not be seen as an event taking place at a certain time; rather, it makes more sense to consider it as a process, albeit a complex one. Hull and Adams (1981) for example, from their study of secondary school science departments, have constructed a detailed model of the curriculum change process, stipulating an entry point (the perception of factors which initiate consideration for change) and an exit point (the change becomes institutionalized), with a number of activities taking place as the change proceeds (e.g. defining the problem, selecting a curriculum package, devising strategies to proceed, commencing certain administrative procedures and evaluating the change). Perhaps a better known model of the change process is one which comprises three broad stages:

1. *Initiation*. The period during which, perhaps after a review of existing practice, ideas for change are suggested, a decision is made to proceed with a change and plans are formulated and developed.

2. *Implementation*. The stage when teachers commence the innovation becomes a routine part of the school or, alternatively, after further review and evaluation, is discarded.

3. *Incorporation* or *Institutionalization*. The final stage when the innovation becomes a routine part of the school or, alternatively, after further review and evaluation, is discarded.

Depending on the significance of the change for those involved, it may take three to five years to complete the process and, because change is invariably a complicated matter, the process is cyclical and does not necessarily follow simply from one stage to the next. The tripartite division of the change process is, however, a useful one and provides a convenient framework in which to analyse the NFER case study data. The first two stages will now be considered, while the third, institutionalization, and evaluation is examined in the next chapter.

Initiation

Where do ideas for change come from?

The initial consideration of curricular and other change can be seen (Hull and Adams, 1981) as originating from any of four main sources:

1. from outside the school (a government initiative, the introduction of a new syllabus by examination boards, an LEA document, an initiative by an external agency such as the MSC);

2. from within the school as a whole (e.g. a decision that all

3.   classes are taught in mixed-ability groups);
from within the department or faculty (e.g. a feeling of
dissatisfaction with a particular programme or course);
4.   from the arrival of a new person, particularly to take a post of
responsibility.

Planned educational change never occurs without an advocate –
a change agent – who perceives that a problem exists and that
something needs to be done in order for it to be resolved. The
change agent need not necessarily be the head of department or,
indeed, a member of the department, although as has been shown,
there was an expectation from senior staff that middle managers
would be curriculum leaders and be proactive rather than reactive
thinkers. This did not mean, however, that they were expected to be
the source of *all* ideas.

It was not always necessary for the head of department to be
the initiator but it was necessary for him or her to offer support and
back-up to departmental colleagues. A phase two head of art remarked
how his staff 'force the pace and keep me on my toes' but thought it
essential for the department head to initiate ideas as well. The situation
of many schools was summed up by a phase one head of faculty who
said of the origins of ideas for change:

It varies from department to department – in my faculty from
one HoD I get no ideas, whereas the other two are not quite so
barren. The head of modern languages has hardly stopped giving
ideas, the head of history has introduced quite a lot of changes,
whereas from the head of English I have no ideas at all!

Another middle manager from the same school said: 'Suggestions
for change come from me, my colleagues or from outside. There are
pressures to change from the school, faculty, the LEA, parents and
governors. We live in a time of tremendous change.'

Teachers, too, expected their department heads to lead from the
front, to be the chief protagonist for the subject, to offer initiatives
and encourage them to be taken up. A scale 2 teacher remarked:
'They need to give direction, weigh up different viewpoints, have
ideas themselves and use the ideas of others.' Another commented
how his faculty head was full of ideas and acted as a catalyst generating
ideas from others.

It was suggested that department heads must allow junior staff to
be innovative and several teachers spoke of departments in which
they had worked where they had been actively discouraged from
introducing anything new. A teacher who taught in a number of
departments and, along with a colleague, had recently completed
probation, thought the suggestions they both had made had been

ignored, adding: 'Perhaps we've made too many and these have been taken as a threat.' Others spoke of probationers in some departments being reluctant to express views and suggest new ideas – encouragement was needed before they were prepared to contribute.

Strategies to promote change

Where individual departments or their heads were not developing, senior staff employed a variety of strategies to combat inertia and ensure staff were exposed to new ideas and made aware of initiatives. Everard (1986) mentions, for example, utilizing weekend conferences, rewarding innovators, seconding staff, seeding ideas for others to pick up, manipulating the situation so that the impetus for change came from the staff and not senior management, encouraging 'dead wood' to retire and making use of outside catalysts. Most of these strategies were referred to in the NFER study – and advisory teachers were seen as good examples of non-threatening outside change facilitators – while the appointment of a strong second-in-command, visits to other schools and the encouragement of greater INSET take-up were others frequently mentioned. A good example of the last strategy involved a phase two head of faculty who was very concerned about one of her department heads and his very old-fashioned approach to his subject. With the support of the head and the adviser she was able to secure for him a place on a ten-week DES course at the local university: 'We managed to persuade him to go on this course and it had a very good effect on him. He came back full of ideas – it was like a new awakening!'

On occasions, it was necessary to overcome conservatism and resistance to new ideas by bypassing the department head altogether and giving responsibility for an initiative to a middle manager from an allied area. This had occurred in several case study schools, particularly in relation to the introduction of technology. A phase one head gave the example of a CDT department which had been extremely reluctant to encourage curriculum development or countenance change, particularly in technology. After several unsuccessful attempts at seeding ideas, the head decided to try an alternative tactic and approached the head of physics who was most keen to introduce technology into the school's curriculum. In fact, since that time, the head explained, the CDT department had made some progress and had been significantly helped by several new teaching appointments and the retirement of a very traditional teacher. Both the CDT inspector and the general inspector for the school had spent a lot of time in the department and it at last appeared as though the head of department was becoming more involved in curriculum development, but as the head said: 'It had taken seven years to change his thinking!'

In some schools, resource allocation was used as a means of stimulating curriculum innovation. One phase one school had a curriculum development fund, in addition to capitation, so departments knew there was money set aside for any initiative they may have wished to implement. Another, where senior staff thought many department heads were rather entrenched in their own subjects and reluctant to consider cross-curricular initiatives, had thought of changing the allocation of capitation from a system based on pupil numbers to one based on planned departmental developments. In this context it is interesting to note the view of an industrialist and management trainer who, when commenting on schools, writes: 'too small a proportion of the available (financial) resources is used to support innovation and development' and available funds are 'over-committed to the support of existing operations, leaving little discretionary resources for dealing with much-needed innovation' (Everard, 1986).

A phase one head commented how he would try to make the 'weaker' heads of department aware of developments and give them time to prepare, by asking: 'How will you tackle this change that is bound to come?' Another tried to encourage the generation of ideas from department heads by saying: 'I've a solution to this particular problem: what is yours?' – thus initiating discussion. If ideas were unforthcoming, the head employed a variety of strategies including encouraging visits to other schools, providing opportunities for INSET and, if possible, appointing probationers with clear instructions to bring in new ideas. The head would ask: 'Why is the department not moving forward? Is it because of lack of resources or time and, if so, in what ways can I help?'

Interestingly, several teachers commenting on change spoke of the benefits of staff movement, especially to take up department headships. A teacher expressed concern at having to work in departments that 'stood still' and noted: 'At this school there are a lot of HoDs who've been in post a long time. I think schools need a certain amount of turnover. At this school there are some dull parts and HoDs need to think about moving on themselves.' Promotion from within the school to middle management was seen as having the benefit of continuity but on occasions it did not lead to sufficient change as 'fresh eyes are sometimes needed'; in general, it was thought to be easier to create changes if appointments were made from outside the school. Another teacher from the same department remarked that it was 'sometimes difficult for an internal promotion to assume a managerial position' but also noted the outsider 'has it hard, too, as they don't want to upset anyone'. Empirical evidence on internal promotion and levels of change is difficult to find, but if large-scale changes were thought to be needed then an external appointment seemed a better way of achieving them (for example see Hoy and Aho, 1973; Gordon and Rosen, 1981; Weindling and Earley, 1987). Certainly in the present study, heads spoke of the need to bring in an external change agent; this was often made clear to applicants at interviews and many newly appointed heads of department saw themselves in such terms. (That internal appointees are able to introduce major changes in their departments can be seen in Example 3 at the end of this chapter.)

Planning for change

Frequent reference was made to the need for department heads to create the right climate in which innovations and ideas could be openly discussed. There was a need for open dialogue between teachers, and heads of department had to work at creating a cooperative working environment. It was important to keep staff fully informed and both formal and informal consultation structures were necessary to enable ideas to be discussed and exchanged. A teacher thought: 'A head of department should try and create an atmosphere whereby staff feel they've been wanting to do something about this or that for some time.' It is no easy task ensuring that departmental staff of differing ages, abilities, experiences and enthusiasms can work together and yet are free to criticize each other's practices and put forward a case for making a change. As Maden (1974) notes, fundamental to curriculum development is a climate whereby cooperation and mutual respect exist: 'Only if this atmosphere exists can departments proceed with the difficult task of dissecting, analysing and reflecting upon what it is they are trying to achieve.' Teachers must feel as though they are able, even encouraged, to put forward ideas for alternative ways of working. It is incumbent upon middle managers to ensure that the department or faculty finds time for deliberation and planning and that they do not, as appears to be so often the case, become preoccupied with the day-to-day detail.

The first step in planning any change is to clarify the nature of the problem to be solved. Why is it thought that change is needed and what action should be taken to improve the pupils' learning experiences? Change can be seen as stemming from two related questions – 'What are the pupils doing?' and 'What could the pupils be doing?' Shared insights about the nature of these become the basis for change. In tackling these questions effective practitioners frequently adopted a participative management style, involving as many staff as possible yet being prepared to take the initiative when necessary. Comments from three middle managers encapsulate what many thought was the effective management of change:

When I came, the department was in a real shambles . . . as a facilitator I must identify areas for change . . . whether I receive messages from colleagues or put things to them I don't know. We had a department discussion about what was bad and we saw one or two developments from various ASE documents. I sent off for a commercially produced package. I liked it and passed it round the staff . . . it soon became evident that we'd adopt it because everybody's reactions were so positive. We also discussed it as a department. There was only one person who wasn't positive and he wouldn't be involved anyway. So we had quite a lot of discussion really. I do try and work on consensus lines.

People must see that there is a need for change and there should be meetings or discussions so that staff are allowed to express their concerns for some things. I would look at something to see why it was not working and get feedback from staff and then bring the matter up at a faculty meeting. There's no point in introducing change for change's sake. You need to ask what needs changing. I would get ideas from the faculty and, along with my own, put them forward in a paper. Ideas would not only come from me, but I might say, 'We need to do something about X.'

I persuaded the staff that a new lower-school science course was a good thing . . . I organized working parties within the science faculty and then we discussed the outcomes of these. Now I'm arranging evenings when a specialist will talk to the faculty and advise. The working parties were small (two or three people) and 'mixed'. They met at lunchtime and after school before [industrial] action intervened. Staff must be involved especially when change is revolutionary. I had to be well prepared and the teachers asked lots of questions – they made me think.

The above approaches used consensus and open discussion, cooperation being engendered by the sharing of concerns and collective problem-solving. It was thought that if teachers contributed to decision-making then they were more amenable to change. Decision-making processes, both within departments and schools, are considered in more detail in Chapter 9, but respondents noted that the greater the degree of participation and sense of ownership of the change by the staff then the more likely it would be successfully implemented. A scale 2 teacher summed it up well when she said:

Because we're all involved in discussing the future plans for the department we therefore feel responsibility for any suggestions. This probably would not be the case if the HoD was making all the decisions.

It is, of course, not always possible to create consensus and it is sometimes necessary to bypass resistance to change and implement new ideas, initially at least, with those staff who are genuinely committed to the innovation. It was thought that change could be introduced once there was a 'critical mass' or a self-sustaining team of committed staff. Department heads were reluctant to implement changes if they felt there were too many dissenting voices: 'If you've not the ability or the interest to do it, then you're battling against a brick wall', or as a head commented: 'The first rule is that you'll only get change if you carry people with you.' There was little point in imposing or forcing changes onto others, as it was admitted colleagues would be so obstructive as to ensure that the ideas would not work. But why are some teachers resistant to change, what forms does this resistance take and in what ways can it be minimized?

Resistance to change

The amount of resistance found within a department or faculty was often related to the levels of involvement in decision-making. As a head of department said:

I'll listen to people and give them their chance to say their piece but at the end I'll say: 'I think we ought to do this.' At the end of the day that's what management is all about. I think that with most people if you're open and honest with them they'll accept a decision although they may not agree with it. If you dictate to people and don't give reasons as to why you're acting in a certain way, then this leads to friction and ill-feeling.

Another remarked:

It's important to do adequate preparation and have lots of discussion but you do need to have a firm direction. It needs to be made clear that this is the way the department is going, but we'll do things slowly and firmly. I think you're always going to get some reluctant staff – staff who are not prepared to change – so if they feel there is a possibility of stopping the change then they won't give it their whole-hearted support.

Resistance itself, as Hull and Adams (1981) state, is not necessarily a bad thing, as it ensures that any plans are carefully thought out and 'There is always the possibility that those who resist a change may in fact be right!' They note that resistance can take a variety of forms both passive ('innovation without change') and active, with teachers campaigning against the change and attempting to get the department to reconsider its plans for implementation.

Various reasons for resisting change were mentioned by NFER respondents. Most commonly stated was a fear of the unknown: seeing change as a threat and 'worrying if I'll be able to cope'. Cross-curricular initiatives were seen as especially difficult to manage because of the threat to teachers' subject identities. Similarly, teachers were often suspicious of change because it normally meant inconvenience and additional work – 'You have to be prepared to spend time thinking, preparing, devising new routines etc.' The costs of innovation must not be forgotten and can add significantly to a teacher's normal workload. Teachers will want to know if the benefits of the proposed change will outweigh the perceived costs. Also, as Watson (1986) has noted, significant change involves 'losers' as well as winners and heads must ensure that the burden of change does not fall disproportionately on any one group. Similarly, the department head has to consider the costs and benefits to individuals within the department. Change will be opposed if teachers feel disadvantaged by its introduction. Alternatively, suggestions for change were spurned if the ideas were simply not liked.

There were, however, strategies employed that were able to help allay staff's fears and minimize concern. Regular briefings and giving of facts and information to teachers before discussing an innovation helped overcome feelings of insecurity and it was noteworthy that some department heads prepared lesson programmes in new areas for staff to try out. Resistance was reduced and cooperation encouraged by department heads – like their senior colleagues – asking staff to help solve particular problems ('I've got this problem, can you help?' If the answer was 'no', then it was necessary to wait – 'they usually come round in the end. If they are wavering they will usually say "OK".'). In fact, many heads of department said that staff were not particularly hostile to change but had to be convinced of its value. The advocacy skills of the department head were crucial and there was a need not only to 'sell' any change in terms of the advantages to pupils' learning, but also to outline the disadvantages, such as the extra work involved. Department heads had to be persuasive and could not ask colleagues to undertake something new unless they were prepared to try it themselves. Where innovations had been partly implemented (e.g. in the lower school) or piloted, it was often the case that teachers' fears diminished as they saw the resulting benefits for themselves and the pupils. In-service education and training was used in new areas so staff could update their knowledge, acquire new skills, allay fears and gain confidence.

On occasions, there were individual teachers within departments and faculties who were simply unprepared or unable to change. In such circumstances it was generally felt best to 'agree to differ' and to permit teachers to continue as before. Others were waiting to retire and did not want to become involved – 'in cases like this you just have to sit things out'. A phase two nominee referring to her last school, in which was found a very traditional teacher who taught very differently from her colleagues, noted:

It would have been stupid of me to attempt to change her practice. What I can do is encourage and lead by example. You must try and show the way, point to the benefits and so on. You can't do this by coercion or by saying to people: 'You must do it this way.' I think any teacher worth their salt wants to improve their practice.

Another, from a different phase two school, remarked:

There was a head of drama who has since left. She was not keen on team-teaching or integrated subjects. I tried to involve her in discussions and we tried team-teaching in blocks of time for those staff who were interested. We tried things out and then looked back on them. With hostile staff it's all to do with timing and with what they want to do. If staff do not want to do something, then it's unlikely to work.

However, some department heads, especially those who saw themselves in the forefront of change, found it difficult to be patient and to give colleagues, particularly more experienced staff, enough time to change.

An example of this was a phase two nominee who had set up a new department from the amalgamation of three schools. The department head said:

I'd like to know successful ways in which I can bring about effective change. As far as successful innovation is concerned my track-record is non-existent. How do I introduce significant change in the department when I have two senior members of staff in terms of age and one in a senior position (a deputy)?

Senior staff within the school noted how 'ideas people' often think that 'if they lead by example, then others will follow. It doesn't always work like that and it can generate impatience.' It is interesting to note that interviews with the two senior departmental staff referred to above showed that neither individuals were resisting the changes; in fact, both were supportive of developments, but as was remarked: 'Old timers like X and myself probably need more training than younger teachers. We need time to stand back and look at what we're doing.' It may therefore be necessary to phase changes in over a number of years and it is to the difficult area of the pace and the timing of change that attention is now given.

The pace of change

Previous NFER research into newly appointed heads established the importance of the optimal pace and timing of change. Similar comments were elicited from those involved in the current project ranging from the teacher who said: 'I don't like lots of discussion and no action' to another who remarked: 'We've moved forward at such a rapid pace.' It is impossible to be prescriptive about the speed of change as this will vary according to circumstances.

A large number of heads of department subscribed to the process of 'evolution rather than revolution' and were reluctant to 'steam-roller' things through if they did not have total support. A phase two nominee remarked that when he first came to the school it appeared as though he did nothing in his first 12 months. The time was spent talking to faculty staff and trying to find out what was happening. Another nominee noted that 'changes evolve over the years. If you try to introduce big changes overnight, then you're asking for trouble', while another spoke of what she had learned from her last department headship:

> My previous experience also helped prevent me from coming in like a tornado and changing everything. With any change it's important to ensure that you've prepared the ground. I respect the experience of my staff and I look towards them for guidance ... I think in my previous post I was too enthusiastic and in too much of a hurry. I've learnt from these experiences.

Senior staff generally agreed that department heads found the change process difficult, especially the pace of change, as 'it's very hard to get the pace right to keep everybody happy'. But it was also noted that middle managers may have less control over the pace of change than do headteachers. (Both, of course, given recent educational reforms and their imposed timescales, are likely to have less flexibility regarding the pace of change.) Senior staff may exert pressures on middle managers to innovate and to introduce change more quickly than they would wish. Department and faculty heads must sometimes resist these pressures and they are in a pivotal role, having to take into account their own views, those of the staff and those of senior management. As a head remarked:

> There may well be, and often is, a dissonance between these three areas that the HoD will find difficult to handle. This is

especially likely if you've got a young, bouncy, upwardly mobile new head who wants to get things going. The reaction from departmental staff may well be to dig in their heels.

Teachers' views

Reference has repeatedly been made to the qualities and skills that educational managers require and it is worth briefly noting here factors concerning middle managers and the change process that teachers perceived as being important. An obvious but key point was the necessity for faculty and department heads to earn the respect of their peers. Where this was so, staff were more prepared to listen to the ideas put forward for discussion and to experiment with them. The head of department had to be sensitive to all viewpoints, to be able to argue for change or defend entrenched positions, to think things through before offering them for discussion, to demonstrate the skills of good judgement and to be able to discriminate between 'the new and the new and useful'. A scale 3 teacher remarked that in his opinion it was necessary to have 'someone who can drag up the traditionalist and bring the wisdom of their experience to bear on those who want to change everything'. They should be able to arbitrate between 'the dinosaurs of the department, like myself, and those who want to shoot ahead'.

Where ideas were in abundance, the department head was responsible for choosing which to adopt and, at times continuity and stability were more important than innovation. There was always the danger of too much change and the need for a period of consolidation. It was important to examine innovations and to decide what was just fashionable and what had real depth – 'the ideal is a combination of the old and the new'. A scale 1 PE teacher noted:

> We're always thinking about curriculum development but I do think that sometimes new courses are introduced just to jump on bandwagons. New initiatives should only be taken on if they are right for the kids at this school and not just for the sake of the initiative itself. There's the danger of always looking for the latest 'in-thing'. So often it's a case of the old method being thrown out in entirety and the new one being taken on lock, stock and barrel – throwing out the baby with the bathwater.

'Change for change's sake' was spurned and some teachers were very critical of middle managers who gave the impression they were looking for rapid promotion. A teacher in a phase two school compared his new head of department favourably with her predecessor saying: 'I'm impressed by the fact that she's interested in the department and not using us as a stepping stone for her career. The sort of changes we've introduced are not just for her curriculum vitae.' This department head had succeeded in creating a climate where changes were discussed 'without the feeling that a bandwagon is rolling merely for reasons of fashion or to enhance an individual's career prospects or personal reputation' (Tyldesley, 1984).

In general, teachers were favourably disposed towards change, provided that it was seen as meeting a need. It was thought important to innovate to provide a stimulus and 'to prevent teachers getting into a rut'. In some departments for example, the introduction of GCSE was seen in terms of being 'a new challenge and good for you as you tend to become entrenched'. Others commented that taking on new initiatives helped to keep teachers motivated – which was particularly important at a time of contraction in the education service. In fact, some commentators (e.g. Tyldesley, 1984) see the most important task of the department head as creating a climate of optimism and motivating staff under difficult conditions – the introduction of change may provide the intellectual stimulation required to help avoid the dangers of a frustrated and immobile workforce.

Summary

This section is perhaps best summarized by quoting from Hull and Adams' (1981) research on the management of change. Between initiation – the period when ideas are discussed and plans developed – and the implementation of a change, departments should aim to achieve each of the following:

1. Each teacher should be favourably disposed towards the planning and implementation of the change, and motivated to take a full part in it.
2. The whole department should feel that the change is the department's own and that it has not been imposed from outside or by individuals from within.
3. Department members should feel supported by senior members of the department and of the school.
4. Participants in the change should not feel that their autonomy or status is unduly threatened.
5. There should be good personal relationships within the department.
6. Each participant should clearly be able to see the intended advantages of the new product over the existing one, for pupils, for him or herself, and for other teachers.

In addition, perhaps there is the need for teachers to believe that they have the skills to effect the change or that they can acquire them.

Implementation

The second stage of the change process, implementation, is when all the discussion and planning become a reality in the sense that the innovation is put into operation and becomes part of departmental or faculty practice. As others have noted, the implementation stage is where many inexperienced managers of change want to commence, but 'successful implementation depends on effective planning and on ensuring that the benefits of the change are recognized by those doing the work' (Bell and Maher, 1986). Nevertheless, it has been suggested that energy spent on elaborate planning can be at the expense of energy spent on implementation. Research into the change process has shown it is better to do a small amount of pre-implementation planning and a large amount of support once the initiative has been introduced rather than *vice versa* (Fullan, 1985).

In an earlier publication, Fullan (1982) made reference to a number of factors which affect the level of success of the implementation stage and these include the following:

1. *Need.* As has already been noted, if teachers do not see the change as addressing a perceived need, then they are unlikely to implement it.

2. *Clarity.* Even when the need for change is agreed it is not always clear what teachers are expected to do differently.

3. *Complexity.* This refers to the difficulty and extent of change required. Recent research suggests that the more significant and extensive the change attempted, the more achieved and that although simple changes are easier to undertake they may not make much of a difference.

4. *History of innovation attempts.* The LEA's or school's track-record affects implementation. The more negative experiences with previous attempts at change, the more cynical or apathetic teachers will be about the next change, regardless of its merit.

5. *LEA and senior staff support.* Such support is essential, and the likelihood of success is enhanced if heads and advisers demonstrate through their *actions* that teachers should take the change seriously.

6.   *Staff development and INSET.* Effective in-service training
     is one of the most important factors related to altering
     teachers' practices (e.g. Joyce and Showers, 1980; Bolam,
     1987). It appears, however, that most of this takes place
     prior to implementation whereas there is a clear need
     for INSET *during* implementation, as it is during the
     initial stages of a change, when uncertainty and anxiety are
     at their greatest and problems become apparent, that
     teachers require further training and support.

Respondents in the NFER research made reference to a variety of
factors relating to the implementation phase. Chances of success were
increased if it was possible to involve only those teachers who were
genuinely committed to the innovation and had developed a sense of
'ownership'. It was stated that teachers would support changes if they
saw them as having beneficial results in the classroom or workshop.
Some department heads did not implement change across the entire
department but rather introduced the change themselves and ensured
that it provided positive results in the classroom. As a phase two
nominee said: 'I like to influence staff by showing them rather than
by telling them; it's best to lead by example.' Another said: 'I will try
as far as possible to do the innovation the first time through, both for
insights and because it gives others confidence to see that I've done it.'
A scale 1 teacher from the same department supported this view when
she said: 'He will never ask you to do anything that he's not prepared to
do himself.' It was thought that teachers were more likely to try out an
innovation if they knew that other members of the department were
already engaged in it.

Views on the magnitude of change that could be achieved differed,
with some respondents believing any amount could be implemented
provided staff felt involved and that their views mattered. Some heads
of department saw the way forward as involving small-scale initiatives
taken on by committed teachers – 'I think a little change regularly
is better than one big hit' – while others thought they had created
difficulties for themselves by trying to introduce too much at once: 'I
could cope with this but could the staff? They did eventually respond
to my enthusiasm but there's been almost 100 per cent change since
I arrived three years ago!' There was a limit to what people could
be reasonably expected to do well and 'innovation overload' was an
important factor to take into account. A teacher in another authority,
nationally known for its involvement in various educational innovations, said: 'If there are any more initiatives we will all go spare!'
Schools and departments had to ensure that they did not overload
themselves with initiatives to the detriment of the pupils.

A further important point concerning the magnitude of change – and again found in the NFER study of headteachers – was the criticism of existing practices implied by large-scale change. There was a need for newly appointed department heads to value what the department offered its pupils and to try to build on existing practice. Confrontation could easily be provoked by a decision to 'sweep clean' and start afresh. As an adviser remarked:

> You need to let the staff know that you think well of them
> and that they are going to help themselves to become better.
> You shouldn't go in as the proverbial whizz-kid with arrogance.
> Nearly everyone wants to do a good job but the implication of
> change is that all that went on before was bad.

It is interesting to note that several respondents made reference to the history of innovation in schools, departments and, in one case, the LEA. A phase two school was described as one that 'always tried to permit you to do what you want . . . the school ethos has created an atmosphere such that we're all concerned with educational change'.

A phase one deputy head noted how change on a whole-school basis encouraged departments to innovate, while as noted above, an LEA's involvement over the years in so many initiatives had, in the opinion of some, meant 'they have become jacks-of-all-trades and masters of none'.

Support during the implementation stage was crucial. As Holt (1981) states:

> It is not enough for a head to support curricular change: the
> head of department must want it to happen and want it enough
> to find time to support his (or her) staff during the difficult period
> when the innovation is being installed and made to work. And
> when this is over, he (or she) must run an 'after-sales' service
> stimulating discussion and underwriting new ideas with moral
> encouragement and the necessary resources.

The role of senior staff was crucial – were they 'enablers' or 'blockers'? The support could be either active or passive (i.e. by not interfering and allowing the department head to proceed), but it was noted by some teachers that 'effective' change would only be achieved if senior staff were involved in classroom visiting to observe innovations at work. There was a need, it was suggested, for senior management to work with their colleagues in a collaborative way.

Similarly, senior staff were seen as playing a key role in coordinating change. Heads thought that change within departments should not be *ad hoc* but, rather, it should fit into an overall school development plan and it should not be assumed that the school is merely the sum of its departments (Maden, 1974). Departmental changes needed to be coordinated, for in the words of a phase one head: 'It's important not to grasp at change for its own sake because change always has knock-on effects.'

Unsuccessful attempts at implementation were often related to lack of support (by both senior staff and department heads), teachers' lack of involvement in decisions concerning change and insufficient INSET both prior to and during implementation. In some instances attempts had been made to introduce a change without the full benefit of INSET. This was true, for example, in a phase one CDT department which had tried to introduce a new technology course. The department head said:

> It was generally felt there was a far greater need for INSET.
> Another teacher, who'd had a little experience of technology,
> and I went on a course – which, incidently, we paid for ourselves.
> The staff's reaction has been mixed. Some have welcomed it;
> others are content with being a woodwork teacher, for example,
> unless they are given the INSET they feel they need.

(Further examples of how in-service training was used to support innovation are provided in the three case studies which follow.)

The third and final stage in the change process, that of incorporation or institutionalization, is considered in the next chapter along with the wider concerns of departmental monitoring, evaluation and review. It is intended to conclude this chapter, however, by considering three examples of how the first stages of the change process were successfully managed in some of the phase two case study schools.

Three case studies

Example 1

Ron Crisp (RC) was head of English and also head of the faculty of expressive arts. In the five years he had been in post, a number of changes had been introduced in English and drama, although music had stayed very much as it was. RC remarked that change was mainly dependent on the person running the area and the significant number of curriculum changes in English and drama was largely due to the individual department heads. The music department did not work as a team and the HoF found it very difficult to encourage development. This was not helped by his lack of expertise in the subject. RC believed strongly in the participative approach and saw any proposed change as unlikely to succeed if it was forced on the faculty.

> Change is always open to modification but very often it can't be
> thrown out completely as it's been put on the agenda by me!

Some things have not been introduced although there is a need for them (e.g. profiling). The problem here is that they are so time-consuming. So some areas have not been put on the table. I think that my staff are doing enough at the moment.

With some changes, RC produced papers which were circulated in advance and discussed at department meetings. He tried to reach a broad consensus, noting that he was often able to proceed to the implementation stage with no real opposition. With the introduction of GCSE he negotiated with a deputy to have eight periods of English and he asked the department if they wanted to have four double periods. It was discussed and organizational problems became apparent. He added:

> When presenting ideas it's important to look at watertight organizational issues – you must look hard at what things will be like on the ground – that is the reality of innovation. Too many educational ideas are good in theory only. In a big school, teachers need a support structure so that they can cope with change. As HoD, I try to have difficult classes and timetable myself across the full range. It's important not only for my credibility but also to keep my feet on the ground – that is to have a realistic sense of what it's like.

Previously, a new 'O' level course had involved a lot of continuous assessment and for this departmental INSET was required. RC made reference to this in his report on 'critical incidents' and wrote:

> The department was very much in favour of the new syllabus in terms of its benefits to their English teaching and pupils' English work. They were, however, very anxious about the assessment at the end of the course which is time-consuming and arduous. We required support from the school in terms of a time allowance.

When asked 'What action did you take', he went on to write:

> I feel this is a key example of an occasion when a HoD needs to support the department and 'fight' for their case. Initially, I had to convince the head that this was a good syllabus. I showed him examples of work produced by pupils . . . The head has been very supportive. Last year, internal arrangements (via supply cover) were made to release staff. This year, because it has become a 'local issue', the permission of the authority had to be sought. Again, the head was supportive and we received some supply cover.

RC also commented that the changes within the faculty had not all been 'top-down' and that in drama there had been extensive innovation. As faculty head, he saw his role as providing a sounding board for the department heads.

Interviews with staff within the department supported the view that most changes had originated with RC but were unlikely to have been implemented without full departmental support. He was seen as being open and honest with his staff, promoting collective decision-making, never forcing anything on the department and, although it was admitted that he could be very persuasive, 'if all of us said "no", he would accept it'.

Example 2

Bill Jones (BJ), as head of Special Needs, had been responsible for the integration of the department's work into the mainstream school. This was a particularly interesting example of change as it had obvious implications for the whole school – all departments and all teachers – rather than being something largely contained within a single department.

BJ's predecessor had been head of a Special School within the mainstream school – the integration had been locational rather than functional. He had made some attempts at integration but had acted in a rather unsympathetic manner and had just said: 'Warnock says integrate, so integrate!' The staff were aghast as they saw the Special Needs unit as a 'sin bin'.

One of the first things that BJ did was to invite the director of education to come out to look at the dearth of resources and materials at the school (what was there was inappropriate). He then put in a claim for £2000.

> I suppose that this was a bit cheeky! I put in an 11-page, fully itemized requisition – which is very hard to argue with! If I had just put in the claim, I would probably have been turned down. With this grant and my generous capitation (the head was fully supportive), I was able to buy, for example, 20 tape recorders, headphones, blank tapes etc.

The department 'shared' secondments – four members of staff each had one term for 'thinking and planning for the future' and produced a joint document. The secondees took one or two departments within the school and looked at the low-ability children in them to see how the Special Needs teachers could help them.

BJ then managed to get Special Needs pupils in Years one to three into 'sympathetic' departments and then into normal tutor groups. One department proved difficult and resented the pupils but: 'The head put his foot down and said that it would have to accept the children. The head's authority was a great support to me.'

The pupils in Years four and five could not be integrated in the same way as they had been separated for so long that they were terrified of going into mainstream classes. However, a Home and Community course with a City and Guilds accreditation was an excellent course run by a very good teacher and some of the 'best' Special Needs pupils were integrated into this. They proved to be the 'stars' of the course: the staff found that the highly motivated Special Needs pupils performed much better than the mainstream pupils and so they welcomed them and the Special Needs department was able to integrate the rest of the pupils in the unit. BJ said that he did not take all and give nothing: if the course took the Special Needs pupils, he would teach on the course and, as he was able to offer things that either no one else could do or no one else wanted to do (residential work, for example), he was a great asset.

Integration was gradual, although it occurred within two years once it got started. BJ maintained a critical eye as he felt that integration *per se* was of no value unless the pupils benefited. Withdrawal continued to be offered alongside in-class support. When they were integrated into a mixed-ability group the Special Needs pupils were always above the bottom ten per cent of the mainstream population; sometimes pupils went into the mainstream for just one subject at first.

Staff in the department spoke of how tactful they had had to be with the mainstream teachers in order to gain their confidence and overcome the reluctance to have someone else in the classroom. That they were successful in this was in no small way accounted for by the atmosphere in the department of open discussion and commitment generated by the head of department.

Example 3

The two years that Bob Penny (BP) had been in post had seen a number of changes made to the PE curriculum. BP had served his probation at the school and on promotion had inherited a fairly traditional curriculum. The department very soon offered mixed PE and introduced, amongst other things, Health-related Fitness and Games for Understanding. BP commented that his biggest difficulty was 'selling' these changes to the parents but he had received lots of support from the head (PE was, for example, part of the upper-school core curriculum). The head of department remarked that ideas within the department did not only come from him, but most notably from his second-in-command and from LEA and national initiatives.

The head of girls' PE, who was second-in-command, commented on the amount of change that had taken place:

We've experienced massive programme changes here and most of them have been new to the department so we've had to learn together and share our expertise. For example, we all came into school early every day for a week to participate in dance as a department and this has helped to unite us. The department's timetabled meeting (during the day) has helped, although this has only happened over the last couple of years . . . There have been a lot of changes and the overall PE syllabus will be renewed in the summer. We will change every few years. I think it's important to keep changing.

The department valued INSET very highly and always tried to send someone on every LEA course. Other members of the department noted that the changes had been well managed because the HoD was both business-like and diplomatic and 'because we constantly get consulted and we're asked what we think'.

A scale 1 teacher explained how changes had been implemented in the department and it is worth quoting her at length:

The HoD had been on a course and informed us that these innovations were taking place and he thought it would be good for us and the pupils if we thought about the changes. He felt that the department had gone a bit stale and was lagging behind. We discussed the idea of mixed PE at some length; we were excited about it, although apprehensive. Personally, I felt as though I was ready for a change. . . The HoD was as concerned as we were about certain aspects of the new programme e.g. creative body management (CBM). I was rather a traditional sports person and it was the new way of thinking that concerned me – the move away from games and towards concepts – but I did welcome the change and I was happy to take the opportunity to go ahead and keep up with trends . . . so the HoD asked each of us to write the bit that related to our own specialist areas. They were in six-week blocks and I did the CBM. We were asked to present our courses to the rest of the department. So it was good that we didn't have to sit down on our own and wade through a whole year's lesson plans. We were contributing to the programme in the best possible way by giving our own expertise. We had a series of INSET sessions: the second-in-command did a session on Games Understanding and later on a Games Invasion course. She presented us with a folder of ideas and lesson plans and she asked for our views. The attitude was, 'You don't have to do it like this but it's there if you want to use it.' I welcomed it with open arms. We also had a couple of evening meetings and we discussed new courses. All of us were games people so it was easy for X (the second-in-command) really, but I think it was more difficult for me and my specialism, dance. As far as the rest of the PE staff went they were complete novices when it came to dance! I gave them a series of six to eight lessons of basic movement. These were lessons that were tried and tested by me over the years. Everyone was appreciative of the literature I gave out but they still didn't feel confident with it, so we decided we'd have a few practical sessions. So for a week, we all came in at 8 a.m. and I taught the lessons and they became the pupils. That seemed to help and it gave them confidence. In addition, X did a fitness course. This was very successful. She produced pamphlets for each year group. These have since been copied by the rest of the county. I think because we all did a bit and shared our work it worked very well.

Both the teacher quoted above and the second-in-command referred to teething problems with the new courses and the latter remarked: 'All these changes may look good on paper but are they making a difference? I sometimes have my doubts.' Both teachers were aware of the need to find the time for evaluation and it is this part of the change process that is the focus of the next chapter.

Summary and discussion

It has been shown that senior staff in schools, together with advisers, expected that department and faculty heads would possess the ability to develop the curriculum incrementally and to facilitate the implementation of innovatory ideas. Middle managers themselves mostly acknowledged their role as curriculum leaders although their perception of what their responsibilities amounted to varied considerably. Evaluation and review (the focus of the following chapter) are, of course, required to ascertain *how* the curriculum should be developed, whether the change be initiated at a national, local, school or department/faculty level, but once the decision to modify has been made, the *way* in which change is introduced largely determines its success or failure.

The process of change was analysed according to the model which divides it into the three phases of initiation, implementation and institutionalization. In the first phase, ideas can come from a variety of sources and middle managers have to consider not only their own ideas but also those of colleagues within the department and the school, as well as those from external agents, local or national. Where there is perceived to be a state of inertia, senior management can employ strategies to promote change within departments: some of these strategies were discussed.

Change has to be planned and, it was suggested, this is best done by open discussion so that all staff can be involved and as many as possible feel a degree of 'ownership' and see the need for change. Middle managers must, however, be aware of how resistance to change arises and how to use it (as, for example, a source of evaluation) or overcome it. They also need the ability to dispel insecurities and to 'sell' the innovation to colleagues. They must also be aware of the appropriate timing and pacing of the change process – these will vary according to the staff and other contextual factors.

Reference has been made to the attitudes of teachers to change. Generally, they respected those department and faculty heads who led by example and who introduced change which was seen to benefit the pupils and the curriculum (rather than their career prospects!)

The implementation phase of the change process requires that those most affected by the change are supported as the innovation becomes accepted into actual practice. Here, the middle manager is in a key position as no amount of planning in the first phase can replace support in the second. It was stated that INSET is more important during implementation than before it and teachers need to be quite clear as to what aspects of their practice need to be modified and to be given confidence as they acquire new skills. Senior staff can play a vital role in supporting departments in the implementation phase, facilitating INSET (by making resources available, for example) and coordinating change.

The third phase in the change process – institutionalization – requires the ability of the department to evaluate the success of the innovation and this is considered in more detail in Chapter 8. The degree of success depends, among other things, on the need to train regularly any new staff involved and to continue to allocate funds to the innovation.

A burgeoning number of substantial, centrally decreed changes, as well as locally sponsored initiatives, are currently on the educational agenda. In addition, with the emphasis on institutional development and the rise of competitiveness among schools – which is likely to increase in the light of the Education Reform Act – many schools are engaged in their own curriculum development initiatives. When schools were selective, and the range ability and interest of pupils within any one school was limited, heads of department did not have to be involved in all the changes that were current. In the present scene, however, middle managers have to take on board the majority of current initiatives, as within their departments they will have pupils of all abilities and interests following a range of courses. Thus the ability to manage both incremental and more radical change is crucial, rather than merely desirable, in the head of department and faculty, and pupil and teacher achievement, performance and satisfaction hang in the balance. Middle managers have to decide what changes need to be made (where these are not obligatory).

In some cases, it is not so much that the direction needs to be changed as that the movement needs to be speedier: here, middle managers need to have the skills necessary to realize this. It would thus, seem imperative that middle managers have a working knowledge and understanding of the change process and that they receive the necessary support as they attempt to put theory into practice. If the right generic skills are acquired, middle managers will be able to meet most demands that are made of them, rather than having to rely on specific training for particular initiatives.

8 How is the Curriculum Evaluated and the Department Reviewed?

The final case study of change in the previous chapter made reference to the need for teachers to find the time to evaluate the success of the curriculum changes introduced in the department. Indeed, both before and during the incorporation or institutionalization stage of the change process, there is a need to evaluate, monitor and review the change. Once a particular course or programme becomes part of the school's curriculum then it needs to be periodically reviewed to determine whether it should continue in its current shape, be modified or be discarded. It is important to remind ourselves that change is best understood as a process, albeit a complicated and cyclical one. The various stages of the change process, outlined in the previous chapter, do not necessarily follow on from each other and, as Bell and Maher (1986) note, 'change is a complex and messy process which will not follow simple linear guidelines'. Curriculum evaluation and departmental review are therefore on-going processes and should not be seen as the exclusive concern of the third stage of incorporation.

It is the intention of this chapter not only to consider how the curriculum is evaluated, but also to broaden the analysis to include the wider issues of reviewing and monitoring the work of the department or faculty and its staff. In this sense the broad definition of the curriculum suggested earlier, to include virtually everything that takes place within a department or faculty, is being utilized. However, before considering the existing literature and the case-study data to see how the processes of evaluation and review were undertaken, it is helpful to define the various terms. The DES pamphlet *Quality in Schools: Evaluation and Appraisal* (1985a) usefully differentiated between evaluation, review, appraisal and assessment. It defined them as follows:

> *Evaluation:* a general term used to describe any activity by the institution or the LEA where the quality of provision is the subject of systematic study.
>
> *Review:* retrospective activity implying the collection and examination of evidence and information.
>
> *Appraisal:* emphasizing the forming of qualitative judgements about an activity, a person or an organization.
>
> *Assessment:* implying the use of measurement and/or grading based on known criteria.

It is the first two activities that will be mainly considered here along with the related notion of monitoring which, in this case, refers to the more general regulatory and surveillance functions of educational managers. To begin with, however, a few general comments are required on the importance of the middle manager's role in curriculum evaluation and departmental review.

The department head's role in evaluation

The job descriptions outlined in Chapter 2 showed that evaluating faculty/departmental progress and regularly reviewing courses were seen by senior staff as key responsibilities of department and faculty heads. A case study school document on the roles and responsibilities of department and faculty heads stated quite clearly that they:

> should regularly evaluate the work being done in the faculty/department in respect of the school's philosophy and the children's needs. If the level of achievement is not satisfactory, the HoD/HoF must assess if the material or approach is wrong, the teaching poor or the pupil motivation lacking, and act accordingly.

The document regarded departmental or faculty evaluation as the responsibility of the head of section with the help of the head and senior staff and noted that it was 'essential that we continue to assess our work'. It regarded departmental evaluation as being clearly linked to both staff and curriculum development. Indeed curriculum development was seen as a part, and a consequence, of evaluation and review.

Senior staff and advisers involved in the NFER project stressed the importance of evaluation and would have concurred with Bloomer (1980) who notes that 'a lively department will keep its schemes of work under continual review, evaluating one or more of the major divisions of its courses each year'. Evaluation was seen as arising naturally out of good departmental practice and as a means of improving that practice. It was a means of knowing, for example, how successful the school or the department had been in meeting its aims and objectives or whether a recently introduced change had achieved what had been intended and/or if there had been any unforeseen outcomes. Its main purpose was one of 'clarifying the discrepancies that exist between goals and practice (intent and actuality)' and of 'providing methods for removing these discrepancies' (Hayman and Napier, quoted in Watts, 1983). Evaluation was seen as crucially important: it helped raise morale, increase professionalism and draw the team together in the pursuit of common goals. Also, as a phase one head of faculty remarked: 'It's good to review because otherwise, if there's no negative feedback, teachers tend to assume all is OK.' Her Majesty's Inspectorate in Wales (1984) go as far as to say that 'whether a pupil achieves or underachieves is largely dependent on the quality of planning, execution and evaluation that takes place within individual departments'.

Despite the importance placed on them, evaluation and review were, in the opinion of headteachers and advisers, activities that heads of department rarely completed systematically, if at all. Indeed, it was suggested by some senior staff that evaluation in education generally is not done well, that it is only paid lip-service and that there is insufficient time for it to be undertaken. Other research studies have noted how educational managers, at all levels and for a variety of reasons, do not undertake systematic curriculum review and departmental evaluation and that there is a tendency to be distracted by routine administration and to be preoccupied with 'the day-to-day' rather than monitoring, evaluating and planning ahead (e.g. see Oxtoby, 1979; Hall et al., 1986). Similarly, Hull and Adams (1981), in their study of science departments, found little evidence of any systematic evaluation of the whole curriculum and the changes that had occurred were mostly modifications, made in isolation, to existing courses. Some department heads regretted this but said (Hull and Adams, 1981) that 'lack of time, and the existence of many immediate day-to-day problems prevented them from developing a rigorous policy of curriculum evaluation'. An analysis of the shadowing days and the observation of meetings carried out as part of the NFER project would support these general findings.

In the experience of a phase one deputy head, departmental evaluation was *ad hoc* and random – 'something that comes out almost as an incidental'. Some department and faculty heads, especially those involved in phase two of the research, were aware of its importance and tried to build it into the year's activities but most would not have disagreed with one nominee who, when asked if the department evaluated what it did, replied: 'Yes, we do, but it's very haphazard and very often it's done when I'm in the bath!'

As HMI and others have commented, evaluation remains largely an intuitive process based on teachers' subjective opinions and there is a clear need for a more structured and formalized approach to departmental or faculty evaluation. Even when evaluation is supposedly practised 'it may amount to no more than a glance at, and an apologia for, the summer's examination results' (Edwards, 1985). Edwards further remarks that much attention has been given to whole-school reviews and the assessment of pupil performance but far less to the evaluation of departments. It appears that most teachers gave low priority to departmental review and curriculum evaluation, with the latter being based on subjective judgements, external examination results often being the only objective criterion. Hodson (1985) states that the major impetus for change is the middle manager's hunch that change is necessary, adding: 'Change should not be precipitated solely in response to personal hunch, 'bandwagon jumping', the propaganda of articulate pressure groups or the glossy advertising of publishers, but in response to a rational appraisal of the existing curriculum and the proposed replacement.' Continuous evaluation of curricular provision is, he suggests, the only means of ensuring that teaching remains effective.

Evaluation was seen as a difficult task for middle managers for a number of reasons. It was thought to be difficult for heads of department to distance themselves from the department and become objective; in the words of a phase one head: 'It is not an exact science . . . it's a highly skilled art and people tend to look for quantitative measures e.g. exam passes, option choices, are the books marked? etc.' Another head in the same authority thought that few department heads evaluated formally, for example by submitting a written report, but most did do it informally. If everything seemed to be going well then matters were left alone, largely because time was scarce and other matters took priority. There was insufficient time to stand back and observe critically. A phase two head of faculty, although wanting to undertake a formal evaluation, was reluctant to engage his staff in this activity as they already 'had enough on their plate and if I ask for extra it might jeopardize what we're doing well at the moment. Also, time spent evaluating Year 4 is time not spent preparing for Year 5.' Some practitioners were more concerned with the future and what needed to be done and, in this sense, evaluating or 'looking back', was given less importance. A deputy head in another school remarked that fulfilling the syllabus together with obtaining the best out of the pupils were topmost in teachers' minds – hence, departmental evaluation was given a low priority. It was also given low priority because 'too many people say "there's nothing wrong" without doing any effective evaluation or thinking how the department could move forward'. In this deputy's view there needed to be evaluation in a structured way but departments should work this out for themselves rather than being given a framework. It did appear that where evaluation was undertaken, departments tended to devise their own means of doing it, often adapting or using the relevant section of whole-school evaluation documents, checklists or aide-mémoires. For example, the phase two head of faculty referred to above had had experience of using the Inner London Education Authority (ILEA) document Keeping the School under Review. The section on reviewing departments and faculties asks a series of questions and was found to have been a useful starting point.

Reviewing and evaluating practice

The discussion so far has tended to perceive the responsibility for review and evaluation as lying with departments themselves, the object being the improvement of existing programmes and practices. However, review and evaluation can, of course, be undertaken by others – whether from within the school or outside – sometimes for reasons of professional accountability rather than departmental improvement. Similarly, a single department may be evaluated independently or it may be part of a much broader school-wide evaluation or review. In turn, the whole-school evaluation may have been initiated by the school itself or be a requirement of the LEA. Examples of all these levels and types of review and evaluation were found in the NFER case study schools and it is intended, for the purpose of analysis, to examine these under the two main categories of external and internal departmental evaluations and reviews.

External departmental evaluation and review

LEA evaluations
Reviews and evaluations of departments or other units within a school may be undertaken by the school's headteacher or SMT or by external bodies such as HMI or the LEA's inspectors or advisers. Inspections by HMI had recently taken place in four of the case study schools and generally they had been welcomed. A phase two nominee had found the experience 'useful and stimulating', while the head of another phase two school noted how the inspection had provided a

necessary catalyst for introducing change in some departments. The head remarked that one head of department had been in post for 21 years and had become very complacent. As a result of the inspection HMI had been able to get the department to reconsider its lower-school curriculum, something which, as a new head, he had not been successful in doing. (The head remarked how different the situation was as regards the modern languages department led by a nominated department head: in fact, if anything, he felt HMI would have learnt from the department!). It was noted that reviews and evaluations undertaken by those outside the school could provide an important and necessary external lever, supply the required detached and objective perspective, and help initiate plans for change. The local authority advisers and inspectors could perform a similar role but, it was stated, so much seemed to depend on the strength and credibility of the individual subject adviser. In some instances advisory teachers were seen as having greater credibility as curriculum change agents than advisers.

The LEAs involved in the NFER project seemed to vary in the amount of time and priority they gave to school and department reviews and evaluations; indeed, different individual advisers within an authority gave these differing emphases. In some instances, advisers had formally evaluated a department or faculty in their own subject specialism; in others, they took part in their capacity as the school's general adviser. An example of the latter was a modern languages adviser reviewing an art department, while in another authority eight advisers had followed first year pupils for two days before reporting to the headteacher on the curriculum offered by the various departments. Evaluations of specific departments or faculties were undertaken by specialist advisers, where possible, in pairs. A PE inspector from a large authority remarked that he and his colleague would carry out approximately two departmental reviews per term – 'We go into the school and look at the PE department in all its aspects and write up possible areas for improvement.'

A PE adviser in another LEA, which had produced a county statement on whole-school review, had given a lot of thought to departmental evaluation and produced a model for the evaluation process. The model was designed to assist in the planning and operation of visits to schools for the purpose of evaluation. The process of evaluation included the careful collection of evidence, the formation of judgements based on evidence and the selection of criteria against which judgements were formed (e.g. stated objective, norms/averages, and other schools' performance). Evaluation was seen as a means of ascertaining departmental effectiveness, implementing improvement or change and providing necessary feedback. The exercise was conducted by the adviser through consultation and the collection of documentary evidence, measurement and observation and usually took two to four days to complete.

Before the visit, the department head was given a copy of the evaluation-process document and was asked by the adviser to provide various pieces of information (for example, programme outline, objectives of work, schemes of work, extra-curricular programme, staff timetable, staff responsibilities and finance). The evaluation-process document gave details of the information the visiting advisers would be seeking. The areas of concern were divided into four sections: resources, the PE programme, extra-curricular activities and the administration of the PE department. These four sections were further subdivided with, for example, Section B – the PE programme – requiring information on schemes of work, presentation of lessons, pupil assessment and programme evaluation. Under the last subheading the advisory team sought information not only on the methods of evaluation used by the staff for assessing both specific courses (e.g. gymnastic courses) and the overall PE programme, but also on decision-making procedures used by the department.

After the visit, a four- or five-page report was produced using the above major headings and areas in need of review were noted. A follow-up visit would be arranged for a later date when the adviser(s) would hold a series of discussions with the head, the head and the department head, the department head alone and with all the department. It was intended that the outcome of the evaluation was to take action on the recommendations: to help solve any problems and to implement ideas and suggestions arising from the evaluation; to review INSET possibilities applicable to identified staff needs; and to retain contact with the school to facilitate further visits and exchanges.

The degree to which the recommendations were implemented and departments improved as a result of the LEA advisers' evaluations was unknown, but it is interesting to note that in a follow-up report of one department produced by the advisers, it was remarked that most of the initial report's suggestions designed to improve the curriculum had been implemented. However, 'few of the recommendations to improve facilities made to the LEA by the Advisers have, as yet, been realised'. (As shall be shown there are some interesting parallels here with evaluations and reviews conducted by SMTs.)

The above LEA had produced a policy statement on whole-school review and evaluation and had been involved in piloting the GRIDS scheme at both school and departmental level. Industrial action by the teachers' unions had meant that little progress had been made with the latter, although it is interesting to note that one adviser was encouraging departments and faculties to review or self-assess their progress and, to this end, had adapted the GRIDS method and incorporated relevant material from subject and advisory association publications.

Other LEAs participating in the research were involved in evaluation and review to varying degrees. Several had produced whole-school review documents, in which participation by schools was voluntary in some authorities yet compulsory in others. In a phase one LEA it was incumbent on schools to demonstrate that they were doing something about review and evaluation. In another, a headteacher remarked that very little formal evaluation had taken place at either whole school or department level, there had been no guidance on this matter from the authority and 'none of the advisers had ever suggested evaluation in that formal sense'.

Senior management evaluations

Heads and deputies, too, differed in the importance and time they gave to formal evaluation and review. In some schools, departments and faculties were reviewed regularly and individual middle managers asked either to submit an annual or termly departmental report or, far less frequently, to be the subject of an in-depth study by the SMT. One case study school had devoted several of its INSET days to considering questions of evaluation and review.

It was, however, much more common for the case study heads to make reference to the informal means by which they monitored and evaluated departmental performance. When asked how he monitored the work of departments a phase two school head said:

> This is quite hard really. You see exam results, you see kids' faces and you see, for example, minutes of department meetings. I do give HoDs the opportunity to come in and talk or I may ask them to come and see me. You also get feedback from parents and you know if the staff are dissatisfied. I think as far as monitoring goes, a lot is done by the seat of your pants . . . I try and encourage a close dialogue with HoDs. I think it may be a gut reaction but it enables one to come to certain conclusions about the department and what it's doing.

In this school it was not school policy for department heads to produce an annual report, annual interviews with the head were not held and, as a deputy remarked, although the head was supposed to receive department meeting minutes, this was not always the case. At another phase two school, the head explained that there was no means of monitoring or evaluating the performance of departments and faculties. He intended to introduce regular reviews based on what he termed 'key result areas' and commented: 'What goes on in the classroom and the departments is never formally reviewed and is all based on hearsay, which is not right.' He expressed a hope that systematic review and evaluation would arise out of teacher appraisal.

Interestingly, this school had been involved voluntarily in a school self-evaluation exercise but both the head and a deputy felt that for the amount of effort that had been invested in the exercise the results had been disappointing. The benefits gained were not commensurate with the energy expended, the school had become preoccupied with the process of review which was seen as cumbersome, long and involved and it was thought that it would not be used again. Elsewhere, heads spoke of the negative feelings towards formal evaluations and reviews that had been engendered by participation in LEA-devised schemes, especially compulsory ones, which were seen in many instances as 'mere paper exercises'. Some were described as far too descriptive, non-judgemental, unchallenging and unhelpful – 'the sort of thing you could safely give to parents without any alterations'. As a result of devoting a lot of time and energy to these unproductive exercises, staff had developed negative views towards the idea of formal evaluations at all levels.

However, a phase one school which had been involved in piloting the voluntary GRIDS scheme found the whole-school review exercise an extremely beneficial one and, among other things, it had led to the school instituting its own voluntary scheme of performance review (see Chapter 6). It was reported that involvement in GRIDS had helped the school develop a team spirit and corporate identity and had gone some way towards breaking down 'departmentalism'. The head did remark, however, that although he would recommend whole-school reviews to others, participation did expose senior staff to the scrutiny of others and autocratic heads might therefore find it difficult to adopt.

Another phase one school had also conducted a whole-school review but in this instance had devised its own set of questions from several existing documents. The review, which encompassed pastoral as well as subject heads, was set up with particular reference to the school's in-service needs and was an attempt to encourage departments and pastoral units to consider critically what they offered pupils. Several members of the SMT were concerned that the curriculum in some areas did not seem to be changing at all and embarking on a review of curricular and pastoral areas was seen as a means by which change might be encouraged and facilitated. It was one way for senior staff to find out what teachers wanted and it was

Figure 8.1: *Curriculum review, with particular reference to curriculum-led INSET needs*

1	What progress has the department made during the last two years? What problems has the department encountered during the last two years?
2	Are you and your department happy in dealing with the new GCSE syllabuses?
3	What changes, if any, have been made to your lower school curriculum?
4	Are you satisfied with the transition from the third year syllabus to your fourth year syllabuses?
5	Are you satisfied with the transition from the 4th/5th year syllabuses to your 6th/7th year syllabuses?
6	How effectively does your department work as a team?
7	What policy does the department have on assessment?
8	What areas of curriculum require further development? What are your priorities?
9	What are your procedures for departmental meetings?
10	Are you satisfied with resources, equipment and accommodation?
11	What liaison/coordination is there between your department and other departments?
12	What contribution does your department make to whole-school activities?
13	What extra-curricular activities are the department involved in?
14	What arrangements does the department have for visits and visiting speakers?
15	What are the INSET needs of: (i) individual members of the department? (ii) subgroups of the department? (iii) the department? (iv) groups within the school? (v) the whole school? (vi) groups at LEA level?
16	Does your department have any method of disseminating information on INSET and curriculum initiatives and developments?
17	Are you satisfied with the quantity of subject-specific INSET at both local and national levels?

hoped the review would start a dialogue between senior and middle management, for it was suggested that only when such a dialogue was engaged in would the school begin to improve.

It was decided that eight members of the SMT (excluding the head) would undertake the review and be responsible for areas different from their own specialisms. For example, a senior teacher who was head of the middle school and taught English was responsible for reviewing Special Needs, mathematics, modern languages, history, English as a second language and Years six and seven. The reviews were voluntary – only one department and one year group decided not to participate – and were produced by senior staff following interviews with heads of department and heads of year. In some cases senior staff had observed the department at work and visited lessons. Before the interviews took place, the school's middle managers were asked to discuss a series of questions in departmental and year meet-ings – they were not required to respond to these questions in writing. For the curriculum review 17 questions were discussed and these have been reproduced in Figure 8.1.

The middle managers were informed which deputy head or senior teacher had chosen their area to review but that an alternative reviewer could be requested: however, none were. After the discussions and the interviews, copies of notes were collated and made available to all staff for discussion. The curriculum and pastoral review document was published approximately six months after the interviews had taken place and was available to all staff, who were encouraged to make written comments. It was then intended to formulate an INSET plan for further discussion and comment. The INSET plan would then be revised, put into action and activities matched to the needs specified. The senior staff also thought it important in conducting the review to identify those areas where they were failing to give appropriate or sufficient support, and in which the school's organization and administration might at times militate against the achievement of goals. The review was seen as a forum for discussion between groups which, it was hoped, would lead to 'the improvement of the educational experience of every child at the school'.

The curriculum and pastoral review was being conducted at the time of the NFER researcher's visit, so it was too early to know how successful it had been. Certainly some middle managers thought the exercise had raised a number of interesting questions, that it had 'made you think about what you're doing' and that it was worth undertaking. However, for many the review was to be judged by what happened as a result and it was very important that it was not seen as 'just another talking exercise'. Contact was made with the deputy head responsible for the review nearly 18 months after the exercise and, in her opinion, it had successfully raised the school's awareness of its INSET needs. As a direct result of the review several workshops had been conducted (e.g. on records of achievement and GCSE). Also 'it was well worth doing' because it had involved other members of the SMT in curricular and pastoral activities. There were plans to repeat the review in three years' time, but on this occasion with more classroom observation. The deputy did suggest that not as much had been achieved by the review as she would have liked, as industrial action had intervened and other concerns had taken priority.

In a phase two LEA, an adviser explained how supply cover had been made available in order for the head and deputies to undertake an evaluation of the school's faculties. The adviser made available copies of two faculty reports from one school in the authority (this was not a case study school) and the following account draws heavily on these. It was decided at the first meeting of the planning committee at this school that the SMT would conduct in-depth studies of all the faculties. It was thought this would be a valuable exercise as, to paraphrase from the first report: it was a useful evaluative tool to assess the faculties' effectiveness; it was a means of reducing the distance between teachers and senior management and, if properly handled, it should lead to mutual understanding; and the head would be in a better position to identify needs and deficiencies if they were witnessed at first hand. The aims of the faculty reports were twofold: to establish at first hand the nature of the faculties' contribution in implementing the aims of the school; and to identify areas of need and to make recommendations. In attempting to fulfil these aims the SMT proposed to take note of a number of elements with respect to classroom activities. These included the following:

1. the nature of the teaching;
2. the relevance of what was taught to the pupils' needs;
3. the deployment of resources (human and material);
4. the arrangements of teaching groups;
5. the aims and objectives of the courses;
6. the schemes of work;
7. the assessment procedures;
8. the facilities available;
9. the work of the pupils;
10. the monitoring of pupil progress;
11. the care and guidance arrangements.

Aspects of organization and management were also reviewed and these included:

1. the effectiveness of the faculty team as a unit in implementing

its pastoral and academic responsibilities;
2. the nature of communications within the faculty and with senior management;
3. the roles and responsibilities of all members of the faculty;
4. the in-service activities of the faculty and the opportunities for staff development;
5. the faculty structure of professional development.

The faculty were informed of the SMT's intentions two weeks prior to the study taking place and at this meeting the above areas were described and any problems and uncertainties resolved. It was agreed that the head of faculty would work closely with the head and accompany him and/or the deputies into the classroom. The report attempted, as objectively as possible, to reflect the state of the faculty as viewed by senior management and to identify future directions which it considered the faculty should take in implementing the aims of the school.

The faculty reviews took two weeks to conduct and involved the head and deputies in discussions with groups of teachers, individual teachers and the faculty as a whole. The intention was that much of the time would be spent inside the classroom, observing teaching methods and pupil progress. A report, which included a series of recommendations, was then made available before being the subject of a day-long faculty meeting when detailed discussion of the issues raised ensued. This meeting took place approximately three months after the review and surveyed general issues before focusing on the specific aspects covered by the in-depth study. Particular recommendations and issues were analysed and in some cases further recommendations resolved. The faculty accepted the report as a fair and accurate assessment of the current situation and it was agreed to submit it in its entirety to the governing body for their consideration.

The first in-depth review undertaken at this school made 11 recommendations, many of which had resource implications. The problem of whether or not the recommendations would ever be implemented was resolved, at least in theory, by the report's final recommendation which said that:

> Evaluation of the effect of the in-depth study of the faculty and the monitoring of the implementation of the recommendations contained in this report will be made at periodic intervals during the course of the next two years (two years being the most realistic time-scale to ensure that all recommendations are implemented).

Of the 21 case study schools involved in the NFER project, only one had conducted formal, in-depth evaluations or reviews of departments or faculties in a systematic manner. In this school – in a different authority from the example given above – the head and deputies had recently completed reviews of the science and design faculties. For a week the SMT visited workshops and laboratories and talked to the department heads about what they had observed. At a later date a full meeting was held with the faculty to discuss matters but, unlike the example above, no written report was submitted. The usefulness of the exercise was, however, problematic and a science teacher commented that although he favoured the idea of a review by senior management, he was not sure how much could be gained from observation. Classroom observation was essential as there was often a mismatch between what people said and what actually happened but there was a need to visit many more lessons than proved possible. A senior teacher in the same faculty thought the review exercise was more useful for the SMT than for the department or faculty as 'it makes them aware; they can be very isolated on the admin side. Also it helped staff to know that the SMT appreciated their problems.' The head was also aware of the limitations of the exercise and was hoping to encourage internal departmental review or self-evaluation. He remarked:

> I think that formal evaluation and review is just so artificial. Any-one who knows SMT are going to be around in week X will put on a good show and SMT can only get snapshots. The interesting thing that came out of the exercise was the interaction between department teams and senior management at the meetings at the end. There was such a mismatch between our perceptions of what was going on and those of the department.

The head added that when he could manage his time better, he was considering spending a week in each department but the logistics of classroom observation were just unmanageable. A head in another authority was trying to timetable one afternoon a week to enable him to visit classrooms.

Some senior staff considered that teachers should expect them to visit their classrooms as such practice was the only way of monitoring what took place. A deputy remarked that it should not be seen 'as a big-brother syndrome', adding that 'the argument that it's not profes-sional to be critical is ridiculous!' A head in another phase two school liked the idea of a review by senior management and thought that staff would not object provided that it was seen as part of a whole-school review, there was feedback and recognition of good work and the emphasis was on improvement and not accountability. As the head remarked: 'One of the problems in education is how do we know if we're doing a good job? We don't!' It was thought teachers would be pleased to see that somebody was interested in their work as, at present, so little feedback was found in schools.

In all the examples of external review and evaluation given so far in this chapter, it has not proved possible to determine with any degree of accuracy what had been their actual effects or outcomes. Given the large amounts of time invested by all parties in whole-school reviews and departmental/faculty evaluations there is a need to know whether the outcomes justify this level of input. How effective and efficient are they for departmental improvement? Reference has already been made to some of the perceived benefits but, unfortunately, a detailed analysis and evaluation of the process was not possible as part of the present study. Other researchers, however, have conducted detailed studies of the process of school and department self-evaluations and have reached some interesting conclusions.

A team from the Open University (OU) have examined critically both voluntary and compulsory LEA school-review schemes, whether initiated for accountability purposes or for purposes of institutional and professional development (Clift et al., 1987). Their detailed ana-lyses found that all the schemes studied showed a lack of clarity as to the purposes of the review activities on the part of many of those involved. In most of the studies undertaken, whole-school evaluation 'did not prove to be an effective means of bringing about substantial and enduring changes in the schools where it occurred and in none did it prove to be a cost-effective one'. Interestingly, they found that voluntary whole-school self-evaluation exercises were more popular with young and junior teachers who liked being involved in matters they were normally excluded from. They were liked least by middle managers who thought they had little to gain and perhaps much to lose as 'they were likely to be the prime targets in any criticism of the status quo'. However, the researchers also suggest that departmental evalu-ation is relatively more effective than whole-school self-evaluation.

One of the OU researchers presents a detailed case study of a review of an art department by the school's senior management (Clift, 1987). Its purpose 'was to establish the extent to which previously determined practices were being adhered to and to maximize their effectiveness'. The review was thus conservative in spirit and not attached to any innovation. The case study of the review of the art department is well worth reading as, unlike the other examples reported in this chapter, it was possible to observe and study the process of the review throughout its duration. Clift (1987) reports that the department review procedure, agreed with the heads of department, had three components: a questionnaire to be completed by the department head prior to a series of meetings between him or her and members of the SMT; observation of departmental staff's lessons by the SMT; and staff appraisal interviews. A draft report was then prepared and given to the head of department and then a revised, negotiated version was presented to a departmental meeting.

Details of the review are given by Clift (1987) but of most relevance here is the degree to which the departmental review was able to meet its objectives. This is examined in detail and it is stated that whereas the teachers in the art department were quick to respond to most of the recommendations addressed to them this was not the case for the SMT. 'In marked contrast with this ready compliance, virtually none of the recommendations for action to be taken by members of the Senior Management Team had borne fruit a year later' although, as Clift admits, some of the recommendations did imply substantial resources which were probably beyond the sanction of the SMT. However, in general terms, Clift judged the review to have been effective and that because 'some of the recommendations were for actions beyond the means of the school does not deny the effectiveness of the review procedure'. Valid and reliable evidence regarding the department had been gathered 'on the basis of which prescriptions for institutional changes might be made, and it provided the necessary motivation for those changes of the most direct importance to the pupils to be acted upon'. Clift (1987) also notes that views differed on whether the review exercise was an efficient means of initiating and implementing change. A member of the SMT voiced concern over the amount of time taken to review a small department, while the head of art saw it as worth while and could not think of any other means as effective.

Reporting to senior staff

As earlier noted, systematic department or faculty reviews were uncommon in the NFER case study schools. Much more frequently found were formal annual reports and interviews with the head and it is proposed to examine these briefly before considering the matter of internal department/faculty review.

In one school, towards the beginning of every autumn term, each head of department spent a minimum of one hour with the head when examination results were considered and a review of the department undertaken. Each department head was asked to produce an annual, open-ended written report. Whereas guidance was given for the review of exam results, by means of a pro-forma, this was not the case for the report although department heads were expected 'to include whatever they think is relevant'.

In another school, the heads of department produced a report for the head; they were asked to set targets for the future and to look back over the year. The department heads themselves had agreed on the report's headings, they were submitted to the head and then individually discussed. The reports in turn were presented to the governors who were appreciative of the extra information and now expected them annually. A deputy from the school stated that the reports to governors were used by senior management as another way of finding out what was going on but 'it was important for the HoDs not to see this as interrupting or interfering with their autonomy'. It was important to build up confidence between middle and senior management and, in the deputy's view, participation in a whole-school review had helped develop this.

A nominated phase two head of faculty remarked that the school used to have an end-of-term departmental review with the head and first deputy. This was seen as a very useful exercise and, it was suggested, there was a need for it to be reinstated. Senior staff from another school, which also required formal reports each term, remarked that there should be very few surprises in these for senior management and that it was important for department heads, when writing the reports, to acknowledge what the staff had done within the department. It provided an opportunity to communicate to others what had been achieved. It was important that staff were seen as accountable and as having responsibilities to another person – someone outside the department or faculty or, indeed, outside the school. A scale 4 teacher remarked that 'department heads should have to answer searching questions from someone', while adding that for his school 'the present review system is unsatisfactory'.

Finally, in another school, the head had drawn up a departmental evaluation form which gave a profile of the effective department as seen from the head's viewpoint. Each department was required to submit an annual report for certain areas of its work. This 'evaluation exercise' was done by the department and time for doing it was timetabled. The head commented that its main purpose was to maximize the use of resources and to promote effectiveness: heads needed to have sufficient knowledge in order, for example, to allocate resources. However, the head also remarked that some teachers saw the exercise as threatening and he thought there was a long way to go before teachers accepted review and evaluation as a natural part of their job.

Internal departmental evaluation and review

Differing views were held by senior staff as to the value of 'top-down' evaluations or reviews and some expressed a preference for these activities to be undertaken by departments and faculties themselves. Internal or peer-group evaluation was seen as generally more effective, especially if the evaluation was initiated as a result of the teachers deciding themselves, through discussion, that this was what was needed. External evaluations and reviews can be quite threatening and it has been suggested that all teachers should be engaged in the process so that they become evaluators as well as being evaluated (e.g. Nuttall, 1981). Not only will participation in, and control of, the evaluation help to allay teachers' fears but 'it also improves the effectiveness of any changes that are implemented. Teachers would understandably resist something they felt was a result of a process they had little to do with, simply a senior management (or headteacher) affair' (McCormick, 1986). As Clift et al. (1987) have argued, the 'notion of giving ownership of the process to the participants is held to be a vital step in promoting effective educational change' and this democratic principle underpins some of the school evaluation schemes currently available (e.g. GRIDS and the IMTEC/NFER *School Development Guide* – see McMahon et al., 1984; and Sumner and Butler, 1985).

As to how much internal or peer evaluation took place, it was noted earlier in the chapter that when it did occur, it tended to be a haphazard and incidental activity on the part of the department head and rarely involved systematic study or the collection and examination of evidence. An analysis of data from the case study schools showed that internal departmental evaluation and review were often given a low priority by both middle managers and teachers, and other concerns were frequently seen as more pressing. However, as HMI in Wales (1984) have noted:

> The extent to which departments undertake a more systematic evaluation depends to a considerable extent on the expectations of the senior staff, and in particular, on the existence of a clear whole-school policy which offers a framework within which to work.

In some of the case study schools it was remarked that senior staff did not lay down sufficient guidance and that there was a need for greater direction from them to encourage middle managers to use their time more effectively. For example, it was suggested that although the latter half of the summer term was perhaps not the best time to embark on any major activity, it was currently 'wasted time' and the extra periods made available due to the departure of examination classes were rarely used effectively by the department for evaluation and development. Senior staff could help facilitate such activities by suggesting meetings take place, attending these and making a contribution to departmental discussions.

In some schools, senior staff were linked to a number of faculties or departments as a sympathetic but not uncritical 'curriculum friend' (Edwards, 1987) usually in areas other than their own subject specialism, and although it was often their intention to attend meetings periodically throughout the year, other matters usually took priority. Depending on the climate found within the department or faculty, senior staff could offer to assist in any evaluative activities, either directly by acting as a non-specialist or indirectly by, for example, providing cover to enable staff to observe each other's lessons. Senior staff could also ensure that middle managers were made aware of any checklists, aide-mémoires or other means by which departments were able to review their performance. Departments may decide to focus initially on only a few of the questions that are raised but such lists did 'provide an agenda to stimulate professional discussion and debate within the department over a substantial period of time' (HMI, Wales, 1984).

Giving advice on the methods and means available to evaluate departmental performance and curricular provision was another way in which senior staff could assist. In one case study school, for example, several INSET days had been devoted to a consideration of questions relating to evaluation and review (the latter to include performance review or teacher appraisal). It is likely to prove necessary to provide departments with technical advice and guidance on how they can evaluate and review their activities because, as has been shown earlier, these were often problematical. (Useful generic advice is given by Hodson, 1985; McCormick, 1986; and Murphy and Torrance, 1987; while advice on evaluating specific subject departments is given by, for example, Hull and Adams, 1981; Allen, 1983.)

Her Majesty's Inspectorate in Wales (1984) have recommended examining and discussing samples of pupils' work at departmental meetings as a method of evaluating provision – a method which has the advantages of being based on direct evidence, involving the whole department and aiding the professional development of teachers, especially the inexperienced and non-specialist. Also, it enables the department head to establish and maintain agreed standards. Such an activity appeared to be increasingly common in the case study schools as they came to terms with the continuous assessment associated with GCSE. There were also found several examples of pupils becoming involved in evaluating particular lessons, courses or units.

In line with developments in the area of assessment, where pupils increasingly are asked to comment on, and take greater responsibility for, their own progress, a few departments were requiring pupils to complete self-evaluation sheets and comment on the new programme offered and, it was noted, their observations could make a significant contribution to departmental evaluation.

Although it could be argued that curriculum review and evaluation should be a permanent item on the agenda of department meetings (see, for example, Watts, 1986), some departments chose to attempt this activity mainly at the end of the academic year. A teacher in a phase two school said that although their timetabled weekly meeting was useful for administration and curriculum review, the latter would be undertaken primarily in the summer term, when there was a lot less pressure and more time 'to sit back and look at what we're offering our pupils – for example, we might spend the entire morning looking at our fifth year syllabus'. It was at this time of the year that departments were more likely to ask whether or not their aims had been achieved or if it was necessary to adapt schemes or introduce new ones. But reviewing the department's achievements was not easy as the criteria of success were not always obvious. Teachers spoke of the need to find the time to evaluate and reflect and this was thought to be particularly difficult when many changes had taken place. In a phase two department which had experienced many innovations, the department head noted his weakness here and said that 'although we move forward at a rapid pace we pay only lip-service to evaluation'. This person was about to be seconded to undertake a curriculum development role for the LEA, and had renegotiated the departmental staff's job descriptions to operate during his absence. Interestingly, the most senior member of the department had been allocated specific responsibility for evaluation and this required him 'to evaluate all aspects of the work of the department and its staff; to communicate his evaluation to the department and where required offer professional help and guidance; and to report to the head and deputies, on a regular basis, the results of his evaluation'.

As noted in Chapter 6, the observation of teachers in the classroom, whether by senior staff, middle managers or departmental colleagues, was not common and was often perceived as impinging upon teachers' classroom autonomy. It could be argued, however, that observation of practice is central to the activity of evaluation and review. Without 'looking at learning', it is difficult to gauge the effectiveness of what takes place in classrooms. As shown in the earlier chapter, some departments appeared to be more ready and willing than others to expose their practice to colleagues for positive review. A notable example was found in a phase one school where the head of PE, after having attended a DES course, had successfully introduced the use of video in the department. Department staff were asked, using a task list, to observe a video recording of a lesson given by the head of department. This was found to be helpful and other members of the department volunteered to be similarly recorded. The department decided to focus on how they communicated information to pupils. They had also recently introduced a new course in basic skills. The programme had been produced by two teachers and the department as a whole discussed how it was to be evaluated. The head of department videoed several lessons and these were the subject of most fruitful discussion. The department head remarked:

> We saw that the interpretation of what had been written down as the programme was very different and this occurred even with people who had worked together. So we analysed the programme and revised it. We then revised other areas of programmes in relation to this.

Clearly, video had been constructively employed by his department but for others not quite ready to use video for evaluative purposes, team-teaching can be a useful means by which teachers can constructively review each other's performance.

Two of the ten LEAs participating in the NFER research project had been involved in piloting the GRIDS scheme of school self-evaluation, and three schools visited (one phase one and two phase two) had been selected to pilot the version of the scheme that had been adapted for the use of departments and faculties. The departmental version of GRIDS was being attempted only in those departments that had expressed an interest but, at the time of the NFER fieldwork, little progress had been made because of teachers' industrial action. Since the time of the NFER research the scheme has been successfully piloted and is now available for general use (Birchenough et al., 1989).

As earlier noted, in one of the authorities, the departmental version of GRIDS had been adapted by an adviser and successfully used in several schools. It was suggested that any review of departments was best carried out in the context of a wider school review and that the aims and objectives of departmental teams needed to be related to those of the school. If this was not the case, then care must be taken to relate the review to the work of other groups in the school.

In reviewing the work of departments and faculties, the GRIDS method uses the same general approach as the secondary school handbook (McMahon et al., 1984) and involves five stages. The first stage is concerned with deciding if the method is appropriate and how it will be managed. Secondly, the initial review involves, inter alia, administering a questionnaire to staff to ascertain their priorities for review. In the third stage a specific review is planned when it is required to identify, by examining statements and collecting evidence, what is existing policy and practice; then to decide how effective present practice is and to agree conclusions and recommendations. The fourth stage focuses on action for development, while the fifth and last stage is to plan the overview and restart the cycle. (Further details are given by Birchenough et al., 1989.)

Essentially, the GRIDS method of departmental review is democratic in principle – it is collaborative and consultative, with curriculum and staff development, together with departmental improvement, seen as the central purposes of the exercise. The aim of GRIDS has been to produce 'process' guidelines for those who wish to review and develop the curriculum and organization of departments and, as with the other schemes, it is recommended that priority areas are identified for specific review and development and that not too much is taken on at any one time. The GRIDS process provides guidelines – not rigid rules – and, it is suggested, the methods may not suit all schools at every stage of their development equally well: it may be necessary to adapt them to the school's particular circumstances. The process takes time and, although not referring specifically to departmental GRIDS, the DES (1985b) pamphlet Quality in Schools suggests one year is the minimum time from identification of a topic for evaluation through the process of review to the initial implementation.

The two phase two faculties which had used the adviser-amended version of departmental/faculty GRIDS had generally positive experiences. In the first, although the initial reaction had been 'Oh no, not another hefty publication!', the experience had been useful and there were plans to use the review process again. The faculty had been able to implement a lot of what they had identified as wanting to do. The LEA had provided some training on how to conduct the review as part of the TRIST scheme. In the second case study school, although senior staff expressed disappointment with their experiences of the whole-school version of GRIDS and would not use it again, the departmental or faculty version had been a lot more successful. The faculty, in conjunction with other schools in the consortium, had reviewed its provision, particularly its lower school programme. Several areas were identified as in need of change specifically as a result of the faculty's involvement in the review process.

It appeared to be very rare for heads of faculty to ask their department heads for an annual written review. A phase one head of faculty expected to receive a copy of the department heads' annual review before it went to the headteacher. The faculty head had previously given the department heads a list of questions he thought they might find useful in preparing their reports. These included questions relating to target-setting and successes achieved. The faculty head explained that 'the HoDs are reasonably effective at this within the faculty, although the new head of RE who was redeployed here, found the change from his last school dramatic to say the least!' A few middle managers produced their own reports, regardless of whether or not it was school policy to do so, because it was seen as a useful exercise, helping to develop a team identity and publicize the successes achieved both by pupils and staff. Department staff were asked to report to the department head on any developments or progress in their areas of responsibility and this, along with information derived from the minutes of department meetings, could be used to help compile the report. A phase two head of PE produced a four-page departmental review after he had been asked to write an imaginary one as part of a course he had completed. The report commented on the curriculum and the changes introduced; the department's administration and staffing; staff development and INSET; the extra-curricular programme; and sporting successes, trips and excursions. It had not proved possible to produce a departmental review every year, however, and it was admitted there was a need for another.

Before concluding this section on internal departmental review and evaluation it is necessary to say something about the means – other than direct classroom observation – by which middle managers monitored the work of departments and faculties. As part of the research, middle managers were asked to discuss ways in which they monitored the work of their colleagues, while teachers were asked if their department heads were aware of what they were doing in the classroom. As might be expected, and in line with earlier comments, the situation regarding monitoring varied considerably from department to department and, occasionally, even within the same department. The following teacher comments give some indication of the levels and range of monitoring undertaken:

> No, the HoD is not aware of what I'm doing. I think to find out what's going on he could look at children's books or folders.
> I'd expect him to. He could talk to me regularly about what I'm doing – he does not!

> He is very aware. We have regular meetings to discuss things – for example a specific year group or worksheet. We share resources. I have a lot of leeway in the way that I teach but the HoD would be aware of what I'm doing.

He is aware informally: for example, the classroom door is left open, and we talk a lot. In the lower school we have set lesson plans. I don't think the HoD inspects books – at least, not to my knowledge.

Yes, my HoD is aware of what I do in the classroom although there is no formal monitoring of my work. There is no looking at record books or anything in either of the two departments I work in. They just leave you to get on with it . . . but HoDs know an awful lot about what's going on – the bush telegraph works very well!

Some department heads were aware of the managerial dilemma between allowing teachers their professional autonomy and being sufficiently aware of what was taking place in the classroom. They wanted to avoid giving staff the feeling that they were being constantly monitored, 'interfered with' or 'checked up on'. This sentiment was rarely expressed by teachers interviewed in the nominated phase two departments and faculties. Very little formal monitoring appeared to take place but through constant individual and group discussion, regular meetings, team-teaching, the sharing of worksheets and various indirect means, effective department and faculty heads were made aware of what was happening – 'you just know what's going on'. A head of department hoped to introduce a new idea (for the department) whereby all teachers were to present six exercise books for other teachers to share and look at. The intention was to look at all the books to ensure that the pupils were getting a balanced curriculum and to introduce a system of record books for staff to record their work. However, in general, informal means of monitoring were more commonly found but middle managers did not wish to be accused – as were some of their senior colleagues – of being unaware of what was going on in the department or faculty.

In some of the phase two departments and faculties the emphasis was on the team monitoring itself rather than being monitored and the climate that had been created, largely through effective leadership, was collegial rather than hierarchical. Senior staff remarked that where such a climate had been engendered, the likelihood of internal departmental review and evaluation being undertaken was increased and important activities such as classroom observation and teacher appraisal were more likely to arise naturally from them and to be accepted as necessary for both institutional and professional development.

Summary and discussion

An attempt has been made to demonstrate how review and evaluation should be central to teachers' activities in schools. Fundamental to the complex process of change, and linked to staff and curriculum development, review and evaluation are thought to affect not only the quality of the curriculum but also pupil achievement. Furthermore, they meet the increasing demands from the community for teachers to be accountable and, it could be argued, strengthen professionalism in that practitioners are seen to be rigorously critical of what they are doing.

Senior staff in schools often cited review and evaluation as indicators of an effective department but, despite this, these were activities which were often given scant attention and accorded low priority when time was limited. In addition, it appeared that practitioners were 'future-driven' and time spent evaluating and reviewing (looking backwards) was time not spent on preparing for the future. What evaluation was found was frequently unsystematic, intuitive and *ad hoc*. Thus, means to ensure that the activities do take place are highly desirable. It is doubtful whether there is any one 'best method' appropriate for all school situations and, very often, the value of a formal procedure lies not so much in its inherent structure as in its catalytic effect and the fact that it generates, and gives space for, reflection, self-evaluation and objective criticism. It is all too easy, when time is at a premium, to assume that everything is all right unless something goes very obviously wrong: however, such a policy does not ensure that the department moves forward.

Various programmes and practices which encourage evaluation and review were also examined. Local authority schemes – systems varying in quantity, quality and kind – sometimes involved isolated initiatives on the part of individual advisers and, at others, a directive from the chief education officer or director of education that all schools participated in some way in examining their performance.

Within individual schools, senior staff may implement formal schemes, either across the establishment or focusing on individual departments/faculties on a rolling programme. It was found that programmes usually involved senior staff observing departments at work and examining documentation before issuing a report which was then discussed with the department concerned. Senior staff may also request annual reports from middle managers and these may cause departments to deliberate on the quality and nature of what they have offered and what they are planning to offer. Such reports were found to be diverse as regards their level of critical evaluation – some were rigorously honest; others were bland. Some schools used externally produced frameworks such as GRIDS; others produced their own.

Some individual departments and faculties were found to have initiated a detailed self-assessment process in which senior staff or other colleagues had varying levels of involvement. Senior staff could support departments reflecting on their work, for example, by providing cover so that the department could meet together in school time or the head of department could visit teachers' lessons. The latter activity was something that was rarely done on anything but a casual basis unless senior staff cooperated in this way. Senior staff could, in fact, help department and faculty heads use their time more effectively by suggesting, for example, that the fifth and sixth year release time in the summer term be used to meet for review and evaluation. It was noted that where senior staff attended such meetings, they were often able to be of considerable help in facilitating and focusing on salient issues. Sometimes, a deputy or senior teacher was allocated to a department to provide a 'curriculum friend' with whom middle managers might reflect upon their practice.

Alongside formal review and evaluation went informal monitoring – facilitated by such features of effective departments as, for example, open-door policies, the sharing of worksheets and the exchange of exercise books.

The efficacy of different schemes for evaluation and review is unproven, and longitudinal and comparative studies are needed to ascertain the effects, outcomes and 'success' (according to multiple criteria) of various schemes. In some situations, it could be that the formidable amount of time expended on full-scale formal review and evaluation might be better spent elsewhere, targeted, perhaps, on a particular area of concern. It was not always clear whether adequate action was taken after a review: although changes initiated by the department were often apparent, senior management did not always realize their responsibilities. Although, ideally, teachers should be constantly evaluating what they are doing and offering in every lesson (and, indeed, some of the effective departments and faculties perceived evaluation to be very much an on-going activity) there was seen to be a need to stand back, take stock and put things in context. Evaluation and review could only be effective, it was suggested, if aims and objectives were clear and these were much affected by context which embraces the needs and aspirations of pupils, parents, the immediate community and society at large, as well as the prevailing educational philosophies. Furthermore, aims and objectives must be able to be realized in the light of the particular situation – so they are not unrealistic – and also take account of 'good practice' elsewhere.

If the greater part of curriculum evaluation and review is done departmentally (which would seem to be the case despite the need for additional evaluation to ensure the coherence of the total curriculum 'package'), considerable demands are made on the middle manager. The activities require both a broad perspective and a fine focus on the details of actual practice and the way this relates to the wider picture. A considerable amount of work is currently being done on performance indicators (see, for example, Wakefield, 1988) and teachers in management positions will need to be familiar with this literature. Furthermore, middle managers need to be able to motivate their staff to participate in the exercise and to be prepared to take action, either individually or as a team as appropriate, according to the findings of the review process. If there are no outcomes from the exercise, teachers are unlikely to take it seriously and will, rather, 'opt out', psychologically at any rate, in much the same way as they do if discussion and consultation procedures do not result in decisions being made – an issue which will be explored in the following chapter.

There is a lack of unanimity about the role of the LEA adviser/inspector and practice varies considerably throughout England and Wales (Stillman and Grant, 1989). It has been suggested, however, that, as a result of the 1988 Education Reform Act, LEA officers will have more of an inspectorial role than an advisory one and will increasingly monitor schools' accountability and performance. This may put them in a new relationship with middle managers who may, thereby, receive less by way of support and services.

Present timetabling structures and use of time within the school day and year may not be the most conducive to facilitating reasoned reflection. Perhaps there is a need for new models here, bearing in mind the critical nature of the activities which are, at present, often squeezed out of departmental life by extraneous circumstances. The recent introduction of five 'contract' days and 'directed' time may mean evaluation and review become a more prominent feature of school life than is currently the case. Inadequate review and evaluation inhibit departmental and school improvement and, it could be argued, leave schools a prey to inertia and staleness on the one hand, and mindless following of fashion on the other.

9 How are Decisions made in Departments and Schools?

The importance of the sharing of decision-making in the furtherance of staff development was briefly referred to in Chapter 6: it is now intended to explore in greater detail this area which impinges on others already discussed (for example, the management of change – see Chapter 7). It is not the intention to adopt a systems approach whereby decision-making mechanisms are analysed – although structures existing in the phase two case study schools will be noted. Neither is it intended to engage solely in an exploration of the *loci* of power in schools and to describe micropolitical activity (what, and how, items get on the agenda; power relations between departments etc. – see, for example, Hoyle, 1982, 1986; Ball, 1987) – although reference will be made to this body of work in the course of the text. Rather, the chapter will look at the part played by middle managers as regards both their own involvement and their furthering of the involvement of others in decision-making within the department and within the school. It will also consider actual practices within schools as perceived by a range of staff.

Edwards (1985; see Chapter 2, Figure 2.1) considers that leadership and communication infuse all the activity engaged in by middle managers whatever the dimension of school life; the dimension of decision-making is no exception and it can, in fact, only be comprehended in the light of a concept of leadership. The NDC categorize management styles, team-building, decision-making and communication as 'leadership skills'. It could be argued that participative decision-making embraces a number of factors identified as contributing to school effectiveness (for example, collegiality, job satisfaction). Rutter *et al.* (1979) found that in effective schools there was clear leadership from the top but teachers felt that their views were represented. Similarly, openness of communication and collaboration were features of schools identified by Fullan (1982) as being good at managing change.

Leadership styles

A useful definition of leadership style is that given by Sergiovanni and Elliot (1975) who see it as the way an individual expresses leadership, uses power and authority, arrives at decisions and in general interacts with teachers and others. Various attempts have been made to draw up typologies of leadership styles (e.g. Lewin, 1944; McGregor, 1960; Likert, 1961; Blake and Mouton, 1964; Etzioni, 1964), some of which, it is argued (Nias, 1980), assume value connotations – for example, delineating the 'autocrat' as caring little for the feelings of others. One of the most useful models – reproduced in Figure 9.1 – is that of Tannenbaum and Schmidt (1958, 1973) which identifies six types of decision-making. Relating this to the contingency theory of Fiedler (1968) which takes account of situational variables, it can be argued that managers (especially school middle managers, who find themselves in such a myriad of situations) need to operate in all seven modes. Indeed, Hull and Adams (1981) contend that the styles of heads of department are usually hybrids. It is how each mode of decision-making is handled that determines its efficacy and the way in which it is perceived. For example, 'tell' and 'sell' decisions are quite acceptable provided that they are communicated in the right way, and the appropriate type of participation is as important as the basic concept of participation itself (Davies, 1983).

Whatever the style, it should be open and clear (Everard and Morris, 1985). Furthermore, Sutton (1985) contends that teachers must be secure in their knowledge of how different issues will be decided – that is, what mode will be utilized: 'What is most important here may not be so much the style itself as its consistency. . . Nothing is more confusing to staff than not to be able to foresee with reasonable certainty how a significant issue is likely to be resolved.' Other factors also need to be considered: the autocratic mode may be quickest at the point of decision-making but has a long implementation time; a decision will take longer to arrive at by a consultative process but will increase commitment and implementation is likely to be faster (Hull and Adams, 1981; Everard and Morris, 1985). Furthermore, there is a limit to the energy of staff (Buckley and Styan, 1988) and an

Figure 9.1: *Types of decision-making* (from Tannenbaum and Schmidt, 1958)

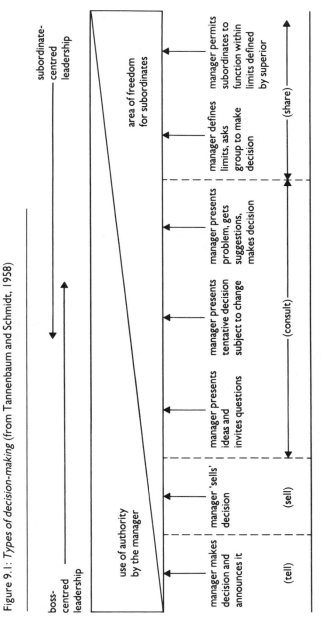

boss-
centred
leadership

subordinate-
centred
leadership

use of authority
by the manager

area of freedom
for subordinates

manager makes
decision and
announces it

manager 'sells'
decision

manager presents
ideas and
invites questions

manager presents
tentative decision
subject to change

manager presents
problem, gets
suggestions,
makes decision

manager defines
limits, asks
group to make
decision

manager permits
subordinates to
function within
limits defined
by superior

(tell)

(sell)

(consult)

(share)

185

expectation that discussion will not drag on interminably (Weindling and Earley, 1987).

In Chapter 2 (see Figure 2.1) routine activities were differentiated from higher level ones, a distinction which would seem to parallel 'transactional leadership' – the 'fixing and dealing which are necessary in administration' – and 'transforming leadership' which involves 'leaders and followers raising one another to higher levels of motivation' (McGregor Burns, 1979). It could be argued that it is in transforming leadership that participative decision-making is crucial and this would explain why this seemed to be a feature of the more effective departments in the NFER study. A middle manager can be extremely *efficient* – as opposed to effective – by operating in the 'tell' and 'sell' modes, for these are perfectly acceptable – and, indeed, probably most appropriate – for administrative tasks. However, essential for *effectiveness*, are two basic leadership functions – task achievement and the fulfilment of colleagues' social needs (Hoyle, 1986) – and it has been suggested that the department head's role needs developing significantly away from focusing purely on administrative tasks to considering the broader needs of colleagues as professionals.

The effective practitioners studied in phase two of the NFER research were not directly asked to describe their leadership style but, on reflection, most considered – and observation and interviews with other parties would confirm this – that they favoured participative decision-making although they were flexible in their approach, being prepared to adopt the most suitable style according to the situation, the available time and the issue.

Attitudes to decision–making

The literature

Hull and Adams (1981) point out that members of a department may have expectations as to how a head of department should approach decision-making. These expectations may be affected by two factors: experience to date and psychological needs. There is some evidence (Knoop and O'Reilly, 1976) that, although favouring a more collaborative role, teachers do not want absolute control. Belasco and Alutto (1972) found that desire for increased participation and levels of satisfaction regarding this were not equally distributed in the teaching population. Primary school teachers in Nias' (1980) study condemned heads who totally devolved responsibility for making decisions which affected the whole school. Nias pointed out that the decentralization of decision-making does not *necessarily* increase the job satisfaction of all teachers. She found that:

> Maximum job satisfaction went hand-in-hand with humane but positive leadership, leadership to which teachers felt they were encouraged to contribute but which gave them in return the chance to perform effectively the main role for which they thought they were employed.

An investigation by Bloomer (1980) identified the desired profile of the head of department as a democrat rather than an autocrat, and evidence from a survey conducted by Howson and Woolnough (1982) suggested similar findings.

The measurement of 'decisional deprivation' (when individuals desire more participation in decision-making than they perceive they actually have) is difficult, but useful in that it underlines the point that it is *perception* of involvement, rather than the actual *degree* of involvement (although, clearly, the two may be concomitant), that determines satisfaction levels. The degree of participation alone does not, of course, reveal very much about the political reality of decision-making in the institution as other factors – for example, the content of decisions and the stage at which various groups and individuals are involved – have to be taken into account (Conway, 1985).

The NFER study

What both the middle managers and the teachers in the NFER study spoke of negatively as regards decision-making were 'rubber-stamping' meetings and 'cosmetic consultation'. Such behaviour was, in fact, more frequently referred to with regard to middle managers' involvement in whole-school decision-making than teachers' involvement within departments. Most department and faculty heads, in both phases, acknowledged the value of open discussion within departments and the following statement by a phase one head of department was atypical: 'I don't think it's the department's job to produce materials or that things are best done in consultation – I'm weary of verbal proceedings.' Generally, it was *outside* departments that discussion became problematic; within departments participative decision-making appeared to be the norm.

Especially in the phase two schools, teachers regarded the part they played in decision-making within the department very positively. They felt that their department head was accessible and that they were able to express their views freely. However, the degree to which they were involved and the quality of participation varied according to the way in which the department head operated and was affected by a number of factors such as the information made available and the 'health' of the team. The 'good' heads of department allowed staff 'to have access to their thinking': they discussed issues and deliberated openly. In the effective departments, it is probably true to say that staff were aware of their own ability to participate and their experience or lack of it. However, in the less effective ones, where staff were deprived of opportunities to widen their horizons, teachers could well perceive that they had a satisfactory degree of involvement but yet be unaware of their own shortcomings and that they were 'speaking in ignorance', opportunities to extend professional experience and expertise having been denied them.

Davies (1983) quotes research evidence which suggests that participation in decision-making can promote better decisions, although an NFER case study headteacher questioned whether the outcome of involvement in decision-making was reinforced emotional commitment to the institution or improved practice. Teachers' participation in decision-making may improve their sense of efficacy and thus enhance morale (Dembo and Gibson, 1985). Many middle managers were aware of the expertise that lay within their departments and wished to capitalize on this. A head of department said: 'If there were a staff disagreement, I would never say "You'll do this anyway." All the staff in my department are older and more experienced than me.' And a faculty head observed: 'I've risen through the department and am not an imported HoF who can come in and pretend they've got all the answers ... I'm learning as much as everyone else.' A head of department who had had industrial experience remarked: 'In education we do not make the most of people who are experienced. In industry they have moved towards corporate decision-making.' A deputy head, referring to one of the phase two nominees said: 'He is prepared to listen even though at times he may appear not to do so. When we were changing from mixed ability to banding, he listened and acted on the department's advice.'

Generally, teachers in the NFER study felt that they had little say in whole-school policy-making; they were either not consulted or were asked for opinions *after* the SMT had decided upon a course of action – the latter situation gave rise to more acrimony than the former. Teachers did not mind decisions being made at a senior level, often saying 'Someone has to decide' or 'That's what they are paid to do', and realizing that a number of decisions were most appropriately made at this level; they were prepared to be 'told' or 'sold' decisions. However, they *did* object to being treated 'unprofessionally' and their time being wasted in pseudo-discussion and cosmetic consultation when decisions had already been made and were unlikely to be modified. Frustrations arising from situations such as these have been identified as causes of stress, which itself leads to underperformance (Dunham, 1984).

The promotion of participative decision–making within departments

Hoyle (1986) identifies four reasons for the increase of pressure for participative decision-making: the change in the socio-political climate of the 1960s; the growing need for greater teacher collaboration for curriculum change; the increasing complexity of schools which undermines the single person kind of leadership; and the growth in management courses which emphasize particular approaches. In the NFER case study schools there was evidence of an assumption that the participative mode was desirable.

If expertise is found within a department, it is logical that a new young department head will wish, out of self-interest if nothing else, to tap it. However, if the expertise is undeveloped, what can the middle manager do to promote participative decision-making which, if it is not to be an 'exchange of ignorance', depends on informed discussion? It is not insignificant that, in the nominated departments, there were a number of related factors which went alongside participative decision-making and, rather than any one leading to another, it is arguable that they were interdependent and coexistent.

The involvement of staff in decision-making – with its perceived benefits in terms of staff development, commitment, willingness to change etc. – cannot just happen. Most of the effective practitioners had worked at it, even if indirectly, largely by generating a climate in which it could flourish. In those departments and faculties where staff had been accustomed to an autocratic leadership style, they had to learn *how* to participate when there was a change of leader. A department head whose own observed departmental meetings were an exemplar of participation, remarked, regarding the situation in the whole school:

> I think that the new head is trying to consult staff now. It's difficult making staff feel some responsibility when they have not been accustomed to it – the previous head was a complete autocrat and never asked anyone about anything.

Another newly appointed faculty head remarked that his staff were longing to get involved in faculty matters but 'did not know how to as yet' as the previous head of faculty had done and decided everything. A phase two head of department similarly observed: 'The first few times we met as a department it was a bit uncomfortable but now everyone expects to express views and there's a very good spirit.'

It was the 'open' departments that practised participative decision-making – not merely because they had a philosophy that placed value on democratic processes *per se*, but because the staff were privy to everything that was going on and were kept fully informed. The teachers had both the necessary information and background knowledge on which to form opinions and make decisions, and the benefit of sharing others' views and experiences, thus broadening their own horizons. Participation was an on-going process and was not confined to organizational structures.

An aspect of the role of the head of department is to encourage and facilitate others to become leaders and, in the view of many senior staff, this was just as important as the middle managers themselves taking the initiative (although, undoubtedly, it is imperative to strike the right balance between devolution and accountability). Yeomans (1987), albeit discussing management in primary schools, wrote: 'The greatest demand on collegial leadership is that the leader as member is sufficiently secure to enable colleagues to lead effectively.' An NFER case study headteacher observed: 'The absolute key to departmental improvement is to involve everyone in everything that goes on. If you can get ideas flowing then you have a structure for making improvement. On the other hand, you have got to have ideas yourself and be seen as a leader.' Another, a newly appointed head, saw the ethos of the whole school affecting what went on within departments:

> There must be ownership of problems in teams and people must not see things in terms of the person above them solving problems . . . When I came here the SMT was not working as a team . . . I felt that there could be no progress until SMT was right. Then I could look at middle management and the process would go down through them for more democratic participation among the teachers.

Collegiality and team–building

Hoyle (1986) writes about 'collegial authority' – the 'pattern of authority which is held to be appropriate to organisations which are staffed by professionals' and which ensures that bureaucracy and hierarchy do not restrict latent expertise. He considers that, largely on account of salary differentials (other than increments for length of service), schools are not characterized by collegial authority and it is not inherent in the system. Those with higher status or salary have power thrust upon them to make decisions. In the NFER research, this feeling was evident: a phase two head of department remarked that he felt it his duty to represent staff at meetings to save their time and a number of teachers interviewed said that they thought that middle managers were paid to make the decisions even if they should consult staff first. The phase one fieldwork – and some phase two – was conducted during industrial action when many of the formal consultative structures had broken down. One department had learnt from the experience. The department head said:

> Before [industrial] action, I'd set up working parties . . . during action, I've written all the courses but now the staff are criticizing them – positively not negatively. It's made them aware of the value of coming together as a group to work things out.

Hoyle (1986) contends that participative decision-making is not a 'right' but something bestowed by a benevolent manager. (For a contrasting view see Watts, 1986.) The arrival of such a benevolent manager at whatever level was often commented upon:

> Decision-making at this school has changed a lot since the arrival of the new deputy. Also, the new HoD has been much keener than his predecessor in getting involved in the school. The same process of democratisation has happened in our department and in the school.

A recently appointed phase two headteacher wrote (in a school document):

> Good communication and participative decision-making is a necessary condition for staff commitment if the school is to move forward. I see the staff of a school broadly as a collegiate group of professionals . . . It is a matter of professional faith in one another.

Arguably, with GCSE syllabuses and the growth of course teams demanding greater interaction among teachers, collegiality within schools could be strengthened. Some of the activities engaged in in connection with GCSE are akin to those identified by Little (1982) as being crucial for the sort of collegiality which results in continuous professional development, namely: frequent, continuous and precise talk about teaching practice; observation and constructive criticism; joint planning, designing, researching, evaluating and preparing of teaching materials; and exchange of good practice.

Research has also been conducted in industry and commerce into the optimum composition of management teams and it has been found that they work best if various ideal types are represented (for example, Belbin, 1981, makes reference to the 'shaper', the 'monitor–evaluator', the 'resource–investigator', the 'completer–finisher'). Interesting though such evidence may be, it is only marginally transferable to schools – where the composition of teams is largely determined more by luck than good management. Appointments are made, primarily, on subject terms, both within the department and at middle management level. Some schools may find themselves in the fortunate position of having a large pool of suitable candidates for a post but others, particularly those in inner cities and those with vacancies in the shortage subject areas (for example, CDT, science, modern languages, mathematics) may find it difficult appointing someone to fulfil curricular needs, let alone having the required characteristics to fill any identified gaps in the team. The situation has often been exacerbated by redeployment and ring fence policies. Furthermore, each member of staff in a school is often a member of a number of teams (academic, pastoral, special issues working parties) in a way that is not comparable to the industrial or commercial situation. Thus, within the department, it is of considerable importance that middle managers have the skills necessary for building a team from the staff they have.

Many of the team-building strategies employed by the effective practitioners were closely related to the ways in which they promoted staff development. However, individuals can be professionally developed without being part of a team or participating in decision-making as a member of a group. Watts (1986) identified three important factors which facilitate a feeling of collectivity: the free flow of information, well-organized meetings and the sharing of responsibilities. These factors were features of the effective departments studied in the NFER research.

Free flow of information occurred when department heads willingly shared their own professional experience (lesson ideas, resources etc.), professional expertise from without the school (professional associations, courses) and information regarding broader curricular and professional matters affecting the whole school community. The effective practitioners were trying to widen the decision-making base, thereby increasing opportunities for alternatives to the curriculum already within the school and thus avoiding the constraints and parochialism to which school-centred innovation can fall victim (Hargreaves, 1987).

Such information can be conveyed both formally and informally. The danger of the latter is that only those who happen to be around at the right moment benefit and acquire the background for subsequent decision-making or involvement in relevant working parties. Thus, although effective departments were notable for their 'rich' conversations, they were very often also recognisable for the way in which formal meetings were conducted (see Chapter 6).

Characteristics of meetings were the communication of information (for example, relaying the main points and the minutes of SMT meetings with middle management) as well as the encouragement of debate regarding issues affecting teachers in the school or the department. The latter issues are, possibly, the more contentious as they affect teachers' day-to-day life for it is, largely, subject-based decisions that impinge most obviously on the classroom practice with which teachers identify most closely. Participation, however, does not necessarily mean that teachers have any more control over the curriculum (Hargreaves, 1987).

At the time of the NFER fieldwork, schools were concerned with the implementation of GCSE. In some cases, the examining board to be used was determined by school policy, though in others, the decision rested with the department and department heads had circulated syllabuses among colleagues, selecting, in the main, the syllabus which was most in line with the type of work in which the department had already been engaged. In many cases, GCSE was spoken of as a facilitator of participation as teachers had to come together to discuss assessment and coursework.

When a head of department was very much in favour of a particular policy for the department or simply wanted participation in decisions regarding implementation, there was often conflict. The effective heads of department were sensitive to this and spent a lot of time in discussing proposals, giving reasons for decisions and trying to overcome feelings of threat by ensuring that staff received the necessary preparation, training and support for any changes in classroom practice. Where opposition was more ideological (for example, a strong feeling for teachers to retain a separate subject identity rather than move towards more integrated work), the problems were less easily resolvable and the department heads had to develop their powers of persuasion.

The effective heads of department tried to promote staff consensus about a proposed change – operating in the 'selling' mode. Middle managers were aware that, in their pivotal position, they had on occasions to 'sell' decisions made elsewhere (by, for example, the SMT, the LEA or the DES). There were limits, however, to the extent to which they would act according to the views of the majority and there was little evidence of totally democratic decision-making (i.e. decisions made according to a majority vote) or radical staff participation such as that earlier found at Countesthorpe (Watts, 1977). Nevertheless, a number of departments were, in fact, 'unanimous' on account of the good 'selling' job of the middle manager or the fact that appointments had been made on the basis of a shared educational

philosophy. Generally, middle managers wanted to make the final
decision should the occasion arise and the department was equally
divided: 'In the department, if I feel someone is very against something I want, I'll drop it *unless it's terribly important to me.*' The words of
one department head is typical of the feelings of many interviewed:

> Most people will accept a decision, though they may not agree
> with it, if you're open and honest with them. If you dictate to
> people and don't give reasons as to why you're acting in a certain
> way, there'll be friction and ill-feeling.

Certainly, there was dissatisfaction when reasons were not given or
thought to have been inadequately explained.

Decision-making within departments has to be seen in the light
of the fact that one of the functions of the head of department is
to establish the department's aims and objectives: 'There is a need to
establish priorities. There is an abundance of ideas in the department
– it's a matter of choosing which to adopt.' Department heads who
were prepared to take the lead, and set an example by doing what
they had decided their staff had to do, were respected: 'The HoD is
very stubborn but he has consulted us all. His attitude is "I'll try it and
if it works you should try it too."'

Staff liked to see *outcomes* and what they reacted to negatively, both
within the department and within the school, was lack of action after
consultation. A head of department remarked: 'It's no good discussing
ideas from probationers and scale 1s if they just get lost'; and a teacher
observed: 'Whatever seems to be agreed, nothing seems to happen
as a result.' A department head admitted to 'rationing' his attendance
at meetings as 'there are endless meetings and nothing is resolved'.
It must be made clear as to when the discussion has ended and a
decision point reached. Teachers did not like uncertainty. In a phase
one school a teacher remarked: 'We put things to our HoD but they
just get lost so there's no point in taking them further. She sometimes
makes an appointment to see the head but he just puts it off so she
doesn't bother any more.' Equally, a head of department commented
that decisions were apparently made by senior staff when teachers
thought that they were in the middle of the consultative procedure.

The effective practitioners spoke of the importance of creating a
feeling of belonging to the department: many organized social events
– a weekly visit to the pub, a meal out together or joint sporting
activities, for example. They felt that it was much easier to help
colleagues, especially older ones, if they had created a social bond. It
was not clear what was the key to the 'happiest departments', the ones
where members worked as a team and where there was the greatest
feeling of belonging. 'We're a keen department . . . Why? Because of

the HoD's approach to the job . . . But all the staff are very nice people . . . It would be no good the HoD taking over the department at X (neighbouring school) because there are two very cynical teachers there.' This teacher implied that the head of department was lucky in having a naturally cooperative and amenable group to work with while, at the same time, acknowledging the part played by the leadership of the department head. Perceptions were often that the personality of individuals was 'given' and middle managers spoke of being fortunate with their staff in this regard. However, it is suggested that the behaviour of the middle manager played an important part, as evidence showed that teachers often fail under poor leadership, motivation declines when there is no professional development and there is a tendency to opt out when professional opinions are not taken seriously or are ignored.

The existence of department or faculty offices was considered to be a great help in creating a feeling of belonging to a team although, of course, there was the problem of 'isolationism' particularly in schools which had departments sited in separate blocks and when there was no central staffroom. A department head said: 'I've painted a room, put a kettle in it and claimed it as an office – there's more discussion now.' It was noticeable that of the faculties studied, those with offices were very often the ones which seemed to be most successful in creating a faculty identity (generally considered to be harder to achieve than a departmental identity) and most successful as regards the cross-fertilization of ideas and collaborative work; individual department rooms within a faculty tended to isolate teachers. As a further communication aid, some departments had a weekly bulletin. One, for example, besides giving administrative information (exam dates and deadlines, for example) announced jobs needing doing in the future so that staff could have time to think about them before the departmental meeting – this was appreciated by teachers in this department.

Problems as regards creating an identity and engendering a feeling of belonging to a team were caused by split sites – teachers were travelling in opposite directions and the valuable breaks and lunchtimes were spent commuting – and the existence of part-time staff. Heads of departments whose staff were likely to change from year to year (often in the 'new' areas like European Studies and PSE and subjects such as RE when there was only one specialist for the whole school) also spoke of the problem of creating identities: 'Social science is a hotch-potch. There are different teachers each year and a number of non-specialists.' In such circumstances, faculty arrangements were often helpful.

Department heads and school decision–making

One of the criteria by which senior staff identified effective middle managers, and a quality which was highly valued, was the ability to take a wide perspective and see subject or area concerns in the context of the whole school. Middle managers who fought for their own corner regardless of the needs of colleagues in other departments and whole-school policies were regarded unfavourably. One phase two practitioner resolved this dilemma by trying to look at the pupils' total curriculum experience and considering the effect of a 'departmental stance'. Refusal to give up a period a week, for example, might mean that the pupils were denied something enriching, and was thus undesirable even if it meant that a department might have to revise its schemes of work if the period were relinquished. Issues involving compromise (which a number of middle managers regarded as inevitable 'once you see things in perspective') very often revolved round resource allocation.

It is with respect to interaction with senior management that the department head's pivotal position is, perhaps, hardest to come to terms with. A deputy head said:

> They would like to take a whole-school view but feel they
> would be betraying their departments. . . They will talk with
> me privately but in meetings they find it uncomfortable to look
> at broad issues. Perhaps it's a 'them-and-us' situation – are they
> seen as siding with the head?

Often it was the case that there was conflict between the different perspectives as to what was judged to be of consequence:

> You have to persist if you want to take up something that is
> deemed low priority by SMT . . . It's best to go direct to the
> head. If you raise something under 'Any Other Business' at HoDs'
> meetings you can be seen as bolshi.

There was some evidence of what would appear to be poorly organized meetings. One practitioner spoke of the fact that although the agenda for heads of department meetings was apparently 'open', the discussion was poor and there was opting out because of apathy. This was because middle management were denied the background information with which they could make informed comment so 'you don't dare open your mouth because you'll look stupid'. At one school a middle manager claimed 'decision-making in this school depends on how "loud" you are and how well you get on with senior staff'.

Some practitioners realized the limited part that they could play in the light of the educational scene outside the school:

The HoFs' meetings have an agenda and papers in advance but both are set by the headteacher and there is no AOB [Any Other Business]. The head is trying to implement tremendous change from the LEA and the government and I think that's why he's taking control of the agenda.

Where agendas were not published in advance of middle management meetings, staff spoke of 'muddling along' and 'having to think on our feet'. The topics for discussion may partly be held responsible for lack of involvement:

The heads of department meetings are chaired by a DH (who rotate annually). They are negative and just turn into a moaning session . . . It was more positive last time . . . Why? Because the agenda was more positive, I think . . . There are no working parties generated from HoDs' meetings.

Where agendas included challenging issues rather than run-of-the-mill administration, commitment was stronger.

There were different committee structures and systems of consultation in the case study schools. In some, only heads of faculty or senior heads of department (usually the 'big' ones – English, science, maths, for example) met with the SMT; in others, all middle managers were included. The former arrangement was prone to accusations of elitism; the latter, of unwieldiness: 'Too large a meeting doesn't allow HoDs to be looked after and stunts growth.' At one school, over 50 per cent of the staff attended heads of department/teachers-in-charge of subject meetings. Department heads not included in meetings with senior staff felt frustrated, especially where they perceived that they were poorly represented by their head of faculty. Some department heads spoke warmly of the way in which their heads of faculty represented departmental concerns at heads of faculty meetings, but others were not so happy and there were instances of the heads of faculty 'blocking' a departmental initiative. A head of PE said: 'It's difficult having someone represent you when they don't care a hoot for PE.' Some schools attempted to overcome the problem by allowing heads of faculty to bring a head of department or faculty representative to meetings on a rota basis. This proved unsatisfactory for the heads of department, however, on account of the lack of continuity: they might become very involved in an issue at one meeting but then not be able to follow it through and, when they next attended, would find themselves in the middle of a new issue for which they had not the necessary background.

Heads of department were not always in the best position to judge how effectively their heads of faculty represented their interests but headteachers spoke of the varying communication skills of faculty heads. At one school there were violent reactions from department heads when new curriculum proposals were announced – an indication, the head thought, that they knew nothing about the lengthy discussion of the curriculum review that should have been passed on to them by their faculty heads. It was not just some faculty heads who seemed to have weaknesses here. A headteacher observed: 'I can think of an HoD who allows staff to discuss matters at meetings but the views he expresses at HoDs' meetings are seen as his own and not those of his department'; and another remarked: 'I always give reasons for my decisions but how far these get filtered down varies according to the HoD.' The effective practitioners were noted for the way in which they satisfied the communication needs of both those above them and those below them.

Furthermore, the 'power' of heads of department was perceived to be reduced by 'baronial' faculty heads: 'HoFs are very powerful people – for example, capitation is dealt with by them. In a sense, the HoD's role is reduced to that of ordering books.' A deputy head's comments are worth citing at length, illustrating as they do the shift in power that often results when middle management structures are modified:

> The faculty system developed because the HoDs/TiCs' meetings became too big and unwieldy. So the previous DH called the HoFs together as a think-tank. Up until that time the HoFs had not had any power. They did a curriculum review. We had presumed that the HoFs discussed various matters within their faculties but they hadn't, so when the review came out, it was a bit of a surprise to many people. Over this review, the HoFs had a lot more power but it's not really recognized. The HoDs and TiCs are quite happy to pass things over to HoFs – the little tasks – but don't like giving them power.

On the micropolitical front, several heads of faculty spoke of the additional power that they had when promoted (power 'won', doubtless, from the department heads who can be the losers when faculties are set up). One said: 'Things have happened which would never have got on the agenda if we had just had departments and not a faculty structure.' Another, a head of science and maths faculty observed: 'I get a more serious hearing from the head than if I'd just been head of science.'

The 'chair' of the faculty rotating between heads of department was something that was discussed and offered as a solution to 'baronial' faculty heads, but the practice was not encountered in any of the schools studied in the NFER project. However, the new incentive allowances could make this possible and give greater responsibility to individuals for a specified period. Clearly, much depended on the management skills of the faculty head. In those cases where heads of faculty took a different view when seeing the needs of the faculty and constituent departments in the context of the needs of the school as a whole, it was important that they gave adequate feedback and explanation to their staff.

Some headteachers were trying to develop the middle management level and this was particularly the case in the phase two schools. Whether or not this was symptomatic of the fact that there were, by happy chance, several very able practitioners at this level, or whether they had become effective on account of senior management support, can only be conjectured but a phase one headteacher did say that he could not involve middle managers more as they were of such poor quality (though, clearly, what he and the deputies could have done to rectify this situation is an important consideration).

A phase two headteacher said:

> In the past, HoFs meetings have been just information giving and a communication channel. I want to give them things to grapple with – for example, capitation, staffing and rooming decisions.
> I was encouraged this morning. An HoD came to me and said: 'Perhaps you could discuss that at the next senior management meeting.' When she came to the school a year ago she would ask *me* for a decision – she saw me as an authority.

At another school, the headteacher said: 'Before, the situation was very much "We can't do anything without first asking the head." I wanted to try to build up cells of several people that would help with team-building.' Elsewhere, a faculty head said: 'In HoFs meetings we used to discuss little things like litter and truancy but we're now beginning to look at curricular issues. We all want a clear decision from each meeting.' A deputy at this school commented that heads of faculty meetings had got out of control because things were being deferred as there was so much to be discussed under matters arising from the previous meeting. So they decided to have one meeting chaired by the deputy and the next without him and with a rotating chair. 'Participation, excitement and involvement are in the blood of the meeting now.'

How did senior staff encourage the involvement of both middle managers and their staff – either as individuals or as departmental representatives – in issues concerning the whole school? At one school, the headteacher identified GRIDS as having helped to develop a team spirit and corporate identity and said that after the exercise, there had been less interdepartmental fighting. The self-review exercise had been well received but it was interesting to note what the head said in this respect: 'If we'd asked for a democratic decision, the staff might have rejected it. We wanted an opportunity to be involved and it was us, the SMT, who had most to lose as it would expose us the most.'

A phase two headteacher who, on taking up post, was concerned about the lack of coherence between committees, the fact that agendas were published at very short notice (if at all), the inertia at major meetings and the low degree of participation by middle managers and junior staff, published a discussion document on communication and decision-making at the school. It was planned to set up a number of working parties (on, for example, information technology, primary school liaison, curriculum development, multiculturalism, INSET). The headteacher hoped that 'all staff would participate in at least two groups according to their own professional interests and the skills and knowledge they have'. The paper continued:

> Each committee or working party would report regularly to the full staff through the committee chair. Debate, if appropriate, would take place, followed by a full staff vote after which, if by voting the committee report had been accepted, it would become school policy.

Senior management, according to this headteacher:

> has the function of leading through exercise of its responsibility to initiate, to facilitate and to implement policy . . . Senior man-agement executive decisions would be made in the light of policy decisions taken by the full staff and would seek the assent of staff and their willingness to act.

At another school, a deputy head went to all departmental meetings to provide the whole-school view and information regarding what other departments were doing. It was felt that it was very important to keep staff informed and enable them to 'be in control of the facts' to stop cliques forming. Another school, for similar reasons, started publishing minutes of SMT meetings because 'people felt that it had an aura of mystery although it has, in fact, always been very open'. A deputy head at a phase one school which strongly believed in participative decision-making attended departmental and faculty meetings and said: 'Sometimes I do not agree with decisions taken but I have to bite my tongue.'

Participation in cross–departmental groups

There was no overall pattern as regards the way in which general working parties were established. In those schools where the staff were divided into mixed groups (subject, sex, age, seniority, etc.) and the groups given a task to do, there was the advantage of ensuring that, theoretically, all staff participated – although, of course, there was the problem of 'passive involvement'. One headteacher felt that it was particularly important to move from the 'volunteer' model to a 'commitment' model – otherwise, as one senior teacher observed, 'the participation of scale 1 teachers in whole-school issues usually depends on the quality of the HoD as representative'. There was no evidence, in the effective departments, of staff being coerced into serving on working parties to try to influence outcomes in favour of the department or faculty, in the way that Bullock (1980) reports. Certainly, teachers' perceptions were that the experience was to their advantage. Sometimes, schools organized staff into groups to work on a task regularly or on a one-off basis (perhaps on an early closure day). One school had, before the industrial action, instituted timetabled curriculum area meetings so that all staff would be included.

There were, none the less, problems as regards staff involvement. The head of a phase two school said:

> I tried to resurrect a curriculum working party to debate issues, get ideas and involve staff, but no one wanted it. It is not that staff are too idle or busy or think that it is the SMT's job: it is just that they trust the SMT. They are very easy, pleasant and hard-working and will do absolutely anything that they are asked. Very few are ambitious as they want to stay in this area and at this school . . .
> The bad side of this is the danger of stagnation.

In another phase two school a deputy commented:

> The staff don't like random groups for discussion . . .they like departmental or year groups . . . They are so predictable – you give up trying to rehearse arguments because you know how they'll react . . . The trouble is that staff don't take things seriously here. They either think that there's a Grand Plan – i.e. SMT have got everything worked out whether they like it or not – or they think 'Oh, they just want our opinions because they don't know what they're doing!'

Some schools were trying, structurally, to widen the decision-making base. In one – a community school – a finance committee was established to deal with capitation. This had previously been done by a deputy on a formula basis. The committee was formed by a representative from the staff association, the community department, heads of year and heads of faculty plus the registrar and an independent staff member.

Such structures should, in theory, break down departmental barriers. However, there was evidence that some practitioners were astute politicians and tried to manipulate senior staff, or school committees, to further their own departmental ends. One head of department said: 'I think that I have a disproportionate amount of influence on decision-making because I'm a member of so many committees.' The importance of 'the word in the corridor' was recognized and several department heads spoke of using the tactic at meetings of asking for twice as much capitation as was reasonable, in the belief that a satisfactory compromise would be reached.

The extent to which such political activity is controlled largely depends on the management skills of the headteacher and deputies. Left to run its own course, it can result in departments erecting further barriers and the development of rigid departmental hierarchies.

Summary and discussion

There is a growing body of knowledge showing that effective schools are those that are good at two-way communication, listen to their teachers and take their views into account before making decisions. Effective management of a complex organization like a school is less likely without real opportunities being created for teachers to participate in decision-making processes. Most teachers like to be consulted about major issues and to have the opportunity to put forward ideas and suggestions. In general, however, many felt they had little say in school decision-making and particularly objected to being consulted after a course of action had been decided on. Senior staff were seen as having the right to make decisions but 'pseudo-democracy' was something to be avoided and could contribute to low morale. But expectations did vary according to the significance of the matter being discussed. Elaborate consultative procedures over matters deemed inconsequential or of minor importance were seen as time-consuming and irritating. Similarly, indecisiveness and slow decision-making were seen as undesirable qualities in school leaders, and teachers liked to see an outcome from the consultative process. There is a need, therefore, for those in leadership positions to create *genuine* opportunities for participation and yet be prepared, on occasions, to make decisions with little or no consultation. A lot will depend on the issue and the level of commitment that is required.

Although, both in the literature and from the NFER research, participative decision-making was generally regarded positively, there were, none the less, dangers associated with it. Having to make decisions on many aspects of school policy may place too much responsibility on class teachers. Indeed, excessive commitment by teachers may result in neglect of their lesson preparation (Bullock, 1980). Some teachers may choose to opt out of working parties or not attend meetings, seeing their first commitment, as teachers, as catering for the needs of pupils and thus giving other matters (e.g. extra-curricular activities) preference. It appeared that job satisfaction was enhanced when teachers were able to contribute at the level they desired yet still perform their main role effectively.

The notion of leadership styles was discussed and a typology of modes of decision-making presented. Effective middle managers, it was suggested, need to be able to operate in all modes – there is no single style that can be identified as the most appropriate for every person in every situation. However, whatever style is used, it should be open and clear and, perhaps above all, consistent. Teachers need to know how decisions, both in departments and schools, are likely to be made and matters of significance resolved. Effective leaders were also shown to have a major concern for achieving tasks and for fulfilling the social and professional needs of colleagues. Leaders had to be adaptable to match constantly changing situations and it was important for department and faculty heads to lead by example and to be a source of ideas. But it was also important for them to encourage and facilitate others to become leaders and take the initiative. For this to happen, middle managers had to feel secure and confident in themselves.

The importance of collegiality was stressed but it was noted that, despite being staffed by professionals, schools tended to be more hierarchical than collegial organizations. Given recent changes, such as the introduction of GCSE and the development of course teams, collegiality within schools may grow but, at present, it has to be worked at and the creation of a feeling of belonging to a departmental team is an important responsibility of its head. Participative decision-making – along with other factors – can help generate such feelings. Whether teachers' involvement in decision-making is seen as a professional entitlement or something given to them by a benevolent manager is a moot point. It could be argued that such an important matter should not be left to the predilections of individuals and that the former view needs to become the predominant one if all schools and departments are to function more effectively.

It was important for department and faculty heads to have the requisite skills in order to create a team from the staff they had. Matters were made more difficult because most teachers did not belong exclusively to one departmental team – they were often members of several teams – and schools were rarely able to appoint the appropriate staff member to enable the department to compensate for any obvious team weaknesses. The team-building strategies employed were similar to the ways in which staff development was promoted and three significant factors were identified: a willingness to share information, experience and expertise; well-organized meetings; and the sharing of department and faculty responsibilities. Also important in generating a sense of belonging were regular social events and the existence of department and faculty offices. The latter were particularly important for faculties – it was generally thought more difficult to create a faculty identity – as they encouraged collaborative work and the sharing of ideas. Team-building and identification with a departmental or faculty unit were not helped by the existence of part-time staff and by split-site schools.

The middle manager's pivotal role was, once again, raised and there was recognition of the difficulties experienced by individuals who wanted to adopt a whole-school perspective yet not be seen as letting down the department or faculty team. It was suggested that department heads' involvement in school decision-making would be greater if the meetings they participated in were better organized, and commitment enhanced if the agenda always included educational/curricular items and was not dominated by administrative concerns. Also, as has been noted elsewhere, there is a need for the teaching profession 'to accept more readily that decisions made at middle-management level are real decisions and not just the start of negotiations, leaving the head with a crisis later' (Brennan, 1987).

Formal consultative structures varied between the 21 case study schools although the differences usually centred on the size of the middle management meeting. In schools where only a few middle managers met with the SMT there were the dangers of elitism or a 'them and us' situation developing, whereas those schools which included all middle managers were likely to be faced with an unwieldy group too large to enable proper discussion and decision-making to take place. It seemed to be quite difficult to achieve the right balance between the two. Where department heads/teachers in charge of subjects were not present themselves in these meetings, the representative function of the head of faculty was seen as of crucial importance. Indeed, the effective faculty (and department) heads were able to satisfy the communication needs of both senior management and their more immediate colleagues.

Finally, mention was made of several attempts to develop both department heads and other staff and to involve them in whole-school issues. The establishment of working parties showed no overall pattern and, in some schools, the staff were divided into mixed groups and allocated particular tasks to undertake. Again, the attempts to widen the decision-making base and involve more staff were not always as successful as the heads had wished.

10 How might Departments and Faculties be Improved?

The focus of this final chapter is on school improvement and an attempt will be made to consider the implications for practice of the main findings of the NFER research. Recommendations will be made as to how departments and faculties might be improved and thus enhance the quality of the learning process. Before this is done, however, and to place these recommendations in context, several issues need to be addressed concerning the organization of schools. Various attempts to minimize the academic/pastoral divide will be noted and the research data used to demonstrate the relative merits of departments and faculties. It will also be asked if conventional departmental structures are best suited to the demands currently being made on schools.

The academic/pastoral divide

What of the academic/pastoral divide at middle management level? In some schools, heads have identified strained relations between academic and pastoral middle managers as being more of a problem than relations between staff and senior management (Baker, 1989). Teachers interviewed in the present NFER study frequently remarked that, in the eyes of pupils, heads of year held more clout than heads of department or faculty; pupils would be able to identify the year heads whereas they would probably not know who the department heads were. In some schools, heads of faculty, having no disciplinary sanctions to resort to, were considered to be 'weak' in comparison with heads of year. Some respondents commented that heads of department and faculty were the 'poor relations' among the middle managers; sometimes the pastoral heads had greater ease of access to senior management and there was some bitterness where pastoral staff overrode subject specialist advice, for example, as regards option take-up. Several department heads, anxious for promotion to deputy headship, felt obliged to take on pastoral posts where these were available – even if they did not really want dual responsibility – in order to enhance career prospects. Some heads of department and faculty found it difficult to play their part in a pastoral team and could not, for example, attend pre-school meetings as this was the time when they were having to make arrangements for cover. In some of the schools, the academic/pastoral rift was further exacerbated by the fact that departments or faculties were accommodated in separate blocks within a fairly spread-out campus so year group meetings were physically difficult to organize.

Such problems, combined with falling rolls and the limited number of incentive allowances made available immediately following the 1987 settlement, have prompted some schools to review their pastoral and curricular arrangements with the consequence that some reorganizations have taken place. One school in the NFER study was planning to link each of its five faculties to a year group, the teams to be run jointly by the head of faculty and the head of year (each with an assistant) until such time as staff movement enabled the headteacher to fuse the two posts and give one person overall leadership of the team. (The sixth-form team was to be drawn from all five faculties.) The faculty teams would move up the school with their year group. In another school with a similar arrangement but with six faculties, it was proposed that teams have a 'fallow year' when they had come to the end of the fifth year so that they could engage in curriculum review and development.

It was not, of course, only for logistical and organizational reasons that such changes were favoured: many respondents spoke of the need to educate the whole child and of the dangers inherent in dividing the pastoral and the academic – a division which has possibly only been a problem since comprehensivization, the emergence of very large schools and increasing social problems among pupils. Faculties were able to take on pastoral responsibility in a way which was not possible for small departmental units.

Departments or faculties?

Faculty structures are of relatively recent origin and, although there are no national statistics to show how prevalent they are, an HMI survey of 185 secondary schools found the main organizational feature to be the subject department (GB.DES, 1988b). Full faculty systems were in operation in under three per cent of schools, while a further 14 per cent had a mixed pattern of departments and faculties. Of the 21 schools in the NFER study 15 had faculty systems, although only seven of these covered all areas of the curriculum.

The observation by HMI in Wales (1984) that, generally, the faculty structure has proved more successful in its administrative than in its academic objectives was one with which many NFER respondents concurred. While the majority, when asked about faculties upheld their educational aims – greater cross-curricular liaison, integration of subject areas, prevention of the duplication of material and topics, provision of a coherent learning experience for pupils – it was considered that it was the right climate and the right people in key positions rather than the form of school organization per se that was of the greatest significance in achieving these aims. (A more recent HMI report (GB.DES, 1988b) has come to similar conclusions.) Faculties were seen as useful for treating 'departmental tunnel vision' but were not the only remedy available. For example, an adviser said:

The faculty system looks good but I'm not sure in reality
if it works. It points the way but perhaps as much can
be done if the head says he wants to set up discussion
groups. The need really is for these broader curricular discussion groups.

Another commented: 'You need a headteacher who creates a cooperative atmosphere supported by lively deputy heads.' It was noted that other strategically placed people could achieve the same ends as faculty heads: 'The head of resources and the head of Special Needs here operate in a cross-curricular way and so the narrow vision of heads of department is no problem.'

Where faculties were considered to be either failing or purely nominal, it was often because other factors in the school organization militated against them. At one school with faculties, the problem was that there was no deputy head responsible for common policies – for example, about homework or assessment – so faculty heads were not encouraged to think along these lines; a coordinator for cross-curricular links was said to be necessary. At another school there was no central staffroom and departments were situated in isolated blocks so teachers rarely mixed outside the department. Where there was no faculty staffroom, departments tended to keep themselves to themselves and there was little social exchange (and in one such situation there were further problems with subdivisions within departments). The importance of matters of location, however trivial they seem, cannot, perhaps, be overlooked. As was noted in

Chapter 3, a deputy head who, before being promoted from within the school, had been responsible for setting up a faculty, said that in the early months, staff would sit in close subject groups in the faculty office. One day the HoF decided to remove the large table from the middle of the room and it seemed as though communication patterns changed instantly: teachers began to interact as faculty members and the subject groupings gradually dispersed.

One of the most obvious problems in establishing faculties is the categorization of subject areas. It is generally accepted that modern languages group easily as do the natural sciences and the humanities but thereafter there are often problems. Should English join a language faculty and maths the sciences or should these two large areas be discrete? Where should CDT be located? In some schools, drama was accommodated in the English or expressive arts faculty; in others, it was considered a performing art. Performing and creative arts are themselves grey areas. Most advisers and senior staff in schools acknowledged that whatever the divisions, there was inevitably a 'last faculty' which was a hotch-potch and difficult to manage. But as a headteacher remarked, this was not necessarily a disadvantage: faculties did not need to be homogeneous and dissimilar departments could learn from each other and be able to recognize each other's difficulties.

The mere existence of faculties did not necessarily guarantee interdepartmental discussion. Although, as suggested in Chapter 5, new faculty heads were generally more confident than new department heads as regards leadership skills, *what they actually did* was not necessarily remarkable, often on account of lack of clarity as to their role: 'Faculties do not work at this school because of inadequate job descriptions. Few staff now are even aware of their existence. One HoD was told that he was a HoF after his appointment!' A head said: 'I'm constrained by the HoFs here who have no concept of what they should be doing. The relationship between them and the HoDs is not clearly drawn.' The rationale behind faculties was sometimes not clearly stated: 'We just drifted into being a faculty and were never told what the expectations would be.' A head of language faculty commented: 'The head said that as HoF I should try to mould a team and give people something to identify with but it isn't that easy – for example, the typewriting teacher has little in common with the modern linguists.'

There was also the feeling that faculties could create, rather than remove, barriers – or at any rate, they could shift them. They might result in more intrafaculty dialogue and liaison within a defined curriculum area (though that depended very much on the leadership of the heads of faculty) but they often restrict interfaculty discussion and communication.

Faculty meetings, noted HMI in Wales (1984), tend to be dominated by organizational rather than curricular matters and, certainly, the NFER study found that in many cases the faculty would only meet together for ten minutes or so for information exchange before breaking up into departmental meetings.

Many of the benefits of faculties would seem to accrue on the one hand to the faculty heads themselves and on the other, to the SMT, especially the headteacher. A number of respondents in the study spoke of faculties being formed for 'administrative convenience'. It is obviously easier for the headteacher of a large school to deal with six or seven heads of faculty rather than with 25 or so heads of department and teachers-in-charge of subjects. At one school the head said he was happy to talk to department heads but remarked: 'I should be the longstop and not the wicket keeper': faculty heads could be a useful intermediary. As was suggested in the previous chapter, there are many problems inherent in holding meetings attended by such a large number of middle managers: for example, it is impossible for all to participate and many matters, although of considerable importance to departments, are irrelevant to the rest of the meeting. However, some heads remarked that, notwithstanding their unwieldiness, such meetings had to be managed as well as possible and were important for 'giving the right message' that all the middle managers were considered important and all subjects of comparable worth. The danger of the head only meeting the heads of faculty is that there is an additional layer in the hierarchy and the heads of department are distanced. One headteacher had, in fact, abolished faculties on account of what he perceived to be their adverse effect on communication (although it could have been, of course, that the problem was that some of the heads of faculty were ineffective). Considerable bitterness was expressed by some 'displaced' heads of department in schools which had introduced faculties and either instigated a 'senior middle managers' meeting (whatever it was called) or eliminated heads of department from any meeting with the senior management team. Heads of department resented the erosion of their power and the possible loss of status.

Some heads remarked that problems of resources could be settled more equitably if they were allocated to faculties rather than departments and in several schools capitation was on a faculty, rather than a departmental, basis. It was noted that when they were more intimately involved in the capitation allocation, faculty heads became more aware of the limits of resources and were more sympathetic to the head's budgeting. A head of department observed that it was important to be on good terms with the heads of faculty 'as they dish out all the money!'

As for benefits to practitioners, headteachers felt that faculty structures helped those promoted to faculty headship, giving them greater awareness of whole-school perspectives and broadening their horizons. References were made to instances of faculties being created in order for the school to retain excellent teachers or those offering shortage subjects. An adviser spoke of this happening with physicists and said that the majority of science faculties in the LEA were purely nominal. There were also, however, instances of effective department heads being promoted in order that their good practice might be shared and standards raised in a curriculum area. An adviser observed: 'If you have a superb head of geography, a poor head of history and an inexperienced head of RE, it makes sense to promote the head of geography to faculty headship.'

Where comments on faculties were positive, it was, as earlier noted, more on account of the particular qualities or skills of the particular head of faculty than because of the mere existence of a faculty structure. Some heads of department spoke warmly of the support given them by their head of faculty, particularly when they were in small or one-person departments which for various reasons were struggling to gain identity in the school or needed a larger group to belong to. The NFER study focused on medium-to-large departments and although not investigating small departments, many respondents spoke of the very real problems of these and one-person departments, and of the need to provide opportunities for such individuals to gain support, either from within the school or the LEA.

As certain teachers blossomed under effective heads of department, so did some heads of department under effective heads of faculty. Some teachers even said that they identified primarily with the faculty area rather than with the subject area – something which is worth commenting on given the widespread tendency of teachers to identify with their specialist subject: 'Before I came here, I considered myself a geography teacher but since working with my HoF, I count myself a humanities teacher.'

Clearly, it is no easy task to modify the perceptions of individual teachers who have been trained in individual subject disciplines although an adviser noted that, in his view, the days of the subject specialist were numbered and, in a falling rolls situation, teachers had to learn to diversify. Heads of faculty committed to integrated work often 'converted' staff by showing good results in the classroom. But even with dynamic, committed and effective faculty heads and successful outcomes in the classroom, entrenched attitudes sometimes remained. It was obvious that some of the faculties in the case study schools would not flourish as faculties, with the opportunity of offering integrated and interdepartmental work when appropriate, until there was a change of personnel – something that is also suggested by Preedy (1988):

> The problems of moving from a departmental to a faculty system are likely to be considerable unless key resignations/retirements occur at opportune times to reduce the scope of territorial self-defence by existing subject departments. Personal and contextual factors, however, are important influences on subject allegiances and the defence of departmental interests.

This 'territorial self-defence' was easily identifiable in comments made during interviews with staff. For example: 'The will for faculties just is not here at this school; too many people are frightened of losing their autonomy.' However, that resistance to change can be healthy (in that it can promote constructive criticism) should not, of course, be forgotten. A number of teachers felt very strongly that faculties created false links in the curriculum and they often had negative attitudes on account of previous experiences. A head of home economics, commenting on a previous school, said: 'We had faculty themes and if the theme of the week was "Green" then we just had to bake green bread!'

There was often an ideological divide between those who saw themselves as teachers of children – child educators – and those who saw themselves as teachers of a particular body of knowledge – subject specialists. Many of the former enjoyed being all-rounders, said that it prevented them from becoming bored and felt quite confident about teaching from another's scheme of work, whereas the following sentiment is typical of the latter: 'Pupils must see the logical, natural development in the subject and here the faculty is weak. I'm a historian and I don't get turned on by teaching humanities.'

There were a number of examples in the phase two schools of faculties working well together over, for example, provision for special needs, problem-solving approaches and common assessment procedures; equally, there were examples of faculties where a concept or process (for example, graphs) was introduced, unintentionally, at different stages in departments within the same faculty and teachers cited the frequent duplication of material (drugs, for example). A relatively new faculty of performing arts (comprising PE, dance, drama and music) in a phase two school had, under the leadership of a dynamic, though inexperienced, faculty head, developed an integrated course for the first year in which all the subject specialists worked to the same theme and put on a common production after each unit 'so the dance group danced to the music group's music'. This had involved new structures within the timetable to allow staff to work to their specialism while collaborating with other disciplines and to give all pupils varied experiences; it had been facilitated by the flexibility and determination of the faculty head.

Alternatives to departments

In recent years a growing number of schools have abolished departments and organized the curriculum into areas with a focus on skills and processes rather than subjects. Many of these units are faculties – in essence if not in name. There are a number of reasons for this trend. In some cases, new developments such as TVEI, CPVE and LAPP have been catalysts for schools to reconsider their curricular structures as staff from a number of disciplines involved with the various initiatives have come together to plan courses. Any one department may have only made a small contribution to a course but such curriculum developments may well see schools moving towards the notion of course teams – made up of subject specialists from a variety of departments – such as are currently found in a number of FE colleges (Tansley, 1988). Similarly, the new INSET arrangements have brought together staff both from across the whole school and within faculties and departments in order to identify common areas for development and discuss common pedagogic approaches. Furthermore, staff have had to consider information technology and multiculturalism which affect all aspects of school life. In many areas, falling rolls, ring-fence policies and redeployment have meant that teachers have had, of necessity, to extend their particular field and become more generalists than specialists. Increasingly, departments have been seen as an unhelpful way of organizing schools.
Tyldesley (1988) argues that:

> It might be better to think in terms of teachers with a range of expertises that are used according to the task in hand working in a range of small clusters in a school that can be redefined and altered according to mutual agreement. The emphasis would be on pedagogy rather than pseudo-managerial tasks.

For Bell and Maher (1986): 'A division into a rigid system of departmental areas may be administratively convenient but mitigates against a cohesive learning experience for the students'; while Buckley and Styan (1988) question whether 'steep hierarchies and tight role definitions' are sufficiently flexible to accommodate the rapid rate of change currently being experienced in schools. Brookes (1987) also identifies a need for 'new, participative team structures which can accommodate present-day needs' and argues that 'departmental organization induces boredom and subject degeneracy, and restricts the flow of new or alternative ideas into or across the curriculum'. At Brookes' school, heads of department meetings had been abolished and all staff opted for membership of one of four standing review groups which delineated school policy. Interestingly, HMI (GB.DES, 1988b) note that teacher enthusiasm for cross-curricular developments appears to be more important than the existence of particular structures. They comment:

> The management of curricular change remains a difficult challenge for most schools, whatever their existing patterns of organization, and there seemed to be no advantage of one structure over another in raising the quality of teaching and learning.

A number of schools have developed modular curricula which have often necessitated the reorganization of departmental structures. Courses acceptable to GCSE examining boards can not only be drawn up within departments but also between departments which are either related (e.g. in the sciences or humanities) or non-related (theme-based 'hybrids'). Watkins (1987) observes that:

> The emergence of cross-curriculum teams preparing modules is a valuable innovation. It can, however, also be a source of resentment if the departmental structure continues, particularly if the loyalties of the most talented teachers appear to be transferred to the cross-curriculum team.

It is possible that the national curriculum introduced by the 1988 Education Reform Act will, on account of its re-emphasis on subjects, rejuvenate departments and prevent further modular developments but, clearly, at the time of writing, it is too early to know. Similarly, notwithstanding the above comments, the introduction of GCSE has, to some extent, reinforced the significance of the subject department. However, regardless of actual structures and organizational arrangements, it is arguable that the same managerial jobs and tasks will have to be done in order that academic and pastoral curricular provision is effective. Whether these activities are shared out or taken on by certain designated individuals, there will have to be some means of both facilitating their execution and ensuring that they have been satisfactorily undertaken. In addition, subject expertise will need to inform integrated courses even if the head of department acts more as a consultant to the whole school. Thus, although the position of head of department may be eclipsed or eliminated, the activities for which the head of department is responsible will not be eradicated: indeed, given recent developments associated with the Education Reform Act, these are likely to become crucial.

Towards better practice

The research project, in deciding to study nominated effective practitioners, wanted to be able to document examples of good practice. It soon became clear, however, that although the focus of the research, and much of the previous discussion, was on heads of department and faculty as individuals, it was increasingly difficult to differentiate, other than conceptually, between individual leaders and their qualities, and departments and faculties and their attributes. Clearly there was a relationship between the two but, as Glatter (1988) notes: 'We do not yet have a precise understanding of the connection between individual and institutional effectiveness.' There is no guarantee for example, that a 'good' department will be led by an effective head of department: indeed, support from senior staff, a strong second-in-command and a team of first-rate teachers were seen as offsetting some of an individual's limitations. However, this situation was considered to be exceptional and a department's potential was more likely to be realized with an able person giving the necessary leadership.

It is leadership that is important but this can emerge from any of a number of levels within schools and departments. As Weindling (1988) in a review of the literature on school effectiveness notes, there is an assumption 'that the head will provide strong leadership, but in secondary schools the issue is leadership not 'the leader' and this is particularly critical to school improvement'. There was some evidence of support for this statement from respondents in the NFER study. LEA advisers were asked to comment on the importance of middle managers and whether or not it was possible to have a 'good school' – whatever that may mean – with a mediocre head (or 'leader') but high-quality department and faculty heads. A senior adviser summed up the views of many of those interviewed when he remarked:

> We should not understrest the value of middle managers. You can, in fact, have a mediocre head and yet still have a very good school and this is because the school will have some cracking good HoDs. I don't think the same is true for HoDs – it's much more difficult to have a mediocre HoD and a good department. Departments can work well without effective assistance from senior management because, by-and-large, subject departments can be autonomous . . . In my view, it's middle managers that drive the school.

Another adviser, in a different LEA, said:

> The success of an organization depends on the quality of leadership. You can find very good leaders in poor schools who run good departments . . . but it's much harder to have an effective department with a lousy HoD and a good headteacher.

Effective leadership at all levels was important but, for many respondents, department and faculty heads were seen as the driving force behind any school and, it was argued, the key to improving the quality of the learning process. Frequent references were made to middle managers as 'kingpins', 'the boiler house', 'the engine room' or 'the hub of the school' and, as noted in Chapter 1, recent HMI statements have gone as far as to say that a school's success relies more on the leadership qualities of department heads than on any other factor. Indeed, although there was a marked tendency for the phase two schools to be considered as effectively managed by senior staff, there were examples where this did not appear to be the situation. In one school, for example, with two nominated practitioners, interviews with staff showed that many did not think highly of the school's SMT, few ideas were forthcoming from it and the head was seen as 'too busy, unable to delegate and in need of a management course'. The school was very 'departmentalized', had no system of working parties or wider discussion about the curriculum as a whole and, although there were found some well-run departments, little interdepartmental discussion took place. In general, the school was not considered to be well managed and, according to many, its leadership left a lot to be desired.

How typical this school was of those found in England and Wales is, of course, difficult to ascertain given the design of the NFER research. However, before considering the lessons that can be learned from the research, it is worth making brief reference to two recent official publications which have attempted to give some idea of the extent of poor management and ineffective leadership in secondary schools, both at senior *and* middle management levels.

The HMI report on LEA provision and the quality of the response to that provision by students in educational establishments in England (GB.DES, 1987a) uses evidence from school visits and district inspector returns and, although it notes that the data collected cannot be taken as statistically representative of the country as a whole, it does state that two issues emerged as crucial to improving educational standards in schools: 'higher expectations of pupils by teachers; and more effective leadership by heads and heads of department'. The report does not state the number of school visits undertaken but shows diagrammatically that, for secondary schools, approximately 15 per cent of heads and approximately 45 per cent of department heads/subject coordinators needed to demonstrate 'more effective leadership' in order to help achieve significant school improvement.

More recently, HMI have published an appraisal of secondary schools (GB.DES, 1988b) based on inspections of 185 English schools carried out between 1982 and 1986. Like previous reports, it points to the importance of leadership and notes that many of those with management responsibility in schools have had 'grossly inadequate' training – middle managers especially were often found to be ineffective and undertrained.

The title of this book – *The Time to Manage?* – is a deliberate attempt to focus attention on the fact that, in terms of time allocation, department and faculty heads had little non-contact time in which to carry out their many tasks. Thus, amongst other things, they have to be effective managers of their own time although there are ways in which additional time might be created or existing time used to better effect. But the title also makes reference to the view of many respondents that, in terms of self-perception, many department heads did not conceive of themselves as managers having responsibilities for others and being in positions of leadership. It is therefore suggested that perhaps the time has come for some practitioners to reconsider what the middle manager's role entails.

The remainder of this final chapter will consider these and other key findings which have implications for effecting departmental and school improvement. The main recommendations emanating from the research can be briefly summarized and these have been reproduced in Figure 10.1. (The necessity of putting these in the form of short sentences means that some may appear to be common sense and rather obvious. For the reader who wishes to see the research base and further discussion related to each recommendation, the relevant chapter(s) is indicated by the number at the end of each statement.)

Creating time to manage

Time is one of a school's most valuable resources and an issue that has come increasingly under scrutiny in the light of teachers' new conditions of service and the '1265 hours' of directed time. How much of that time should be allocated to actual teaching has not been precisely spelt out and class-contact ratios will continue to vary from LEA to LEA and from school to school. Middle managers in the case-study schools were found to have non-contact ratios varying between 0.15 and 0.35 of a weekly timetable, with faculty heads (at least in theory) having slightly lower teaching loads. As with other staff, there was a

Figure 10.1: *Recommendations for improving departments (and faculties)*

- More time should be made available to enable HoDs to perform their managerial tasks more effectively. (3,4,5)

- Opportunities should be created for HoDs to reflect on and gain a better understanding of the full range of their responsibilities. (2,3,6–9)

- HoDs need to acquire the leadership and management skills/knowledge necessary to facilitate desired outcomes and ensure effective departmental performance. (3,4,6–9)

- Consideration should be given to middle managers' training needs and how these might best be met by a process of management–development activities in schools and LEAs. (5,6,10)

- Senior staff in schools and LEAs should fully recognize and enact the key role they play in supporting and facilitating the effective functioning of departments. (3,5–9)

requirement, at times, for them to cover for absent colleagues and obviously this made further inroads into the few 'free' periods that they had been allocated.

The suggestion that schools are 'busy' places and that more time is needed for middle managers – and, indeed, other staff – to carry out their responsibilities is, of course, not new. The DES (1985a) noted, in *Better Schools*, how department heads commonly had 'too little time and scope for managing the planning and development of the curriculum and optimising the use of staff and other resources', while the Cockcroft Report (1982) pointed to the demanding nature of the heads of mathematics' job and the fact that they were given so little time to carry out their duties. The report suggested that 'although it was possible to carry out some of the duties outside normal school hours, certain of them can only be performed while teaching is in progress and the necessary time needs to be provided within the timetable'. Unsurprisingly, the vast majority of middle managers involved in the NFER research made reference to lack of time as a major constraint on the performance of their duties and, as earlier noted, tasks which required long, uninterrupted spells were, of necessity, under-taken at home.

Ideally, the allocation of non-teaching time to middle managers should reflect their individual situations – for example, some may have a large number of part-time teachers within the department and this will often affect the department head's workload and the degree to which tasks can be delegated. (Alternatively, teachers with commitments to several departments could be allocated fewer teaching periods to enable them to make a greater contribution to departmental activities.) Also, in those subjects where there is a shortage of well-qualified staff, department heads will, necessarily, spend a considerable amount of time giving support and guidance. (For a discussion of this in relation to heads of mathematics departments see Straker, 1987.) Similarly, careful consideration should be given to the allocation of additional commitments and responsibilities to department and faculty heads. In the case study schools most middle managers were also form tutors, while only a few were pastoral heads (heads of house or heads of year) or had school-wide responsibilities (e.g. examination entries or staff development).

Although it is being suggested that additional commitments should be avoided as they are likely to impinge upon the effective performance of the department head's role, it was noted rather ironically that, in order to achieve promotion within schools, there was a need to widen experiences and gain new skills. Senior staff are therefore in a difficult position and need to be convinced of the capabilities of individuals before they are given responsibility for dual roles or are given wider commitments. If possible, additional responsibilities should be allocated to others within the department (or pastoral unit) to offset some of the middle manager's increased workload. Of course, heads and deputies may be limited in the actions they can take – for example, a falling rolls situation, staff redeployment, the freezing of posts and a shortage of points (or incentive allowances) may mean there is little choice.

Conversely, the difficulty of running a department or faculty well and yet remaining an effective teacher was also noted. To undertake the full range of departmental responsibilities and continue to be an able classroom practitioner was, given existing contact ratios, not easy. Some middle managers commented that if teaching was given first priority and departmental concerns second, then it was likely that they would be perceived as inefficient and as 'poor' department heads. The dilemma of how to be a good manager and yet ensure that this did not have a detrimental effect on one's teaching was, for some, difficult to resolve and would be helped considerably by a greater allocation of non-contact time. It should be noted, however, that a key assumption underlying much of the recent interest in school leadership –

and something that the research findings would endorse – is that effective management, at all levels, is necessary in order to improve the quality of teaching and learning. The observation days and the other data recorded gave some indication of the degree to which an individual's classroom practices were affected by 'management tasks' – the extent to which an individual department head's teaching and that of colleagues within the department would 'improve' if the former was given additional time for these tasks is unknown. What is more certain, however, is that in the majority of cases improvements would take place.

At present there is little or no 'slack' time in schools – a condition which research into industry and commerce suggests is not conducive to excellence (e.g. Peters and Waterman, 1984) – and this state of affairs is likely to result in there being little enthusiasm from staff to embark on any changes if they believe they are already 'overcommitted'. As has been shown, developing new initiatives involves a considerable commitment of time from all parties and one of the department head's tasks is to convince colleagues of the merits of any proposals. How then might more time be created to enable departmental improvements to occur?

There are two obvious ways in which the amount of time devoted to activities likely to lead to improvements could be increased. Existing contact ratios could be decreased by extra staffing from the LEA, or non-teaching time used to better effect by individuals becoming more effective managers of their time. The former option is, at the time of writing, an unlikely possibility, whereas the latter, as has been shown, was recognized as an important training need of middle managers. Although not referring exclusively to middle managers, Evans (1984) has made several other suggestions as to how time can be made available for school-based curriculum development. It may be necessary, he notes, to decrease the school's contact ratio to produce 'extra' non-teaching periods which can then be allocated for developmental activities. Obviously, a full analysis would be needed to ensure any reductions made did least damage to the school's curriculum provision. (Evans gives the example of the possibility of increasing group sizes and saving lessons by removing unpopular option courses in Years four and five.) Similarly, periods could be reduced by providing 'more "lead" lessons where two or more classes are combined for an introductory lecture or film'. Alternatively, if the existing curriculum and teacher contact ratios are to remain unaltered, then the only other way to create additional time is to increase the teaching load of some staff to enable others to do less. Evans (1984) suggests various ways in which this could take place in schools, noting that where possible, the subject teachers who will benefit from a particular curriculum development programme (e.g. the development of a science course for less-able upper-school pupils) should be prepared to forfeit some of their 'free' periods to enable others to undertake this work. Also, it is suggested that senior staff can be used as a pool for curricular-support lessons or, as was found in some of the NFER case study schools, to enable other desired activities (e.g. classroom observation) to take place.

The introduction in 1987 of the five 'contract' days may also provide much needed time to engage in professional activities and it will be interesting to see how schools respond to this and to the other recently introduced notion of 'directed time' or '1265 hours'. Adams (1988), in an account of how schools have managed the latter, suggests that successful directed time management will become a key factor in school effectiveness and there is no reason why this should not also be the case for 'contract' days. Both areas are in need of further investigation.

The NFER research has given some indication of the nature of the middle manager's job – they are 'busy' people – but as has been noted, little time was found for planning, evaluating, reflecting or observing: key activities that need to be undertaken if departments and faculties are to ensure the continuing relevance of their curriculum provision. The research also found a need for more technicians and ancillary staff to support the work of schools. Such support, it was suggested, is required for a greater number of subject areas than hitherto – departments are increasingly producing their own materials and resources and this, along with developments associated with the new forms of pupil assessment, has led to increased pressures on staff. There is a need to ensure that teachers' valuable non-contact time is not regularly used in carrying out low-level, non-professional and routine activities (e.g. photocopying).

Even the more effective managers of time found it difficult to carry out their duties well and, as has been suggested, there were aspects of the department head's job that were not being carried out effectively. There were rarely occasions when practitioners could say that they had done everything and the observed middle managers often listed the things that were 'waiting to be done'. Clearly, there was a need for them to prioritize – some matters should be defined as more important than others – and, where possible, to delegate. Delegation is one area that needs developing and the research supports Straker's (1984) conclusion that 'there is room for considerable delegation of responsibility in some areas of work which heads of department feel are carried out well', thus allowing more time to be focused on other responsibilities. Interestingly, Busher (1988) has given an account of how, as a head of department, he attempted to reduce his problems of role overload by introducing a scheme of staff development. The process of departmental management was analysed and divided into five areas; these in turn were subdivided into task areas and differentiated according to level of difficulty and likely impact on the department. Departmental staff were then invited to undertake some of the identified tasks and were able to volunteer for others. Although Busher noted that it was difficult to evaluate the success of the scheme, it was, in his view, a useful means of promoting staff development and reducing the role overload of department heads.

Adequate role perceptions

Shortage of time meant activities such as curriculum evaluation, departmental review and staff development were not always undertaken or were carried out partially as more immediate and pressing matters and 'the day-to-day' took precedence. However, it has also been suggested that some of the responsibilities of department heads were not carried out, not because of the very real constraints of time, but rather because they were seen as problematical. There were some aspects of the middle manager's role that individuals were reluctant to embrace and this militated against departmental improvements. Ineffective department heads were seen, amongst other things, as having a conception of the role different from that of their effective counterparts. It was a limited and an inadequate view, with such individuals not seeing themselves as leading a team or as managers of others – rather there was a tendency for them to see themselves as senior subject teachers.

Again the research findings would support Straker's (1984) conclusion that, even if they were allocated extra non-teaching time, many department heads would not use this for classroom observations or to improve the overall performance of the team. As earlier noted, the whole issue of mutual visiting and observation of colleagues was complicated by the notion of classroom autonomy and teacher professionalism and, it was suggested, there was a need for all teachers to have their performance reviewed – which might include 'looking at learning' – as part of a programme of institutional and professional development. Also noted was a perceived conflict between the department head's leadership and management function, and the notion of developing collegiality and a team spirit. The managerial dilemma, supposedly, was between allowing teachers their professional autonomy yet being fully aware of what was going on within the department. For some department heads there was a reluctance to criticize or reprimand (or conversely to thank and praise) and it was felt relationships with colleagues would somehow suffer if the management role was fully embraced. It was apparent that the more effective department heads were able to foster a collegial climate, which in turn enabled the team to monitor itself and from which observation and appraisal seemed to arise naturally. The inability of teachers to be able to expose their own weaknesses and build on the strengths of others was clearly a barrier to staff development and departmental improvement. Yeomans (1987) reporting on the results of a study of staff relationships in primary schools – which in many ways are not dissimilar to the medium-to-large departments studied in the NFER research – encapsulates this dilemma neatly in the title of a paper – 'Leading the team, belonging to the group?' Learning to work in a group is an important attribute of leadership and effective leaders are able to be both leaders and members of the group without experiencing any psychological discomfort or role conflict.

Another factor identified as impinging upon effective performance was uncertainty as to what the role of the head of department entailed. An effective middle manager was defined as someone who was aware of the demands that the role made and had, or was developing, the necessary skills and strategies to meet these. The effective practitioner understood what the job involved and was able to translate this into action. The research showed that it was felt many practitioners had not thought clearly about the role and what it involved in its entirety. It was suggested, for example, that perceptions varied regarding the department head's role as curriculum leader and change agent/facilitator. It was also noted that heads of department were reluctant to act as staff developers and that there was a need for them to see themselves as responsible for evaluating the work of their departments. Evaluation was seen by senior staff as an important means of raising teacher morale and increasing professionalism, helping to create a team and generally leading to departmental improvement. However, according to many, department heads rarely completed systematically the process of evaluation or review that was crucial for improving departmental practices.

For Edwards (1985), role uncertainty was the greatest obstacle to more effective departments and there was a need for greater clarity and a stricter definition of boundaries between roles. Other research- ers have shown how a lack of role clarity can be a significant cause of stress and hence reduce levels of effectiveness (e.g. Dunham, 1978, 1984). Job descriptions can be of some assistance and there is a need for schools to produce for all their staff clear and detailed specifications so that individuals know what is expected of them and what they can expect from others.

Developing requisite skills

Reference has been made to the skills and knowledge required in order to become an effective practitioner. The nature of the requisite managerial skills becomes apparent when it is recalled how respondents defined the 'effective department head' and 'effective departmental practices'. There was a considerable degree of consensus here and the former was expected to exhibit purposeful leadership, to encourage and motivate staff, to facilitate change, to offer support and guidance and constantly to review and evaluate departmental practices. Effective department heads were seen as team leaders having the ability to create a departmental identity, yet able to encourage and facilitate others to become leaders. A key criterion was flexibility and they had to be aware of the range of styles available and be willing to share information, experience and expertise. They were expected to develop their staff professionally, to share departmental responsibilities, to conduct well-organized meetings, to have an educational vision beyond the confines of the department, to keep staff well informed and to involve them in the decision-making process. There was a need for them to have an understanding of the 'gadfly' nature of school management, to reconcile possible conflict between their role as manager and as team member, and to encourage and facilitate individual and group evaluation and appraisal. It was also important for department heads to have a working knowledge and understanding of the change process, to create the right climate for change, to create a sense of 'ownership' and to be able to manage both incremental and radical change. Advocacy skills were essential for these and other areas of the department head's job. Frequent reference was made to their pivotal role and the need for them to take into account the views of both department members and the SMT; while for teachers the ability to offer support, to listen and to be prepared to change opinions were important factors.

Indicators of effective departmental practices included the obvious criterion of examination performance (relative to pupil ability and performance in other subjects) but also, for example, team identity, a purposeful curriculum, a positive attitude on the part of pupils to the subject, option choices, a lack of discipline referrals, agreed aims and objectives (consistent with those of the school) which were reflected in department-produced schemes of work and an exploration of cross-curricular issues.

Individual practitioners required a wide range of interpersonal, management and administrative skills as well as, ideally, many desired personal qualities. (The individual qualities of effective department heads and the attributes of successful departments were presented in Figure 3.1.) One of the LEAs involved in phase two of the research had produced a management development policy for secondary schools, which outlined alphabetically the personal attributes and skills that were needed for effective management. These were: awareness, communication, decisiveness, delegation, evaluation, flexibility, innovativeness, job commitment, knowledge of self, leadership, management identification, planning and organization, problem analysis, professional development of colleagues, stress tolerance and team work/team-building. What was of interest to this authority (and an increasing number of others) was the process by which such skills are acquired.

These were the skills, knowledge and attributes required of effective school managers but what were department heads' main training and development needs and how could these be most effectively met? Some of them will be obvious from the preceding discussion but, identified by senior staff as of paramount importance and an issue that subsumes or incorporates many of the others, was the ability to manage people. The most successful department heads were seen as those who had completed the difficult transition from 'a manager of children' to 'a manager of adults'. Department heads themselves often identified 'survival strategies' (e.g. the effective use of time or personnel management) and the latest innovation (e.g. GCSE) as major training needs, while senior staff made frequent reference to the two broad themes of interpersonal relations and an understanding of current educational issues. It was thought necessary for heads of department in-service courses to include coverage of the 'nuts and bolts' of running departments (e.g. resource management, requisitions etc.) along with the more generic management issues commonly found on courses for heads and deputies (e.g. people management, decision-making, communication, delegation, stress resolution, managing change, team-building etc.). Generally, there was a need to gain a broad understanding of the nature of appraisal, classroom observation, evaluation and staff development and these areas were seen as those in which training and guidance would be welcomed.

The NFER research attempted to identify the main training and development needs of department heads by means of semi-structured interviews with various parties. Others have used more structured approaches and it is interesting to note the findings of a small-scale research study in one LEA. The Dorset Education Management Development project (1986) tried to identify the management needs of teachers by asking a small sample of them, following an interview, to complete a questionnaire which included a checklist of 30 management tasks. Respondents were asked to note, in order of priority, their most important areas of training need. As far as middle managers were concerned, the highest estimated needs were monitoring and evaluating; developing procedures for pupil assessment skills; managing change (these were also the top three estimated needs of senior staff); and planning the curriculum. Their lowest estimated needs (i.e. tasks which received nil scores) were: working with non-teaching staff; relating to the community; relating to governors; and dealing with the media. The survey took place before the content of the Education Reform Act became clear and it could be argued that external relations (especially dealing with parents and governors) will become a more pressing concern for middle managers.

The Dorset project team also asked for details of training that teachers had found particularly effective and, according to the questionnaire returns, nearly half made reference to short courses especially on specific skills. Also of interest was how staff learn best and – within schools – working as a trainer of other staff, job rotation, working alongside others, job enhancement, involvement in appointment procedures and working with advisory teachers were most frequently mentioned; while – with other schools – observation visits (with a specific object) and meeting with staff in similar posts were most popular.

The above education authority is one of eight which have been working with the NDC in a pilot project to determine needs for management development and to produce guidelines and advice on how these might be met. Management development – a form of staff development for those teachers with management responsibilities – has been defined as 'the process whereby the management function of an organization is performed with increased effectiveness' (McMahon and Bolam, 1987). It encompasses individuals trying to improve their own performance as managers and ways in which they work together to manage the school. Its purpose, in helping managers to develop a range of skills, is to enable schools to develop and thus improve the education of the pupils within them. However, as the DES (1988a) notes:

Current arrangements for management development are fragmentary. Many individual heads and LEAs take care to ensure that teachers experience developmental opportunities and training in preparation for increasing management responsibilities, but such practices are far from universal.

Management development – like other forms of INSET – consists of more than external courses; it includes a variety of structured opportunities and activities which can take place in a number of ways. These opportunities can usefully be subdivided according to the degree of closeness to an individual teacher's actual job. The two categories of 'on-the-job' and 'close-to-the-job' correspond to school-based/school-focused activities, while an 'off-the-job' activity usually refers to an external in-service course (McMahon and Turner, 1988). According to the NDC, external courses – which, in their view, are the most expensive and least effective method of bringing about change – are the most common form of management development but other examples of off-the-job activities would be fellowships, secondments, visits to schools and job exchanges. On-the-job activities 'focus very directly on an individual's own job and they can be carried out within the job almost as part of it' (e.g. job enhancement, job rotation, appraisal, mutual observation and coaching). Close-to-the-job activities 'relate closely to the actual job . . . but the focus is not so directly upon the individual member of staff' (McMahon and Turner, 1988). Examples of management development activities in this category would include team building, self development work, school-based consultancy and workshops, and selection and appointment experiences. (For an overview of the various forms of management development activities and resources see Wallace, 1986.)

The NDC (McMahon and Bolam, 1987) also draws attention to the fact that individuals

learn through experience, through reflecting on that experience and through receiving constructive criticism about their performance. It follows that management development programmes must take account of this by creating opportunities for effective learning to take place as close-to-the-job as possible.

In addition, it is noted that the management development needs of individuals and groups may well vary according to age, gender, school type and job stage. Regarding the latter, for example, different needs are likely to be experienced by teachers during the preparatory, the appointment, the induction, the in-service and the transitional stages. It is therefore necessary for LEAs to show clearly, by policy statements and practices, that management development is central to school effectiveness and the NDC, through its research and development work, has made a major contribution in helping LEAs bring about coherent management development policies.

The NFER research has shown that some middle managers did not feel very well prepared for the post and that adequacy of preparation so often depended on the person with whom one had previously worked. Effective preparation for the next stage appeared to be fortuitous and most off-the-job training that was available was invariably offered after the appointment had been taken up. Also, providing management development opportunities for staff was an ad hoc activity – it was rarely deliberate school or LEA policy – and, as was earlier noted, some department heads found fulfilling their staff development role difficult or problematic. The Dorset team suggested that many management development needs could be met by school-based INSET and they recommended that schools should provide more on-the-job opportunities and organize specific courses or workshops on particular topics – the latter, they state, being effective vehicles for innovation. The process of management development should assist individual practitioners and the units in which they work to become more aware of their strengths and weaknesses as well as providing them with the knowledge, skills and understanding necessary for effective school management.

Support from LEA and senior staff

It is the view of the NDC that each LEA and school should have a management development policy and programme but, as was earlier noted, the DES saw such practice as far from common. The NDC also states that there is a need to balance the professional development needs of the staff with the institutional development needs of the school as identified in a development plan. It is incumbent upon senior staff in schools and LEAs to ensure that development, including management development, does take place and there is a need for coherent rolling programmes of management development and training. But what are the other ways in which senior staff and LEA advisers can support improvement efforts and ensure departments function effectively?

The research has shown that the levels of support received from advisers varied, as did the INSET opportunities the LEAs provided for department and faculty heads. Some subject advisers were able to arrange annual conferences and termly meetings, and these were found to be especially helpful for single-person departments where 'loneliness' could be a real problem. Newsletters, too, were a useful means of communication, but increasingly, for a number of reasons, advisers were finding it difficult to visit schools and their curriculum development role was, in some instances, being undertaken by advisory teachers. Also, on occasions, advisers were able to participate in department and faculty reviews which were found to be helpful.

However, even when advisers were able to provide in-service courses for department and faculty heads or create opportunities for them to meet, these invariably had to be offered after school hours or at weekends as heads were increasingly reluctant to release staff if cover could not be found. In some of the case study schools and LEAs, the problem of cover was very real and, even if supply teachers were available, the resulting disruption to pupils' learning and the additional work created often meant costs outweighed the perceived benefits of attending INSET or meetings. There are no easy solutions to this problem and there have been various attempts made by LEAs to solve it – for example, by increased staffing, the setting up of a permanent pool of supply teachers, 'paying' teachers to attend courses in their own time (see Earley and Baker, 1989; Hall and Oldroyd, 1988). There is little doubt that solving this problem, or at least reducing its most harmful effects, could lead to considerable improvements being made in the quality of learning experiences. Department heads have a very important duty to ensure their pupils do not suffer unduly from staff absence and they can facilitate this by, for example, asking colleagues to set and mark work for planned absences and be prepared to change classes if necessary, create a bank of worksheets for emergencies and ensure supply teachers working within the department are adequately supported (Earley, 1986). In some schools, departmental staff cover for each other to enable colleagues to attend activities during school time, while rates of teacher absence may be reduced if internal cover is departmentally based rather than school based. Senior staff can support their department heads by ensuring that the school has equitable cover arrangements and that those teachers with heavy commitments are least called upon. They can also make sure supply teachers are made aware of all relevant school information (or know where to find it) and that department heads recognize the important responsibility they hold with regard to cover arrangements. (These were rarely specifically spelt out in job descriptions.)

Heads and deputies could aid departmental effectiveness in other ways, too. Where possible, they could arrange that the department had a suite of rooms or at least was geographically close and thus help the development of a team identity. Also, as earlier noted, there was a growing need for ancillary support. Senior staff should also try to ensure that there are no timetable or organizational arrangements which hinder performance.

There was a need to create the right environment for middle managers to flourish and achieve their potential. As with pupils, if high expectations were set, there was a greater likelihood that they would be delivered. (Some examples were given of senior staff who had not encouraged department heads to conceive of themselves as managers having responsibilities for other adults.) Job descriptions for middle managers and their staff can help clarify the nature of an individual's responsibilities. In some instances it was suggested there was a need for greater direction and guidance from the SMT to ensure key departmental activities were carried out. Senior staff could perhaps facilitate development and evaluation by suggesting these activities take place and arranging meetings which they can attend and contribute to. Heads and deputies could offer their assistance in any departmental evaluation activities either directly (e.g. by informing staff of relevant evaluation instruments) or indirectly (e.g. by providing cover to enable classroom observation to take place). The notion of a 'curriculum friend' was also thought to have value.

Senior staff were found to differ in the importance and the time they gave to formal evaluation and review, but when this did take place – especially departmental rather than whole-school review – it was found to be a helpful means of encouraging change and effecting improvements. Reviews were seen to be particularly useful for the SMT as they were made more aware of the lot of the teacher and it helped break down isolation and encourage a dialogue between the various parties. It was important for heads to inform middle managers that they were accountable to others and the SMT should try to encourage internal evaluation/review as this was generally seen as more effective than the 'top-down' versions. Perhaps evaluation exercises could be built into 'directed time' or some of the 'contract' days be used for departmental review, evaluation and development. There was a need for something more than the termly or annual report/interview with the head.

A few heads were able to allocate some weekly time to enable observation to take place and the view was expressed that effective or 'real' change was only achieved if senior staff were involved in classroom visiting to observe innovations 'at work'. The SMT played a key role in supporting and resourcing change efforts, facilitating INSET, ensuring funding continued and that new staff were 'trained up'. Change needed to be coordinated and heads had to ensure that departmental changes were not *ad hoc* but part of the school's overall development plan.

Senior staff could, of course, provide positive role models by exhibiting the desired qualities of managers (e.g. giving praise, showing interest, being accessible etc.) and by ensuring they themselves functioned as a team and were giving the school adequate leadership and direction. They should have a clear idea of where they wanted the school to go and be able to articulate that 'vision' and motivate others to work towards it. They could encourage middle managers to meet and discuss their concerns. Where systems of staff appraisal were found they were seen as an important source of support.

Senior staff could also ensure that school meetings were well organized and effectively used and that the latter did not attend to routine administrative matters to the detriment of educational concerns. There was a need to create opportunities for teachers to participate in the decision-making process at all levels and for there to be genuine systems of consultation. Effective schools are collaboratively managed by their staff, there is excellent communication within them and teachers' views are given serious consideration before decisions are made. Senior staff need to involve and develop department heads and ensure that decisions reached at middle management meetings are real and will be implemented. Other research studies (e.g. Farrar, 1987) have shown that schools that have been most successful in implementing improvements are those which, among other things, have been willing to share responsibility for school management by increasing the authority of others. An effective management strategy was to devolve decision-making to the unit where implementation occurred. Managing change within schools and departments is no easy task but the chances of success are increased considerably if educational leaders are able to secure a sense of 'ownership' and commitment on the part of those who are expected to carry them out. This is more likely to occur if staff feel they are involved in decisions affecting them. Also, as Peters and Waterman (1984) and others have shown, the organizations most successful in adapting to change tend to be characterized by 'loose–tight' properties – their leaders kept some things under tight control whereas other things were loose, thus ensuring flexibility and scope for others whilst maintaining autonomy and control.

Summary and discussion

The key findings of the NFER research have been discussed under the general headings of creating time, role perceptions, management skills and support from senior school and LEA staff.

As earlier noted, there has been an increasing recognition that those who have responsibilities for school management need assistance in developing the requisite skills and knowledge. It was also pointed out that management is concerned with the achievement of goals; in education it is about bridging the gap between the intentions of educational policies and their implementation. However, as Glatter (1988) has argued, educational management should not be confused with 'managerialism' – a situation where the needs of managers and organizations are given priority over others. It is pupils who are intended to be the prime beneficiaries of effective school management and it 'should be viewed as an integral part of the educational process as a whole' while necessarily avoiding 'creating two separate worlds of 'education' and of 'management' (Glatter, 1988). It is unwise and divisive, in a professionally staffed organization like a school, to make too great a distinction between the managers and the managed. Of course, management skills are required at all levels – to manage both learning within the classroom, and staff and resources within the school. However, the adverse effects of poor management will be more widely felt if those designated individuals holding management responsibility do not possess some of the characteristics and skills thought necessary for effective leadership.

Some educationists have argued that teachers should receive certain *entitlements* from their school managers. Watts (1986), for example, has listed five rights that department members have from their department heads: the right to gain increased professional expertise; the right to be challenged; the right to a proper role in decision-making; the right to be kept in the picture; and the right to know the department head's view of individual performance. As professionals, teachers have every justification in demanding these rights and ensuring schools and their subunits – departments, faculties and year groups – are well run and administered. It is hoped that the research reported here, which has largely focused on nominated good practice, will go some way towards helping school managers, especially department and faculty heads, become more aware of the nature of their jobs and the skills and qualities required in order for them to be most effectively performed. In so doing, it may help to improve the quality of teaching and learning and thus lead to better schools. For those readers who are department or faculty heads, perhaps now is the time to start managing.

Appendix
Advisory Committee
Members

The project team have been guided and supported by an advisory committee consisting of the following people:

Sue Bullan	Deputy Head, Berkshire LEA
Jenny Crocker-Michell	Head of faculty, London borough of Ealing
Tony Dillon	Her Majesty's Inspectorate
Brian Fidler	Senior Lecturer, Bulmershe College of Higher Education
Ivan Harman	Head of department, Buckinghamshire LEA
Roy Kennard	Head of department, Hampshire LEA
Ray Tolley	Advisory teacher, London Borough of Croydon
Rod Usher	Secondary Management, Inner London Education Authority
Helen Whiter	Subject Adviser, Cambridgeshire LEA

References

ACAS (1986). *Teachers' Dispute ACAS Independent Panel: Report of the Appraisal Training Working Group.* London: ACAS.

ADAMS, P. (1988). 'Time's up', *Times Educational Supplement.* 29 July.

ALLEN, D. (1983). *Evaluating the English Department, Booklet Two.* Abbots Bromley, Staffs: Evaluation in Education Series.

ASSOCIATION FOR SCIENCE EDUCATION/BRITISH GAS. (1986). *Management in School Science Departments.* London: British Gas.

BADLEY, G. (1986). 'Appraising heads of department', *British Journal of Inservice Education,* 13, 1, 9–14.

BAILEY, P. (1981). 'Appraising the performance of departments in maintained secondary schools: concepts and approaches.' In: RIBBINS, P. and THOMAS, H. (Eds) *Research in Educational Management and Administration,* 106–114. Birmingham: BEMAS/SSRC.

BAKER, L. (1989). 'The academic/pastoral divide', *Topic,* Issue 2. Windsor: NFER-NELSON.

BALL, S.J. (1987). *The Micro-Politics of the School.* London: Methuen.

BELASCO, J.A. and ALUTTO, J.A. (1972). 'Decisional participation and teacher satisfaction', *Educational Administration Quarterly,* 8, 1, 44–58.

BELBIN, R.M. (1981). *Management Teams: Why They Succeed or Fail.* London: Heinemann.

BELL, L. (1987). 'Appraisal and schools', *Management in Education,* 1, 1, 30–34.

BELL, L. and MAHER, P. (1986). *Leading a Pastoral Team.* Oxford: Blackwell.

BIRCHENOUGH, M., ABBOTT, R. and STEADMAN, S. (1989). *Reviewing School Departments.* London: Longman.

BLACKBURN, K. (1986). 'Teacher appraisal.' In: MARLAND, M. (Ed.) *School Management Skills.* London: Heinemann.

BLAKE, R. and MOUTON, J. (1964). *The Managerial Grid.* Houston: Gulf.

BLATCHFORD, R. (Ed.) (1985). *Managing the Secondary School.* London: Bell and Hyman.

BLEZARD, D. (1985). 'The head of department as an agent of change.' In: *The Role of the Head of Department,* Part One, FEU Staff Report, 17, 4. Coombe Lodge.

BLOOMER, R.G. (1980). 'The role of the head of department: some questions and answers', *Educational Research,* 22, 2, 83–96.

BLUMBERG, A. and GREENFIELD, W.D. (1980). *The Effective Principal: Perspectives* on *School Leadership*. Boston: Allyn and Bacon.

BOLAM, R. (1987). 'What is effective INSET?' In: *Professional Development and INSET: Proceedings of the 1987 NFER Members' Conference*. Slough: NFER.

BRENNAN, J.A. (1987). 'The emotional aspects of sustaining secondary headship', *International Journal of Educational Management*, 1, 2, 3–5.

BRIDGES, E.M. (1986). *The Incompetent Teacher*. Lewes: Falmer.

BROOKES, W. (1987). 'Structural defects', *Education*, 6 February.

BRYDSON, P. (1983). Head of department and self-evaluation. Paper for invitation seminar on Curriculum Problems and Issues, University of Hull Institute of Education.

BUCKLEY, J. (1985). *The Training of Secondary School Heads in Western Europe*. Windsor: Council of Europe/NFER-Nelson.

BUCKLEY, J. and STYAN, D. (1988). *Managing for Learning*. London: Macmillan.

BULLOCK, A. (1980). 'Teacher participation in school decision-making', *Cambridge Journal of Education*, 10, 1, 21–28.

BULMAN, L. (1986). 'Arranging and chairing meetings.' In: MARLAND, M. (Ed.) *op. cit.*

BUNNELL, S. (Ed.) (1987). *Teacher Appraisal in Practice*. London: Heinemann.

BURNHAM REPORT. GREAT BRITAIN. MINISTRY OF EDUCATION (1954). London: HMSO.

BUSHER, H. (1988). 'Reducing role overload for a head of department: a rationale for fostering staff development', *School Organization*, 8, 1, 99–104.

CAPELL, A., MILLS, D. and POSTER, C. (1987). *Training and Development Needs Questionnaire: Handbook for Schools*. Bristol: NDC/SMT.

CHILVER, Lord (1988). *Report of the Interim Advisory Committee*. London: HMSO.

CLIFT, P.S. (1987). 'The Art Department.' In: CLIFT, P.S. *et al. op. cit.*

CLIFT, P.S. *et al.* (1987). *Studies in School Self-Evaluation*. Lewes: Falmer.

COCKCROFT REPORT (1982). *Mathematics Counts*. London: HMSO.

CONWAY, J.A. (1985). 'A perspective on organisational cultures and organisational belief structures', *Educational Administration Quarterly*, 21, 4.

DADDS, M. (1987). 'Learning and teaching appraisal: the heart of the matter', *School Organization*, 1, 1, 253–259.

DAVIES, B. (1983). 'Head of department involvement in decisions', *Educational Management and Administration*, 11, 173–176.

DEAN, J. *et al.* (1979). *The Sixth Form and its Alternatives*. Slough: NFER.

DEMBO, M.H. and GIBSON, S. (1985). 'Teachers' sense of efficacy: an important factor in school improvement', *Elementary School Journal*, 86, 2, 173–184.

DIFFEY, K. (1986). 'Upward Appraisal', *School Organization*, 6, 2, 271–276.

DIFFEY, K. (1987). 'How to conduct a teacher appraisal interview', *School Organization*, 7, 1, 225–234.

DIXON, P. (1987). 'Towards a practical model for the review, evaluation and improvement of classroom methodology', *School Organization*, 7, 1, 235–242.

DORSET LEA (1986). Dorset Education and Management Development Project Report 1985–86 (mimeograph).

DUNHAM, J. (1978). 'Change and stress in the head of department's role', *Educational Research*, 21, 1, 44–47.

DUNHAM, J. (1984). *Stress in Teaching*. Beckenham: Croom Helm.

EARLEY, P. (1986). *Questions of Supply*. Slough: NFER.

EARLEY, P. and BAKER, L. (1989). 'The demand for supply: finding solutions to the problem of cover', *Education*, 5 May.

EDWARDS, R. (1985). 'Departmental organization and management.' In: EDWARDS, R. and BENNETT, D. *Schools in Action*. Cardiff: Welsh Office.

EDWARDS, R. (1987). *Curriculum in Action: Case Studies from Wales*. York: Longman SCDC.

ETZIONI, A. (1964). *Modern Organizations*. Englewood Cliffs, NJ: Prentice-Hall.

EVANS, T. (1984). 'Providing time for school-based curriculum development', *School Organization*, 4, 2, 109–116.

EVERARD, B. (1986). *Developing Management in Schools*. London: Blackwell.

EVERARD, B. and MORRIS, G. (1985). *Effective School Management*. London: Harper and Row.

EXTON, R. (1986). 'Organizing the English department team.' In: BLATCHFORD, R. (Ed.) *The English Teacher's Handbook*. London: Hutchinson.

FARRAR, E. (1987). Improving the urban high school: the role of leadership in the school, district and state. Paper presented at American Educational Research Association, Washington, D.C.

FELLOWS, T.J. and POTTER, H.L. (1984). 'Characteristics of job specifications for heads of science departments in secondary schools', *Research in Science and Technological Education*, 2, 1, 31–35.

FIDLER, B. and COOPER, R. (Eds) (1988). *Staff Appraisal in Schools and Colleges: A Guide to Implementation*. Harlow: Longman.

FIEDLER, F. (1968). 'Personality and situational determinants of leadership effectiveness.' In: CARTWRIGHT, D. and ZANDER, A. (Eds) *Group Dynamics*. New York: Harper and Row.

FLETCHER-CAMPBELL, F.J. (1988). *Middle Management in Schools – Pastoral and Academic Heads: An Annotated Bibliography*. Slough: NFER.

FLISHER, B. (1986). 'How heads and deputies use their time – a time task analysis.' In: DAY, C. and MOORE, R. (Eds) *Staff Development in the Secondary School: Management Perspectives*. Beckenham: Croom Helm.

FREEMAN, A. (1987). 'Pastoral care and teacher stress', *Pastoral Care in Education*, 5, 1, 22–28.

FULLAN, M. (1982). *The Meaning of Educational Change*. New York and London: Teachers College Press.

FULLAN, M. (1985). 'Change processes and strategies at the local level', *Elementary School Journal*, 85, 3, 371–421.

GLATTER, R. (1988). 'Changes and continuity in school management.' In: *Managing Schools*, Block 7, E325. Milton Keynes: Open University Press.

GLATTER, R. et al. (Eds) (1988). *Understanding School Management*. Milton Keynes: Open University Press.

GOODSON, I. (Ed.) (1985). *Social Histories of the Secondary Curriculum*. Lewes: Falmer.

GORDON, G.E. and ROSEN, N. (1981). 'Critical factors in leadership succession', *Organizational Behaviour and Human Performance*, 27, 227–254.

GREAT BRITAIN. DEPARTMENT OF EDUCATION AND SCIENCE (1983). *The In-service Teacher Training Grants Scheme* (Circular 3/83). London: HMSO.

GREAT BRITAIN. DEPARTMENT OF EDUCATION AND SCIENCE (1985a). *Better Schools*. London: HMSO.

GREAT BRITAIN. DEPARTMENT OF EDUCATION AND SCIENCE (1985b). *Quality in Schools: Evaluation and Appraisal*. London: HMSO.

GREAT BRITAIN. DEPARTMENT OF EDUCATION AND SCIENCE (1987a). *LEA provision for Education and the Quality of Response in Schools and Colleges in England, 1986. A report by HMI*. London: HMSO.

GREAT BRITAIN. DEPARTMENT OF EDUCATION AND SCIENCE (1987b). *School Teachers' Pay and Conditions Document, 1987*. London: HMSO.

GREAT BRITAIN. DEPARTMENT OF EDUCATION AND SCIENCE (1988a). *School Management Development. Teacher Supply and Training Branch*. London: DES.

GREAT BRITAIN. DEPARTMENT OF EDUCATION AND SCIENCE (1988b). *Secondary Schools: An Appraisal by HMI*. London: HMSO.

HALL, V. and OLDROYD, D. (1988). *Managing INSET in Local Education Authorities*. Bristol: MSC/NDC.

HALL, V., MACKAY, H. and MORGAN, C. (1986). *Head Teachers at Work*. Milton Keynes: Open University Press.

HALL, J.C. and THOMAS, J.B. (1978). 'Role specifications for applicants for heads of maths departments in schools', *Educational Review*, 30, 1, 35–39.

HANDY, C.B. (1981). *Understanding Organizations*. 2nd edn. Harmondsworth: Penguin.

HANDY, C.B. (1984). *Taken for Granted? Understanding Schools as Organizations*. Schools Council Programme One. York: Longman.

HARGREAVES REPORT (1984). *Improving Secondary Schools*. Report of the Committee on the Curriculum and Organization of Secondary Schools. London: ILEA.

HARGREAVES, A. (1987). 'The rhetoric of school-centred innovation.' In:

HEWTON, E. (1988). *School-Focused Staff Development: Guidelines for Policy Makers*. London: Falmer.

MURPHY, R. and TORRANCE, H. (Eds) *Evaluating Education: Issues and Methods*. London: Chapman.

HMI (WALES) (1984). *Departmental Organization in Secondary Schools*. HMI (Wales) Occasional paper, Welsh Office.

HODSON, D. (1985). 'Evaluation: the neglected phase of curriculum development', *School Organization*, 5, 4, 331–342.

HOLT, M. (1981). 'The head of department and the whole curriculum.' In: MARLAND, M. and HILL, S. (Eds) *Departmental Management*. London: Heinemann.

HORD, S.M. and DIAZ-ORTIZ, E.M. (1986). Beyond the principal: can the department head supply leadership for change in high schools? Paper presented at the International Research Seminar on Internal Change Facilitators. Centre for Educational Policy and Innovation, University of Leuven, Belgium.

HORD, S.M. and MURPHY, S.C. (1985). The high school department head: powerful or powerless in guiding change? Paper presented at the annual meeting of the American Educational Research Association, Chicago, Illinois.

HOUGHTON REPORT. GREAT BRITAIN. DEPARTMENT OF EDUCATION AND SCIENCE (1974). Report of the committee of inquiry into the pay of non-university teachers. London: HMSO.

HOWSON, J. and WOOLNOUGH, B. (1982). 'Head of department – dictator or democrat?', *Educational Management and Administration*, 10, 1, 37–43.

HOY, W.K. and AHO, F. (1973). 'Patterns of succession of high school principals and organizational change', *Planning and Changing*, 4, 2, 82–88.

HOYLE, E. (1980). 'Professionalization and deprofessionalization in education.' In: HOYLE, E. and MEGARRY, J. (Eds) *The World Yearbook of Education: The Professional Development of Teachers*. London: Kogan Page.

HOYLE, E. (1982). 'Micropolitics of education organizations', *Educational Management and Administration*, 10, 2, 87–98.

HOYLE, E. (1986). *The Politics of School Management*. London: Hodder and Stoughton.

HULL, R. and ADAMS, A. (1981). *Decisions in the Science Department*. Hatfield: Schools Council/Association for Science Education.

JOYCE, B. and SHOWERS, B. (1980). 'Improving in-service training: the messages of research', *Educational Leadership*, October, 4–10.

KERRY, T. (1982). *New Teacher*. Teacher education project. London: Macmillan.

KING, C. (1986). 'The burden of appraisal'. *Times Educational Supplement*, 8 August.

KNOOP, R. and O'REILLY, R. (1975). 'Participative decision making in the curriculum', *High School Journal*, 59, 4, 153–158.

KYRIACOU, C. (1987). 'Teacher appraisal in the classroom: can it be done successfully?', *School Organization*, 7, 2, 139–144.

LACEY, C. (1970). *Hightown Grammar*. Manchester: Manchester University Press.

LAMBERT, K. (1975). 'Research report: the role of the head of department in schools', *Educational Administration Bulletin*, 3, 2, 27–39.

LATCHAM, J. and CUTHBERT, R.E. (1979). *Analysing Managerial Activities*. Bristol: Coombe Lodge.

LAWLEY, P. (1985). 'The changing curriculum 14–19: implications for the subject department', *Secondary Education Journal*, March 19–21.

LEWIN, K. (1944). 'The dynamics of group action', *Educational Leadership*, 1, 195–200.

LIKERT, R. (1961). *New Patterns of Management*. New York: McGraw-Hill.

LITTLE, J.W. (1982). 'Norms of collegiality and experimentation: workplace conditions of school success', *American Educational Research Journal*, 19, 3, 325–340.

MADEN, M. (1974). 'The departmental meeting: its role in curriculum reform', *Secondary Education*, 4, June, 102–104.

MANASSE, A.L. (1985). 'Improving conditions for principal effectiveness: policy implications for research', Elementary School Journal, 85, 3, 439–463.

MARLAND, M. (1971). Head of Department: Leading a Department in a Comprehensive School. London: Heinemann.

MARLAND, M. (Ed.) (1986). School Management Skills. London: Heinemann.

MARLAND, M. (1987). 'Appraisal and evaluation: chimera, fantasy or practicality?' In: BUNNELL, S. (Ed.) Teacher Appraisal in Practice. London: Heinemann.

MARLAND, M. and HILL, S. (Eds) (1981). Departmental Management. London: Heinemann.

McMAHON, A. (1987). Report on the First National Conference for LEA Co-ordinators of Teacher Appraisal Pilot Schemes. Bristol: NDC/SMT.

McMAHON, A. and BOLAM, R. (1987). School Management Development: A Handbook for LEAs. Bristol: NDC/SMT.

McMAHON, A. and TURNER, G. (1988). 'Staff development and appraisal.' In: 'Managing staff in schools' E325, Block 4, Managing schools. Milton Keynes: Open University Press.

McMAHON, A., BOLAM, R., ABBOT, R. and HOLLY, P. (1984). Guidelines for Review and Internal Development in Schools (GRIDS). Secondary Schools Handbook. York: Longman/Schools Council.

McCORMICK, R. (1986). 'Self-evaluation.' In: MARLAND, M. (Ed.) School Management Skills. London: Heinemann.

McCORMICK, R. and JAMES, M. (1983). Curriculum Evaluation in Schools. Beckenham: Croom Helm.

McGREGOR, D. (1960). The Human Side of Enterprise. New York: McGraw-Hill.

McGREGOR BURNS, J. (1979). Leadership. London: Harper and Row.

MILLER, J. et al. (1986). Preparing for Change. York: Longman/FEU.

MINTZBERG, H. (1973). The Nature of Managerial Work. New York: Harper and Row

MISKEL, C. and COSGROVE, D. (1985). 'Leader succession in school settings', Review of Educational Research, 55, 1, 87–105.

MONTGOMERY, D. (1985). 'Teacher appraisal: a theory and practice for evaluation and enhancement', Inspection and Advice, 21, 1, 16–19.

MURPHY, R. and TORRANCE, H. (Eds) (1987). Evaluating Education: Issues and Methods. London: Chapman.

NIAS, J. (1980). 'Leadership styles and job-satisfaction in primary schools.' In: BUSH, T. et al. (Eds) Approaches to School Management. London: Harper and Row.

NIAS, J. (1984). 'The negotiation of decision-making roles in a new school.' In: GOULDING, S. et al. (Eds) Case Studies in Educational Management. Milton Keynes: Open University Press.

NUTTALL, D.L. (1981). School Self-Evaluation: Accountability with a Human Face? York: Longman/Schools Council.

OLDROYD, D. and HALL, V. (1988). Managing Professional Development and Inset: A Handbook for Schools and Colleges. Bristol: NDC/MSC.

OXTOBY, R. (1979). 'Problems facing heads of department', *Journal of Further and Higher Education*, 3, 1, 46–59.

PETERS, T. and WATERMAN, R. (1984). *In Search of Excellence: Lessons from America's Best Run Companies*. New York: Harper and Row.

POCKLINGTON, K. (1987). *TRIST – A Strategy for Professional Improvement. Evaluation Report*. London: ILEA.

PREEDY, M. (1988). 'Managing curricular and pastoral processes. Approaches to curriculum management'. In: *Managing Schools: A Third Level Course*, 3, 1. Open University School of Education. Milton Keynes: Open University Press.

REYNOLDS, D.(1982). 'The search for effective schools', *School Organization*, 2, 3, 215–238.

RIBBINS, P. (1985). 'The role of the middle manager in the secondary school.' In: HUGHES, M. *et al.* (Eds) *Managing Education: The System and the Institution*. London: Holt, Rinehardt and Winston.

RIBBINS, P. (1986). 'Subject heads in secondary schools: concepts and contexts.' In: DAY, C. and MOORE, R. (Eds) *Staff Development in the Secondary School: Management Perspectives*. Beckenham: Croom Helm.

RICHARDSON, E. (1975). *The Teacher, the School, and the Task of Management*. London: Heinemann.

RUDDOCK, J. (1981). *Making the Most of Short In-service Courses*. London: Schools Council/Methuen.

RUTTER, M. *et al.* (1979). *1500 Hours: Secondary Schools and their Effects on Children*. London: Open Books.

SERGIOVANNI, T.J. and ELLIOT, D.L. (1975). *Educational and Organizational Leadership in Elementary Schools*. Englewood Cliffs, NJ: Prentice-Hall.

SIDDLE, J. (1978). *Head of Science and the Task of Management*. Hatfield: Association for Science Education.

STILLMAN, A. and GRANT, M. (1989). *The LEA Adviser – A Changing Role*. Windsor: NFER-NELSON.

STRAKER, N. (1984). 'The teaching load of a head of mathematics, and consequent effects on the department.' *School Organization*, 4, 3, 221–229.

STRAKER, N. (1987). 'Mathematics teacher shortages in secondary schools: implications for mathematics departments', *Research Papers in Education*, 2, 1, 126–152.

SUMNER, R. (Ed.) (1988). *Quality in Schools: Papers from an NFER Conference*. Slough: NFER.

SUMNER, R. and BUTLER, R. (1985). 'School development through survey feedback.' In: *From Research to Practice: Proceedings of the 1984 NFER Members Conference*. Slough: NFER.

SUTTON, J. (1985). 'Staff Management II.' In: FRITH, D. (Ed.) *School Management in Practice*. Harlow: Longman.

TANNENBAUM, R. and SCHMIDT, W.H. (1973). 'How to choose a leadership pattern', *Harvard Business Review*, 36, 2, 95–101.

TANSLEY, P. (1988). *Course Teams – the Way Forward in FE?* Windsor: NFER-NELSON.

TAYLOR, W. (1980). 'Professional development or personal development?' In: HOYLE, E. and MEGARRY, J. (Eds) *The World Yearbook of Education: The Professional Development of Teachers.* London: Kogan Page.

TORRINGTON, D. and WEIGHTMAN, J. (1982). 'Technical atrophy in middle management', *Journal of General Management,* 7, 4, 5–17.

TORRINGTON, D. and WEIGHTMAN, J. (1985). 'Teachers and the management trap', *Journal of Curriculum Studies,* 17, 21, 197–205.

TORRINGTON, D. et al. (1987). 'Doing well but could do better', *Times Educational Supplement,* 30 October.

TRETHOWAN, D. (1987). *Appraisal and Target Setting.* London: Harper and Row.

TURNER, G. and CLIFT, P. (1988). *Studies in Teacher Appraisal.* London: Falmer.

TYLDESLEY, N. (1984). 'New directions in departmental leadership.' In: HARLING, P. (Ed.) *New Directions in Educational Leadership.* Lewes: Falmer.

TYLDESLEY, N. (1988). 'A catalyst for change', *Education,* May 27.

WAKEFIELD, B. (1988). 'Performance indicators for secondary schools: some practical considerations.' In: SUMNER, R. (Ed.) *Quality in Schools: Papers from an NFER Conference.* Slough: NFER.

WALLACE, M. (1985). 'Promoting careers through management development', *Education 3–16,* 13, 2.

WALLACE, M. (1986). *A Directory of School Management Development Activities and Resources.* Bristol: NDC/SMT.

WALLACE, M. (1988). *Towards Effective Management Training Provision.* Bristol: NDC/SMT.

WATERS, D. (1987). 'No bloody meetings', *Management in Education,* 1, 1, 1–2.

WATKINS, P. (1987). *Modular Approaches to the Secondary Curriculum.* York: Longman/SCDC.

WATSON, L. (1986). 'The "loser" and the management of change', *School Organization,* 6, 1, 101–16.

WATTS, J. (Ed) 1977. *The Countesthorpe Experience: the first five years.* London: Allen and Unwin.

WATTS, M. (1983). 'Developing instruments of policy for faculties and departments in secondary schools', *School Organization,* 3, 2, 169–175.

WATTS, M. (1986). 'Leading the English department.' In: BLATCHFORD, R. (Ed.) *The English Teacher's Handbook.* London: Hutchinson.

WEIGHTMAN, J. (1988). 'The managing and organizing balance: collegiality, prescription or leadership?' Paper presented at BEMAS Research Conference, Cardiff.

WEINDLING, D. (1987). 'Diagnosing INSET needs: a review of techniques.' In: *Professional Development and INSET: Proceedings of the 1987 NFER Members' Conference.* Slough: NFER.

WEINDLING, D. (1988). 'The process of school improvement: some practical messages from research.' In: SUMNER, R. (Ed.) *Quality in Schools: Papers from an NFER Conference.* Slough: NFER.

WEINDLING, D. and EARLEY, P. (1987). *Secondary Headship: The First Years.* Windsor: NFER-NELSON.

WEST SUSSEX COUNTY COUNCIL (1981). Handbook for heads of department in secondary schools in W. Sussex. Education Department, County Hall.

WINROW, W.K. (1985). 'Professional development.' In: BLATCHFORD, R. (Ed.) *op. cit.*

WRAGG, E.C. (1987). *Teacher Appraisal.* London: Macmillan.

YEOMANS, R. (1987). 'Leading the team: belonging to the group?' In: SOUTHWORTH, G. (Ed.) *Readings in Primary School Management,* Lewes: Falmer.

Index

academic/pastoral divide, 5, 205–6
accessibility, 54–6
accommodation, 54–5, 70, 78
   see also schools – split-site
Adams, A., 131, 133, 139, 144, 158, 173, 184, 186, 220
administration *see* school management
advisers, 46–7, 78–9, 95–6, 102, 161–3, 227–8
Advisory Conciliation and Arbitration Service (ACAS), 117–18
after-school activities, 25–6
Aho, F., 137
Allen, D., 174
Alutto, J.A., 186
appraisal, 44, 72, 98, 116–24
Association of Science Education (ASE), 68, 115

Badley, G., 122
Baker, L., 205, 228
Ball, S.J., 183
Belasco, J.A., 186
Belbin, R.M., 191
Bell, L., 2, 111, 115, 116, 117, 145, 156, 212
Bennett, D., 33
Birchenough, M., 93, 176, 177
Blackburn, K., 71
Blake, R., 184
Blezard, D., 130
Bloomer, R.G., 157, 187
Blumberg, A., 9
Bolam, R., 3, 90, 92, 225, 226
Brennan, J.A., 204
Bridges, E.M., 118
British Gas, 115
Brookes, W., 212
Brydson, P., 32
Buckley, J., 24, 184, 212
Bullock, A., 201, 202

Bulman, L., 115
Bunnell, S., 116
Burnham report, 6, 7
Busher, H., 221
Butler, R., 173

Capell, A., 93
case studies - *see* research
change – as a process, 133
   case studies, 148–53
   implementation of, 145–8, 154
   initiation of, 133–5
   institutionalization of, 133, 154
   pace of, 142–3
   planning for, 137–9
   resistance to, 139–42
   strategies to promote, 135–7
   teachers' views on, 143–4
collegiality, 72, 114, 190–5, 203
communication, 54–6
consultation, 56–7
critical incidents, 79–85
curriculum
   development and change, 4, 5, 6, 68, 92, 105, 110, 129–56
   evaluation, 157–83
   national, 76, 78, 95, 213
Chilver, Lord, 126
Clift, P.S., 117, 170–1, 173
Cockcroft report, 36, 217
Conway, J.A., 187
Cooper, R., 117
Cuthbert, R.E., 2

Dadds, M., 116, 117
Davies, B., 184, 187
decision-making
   involvement of staff in, 53, 113–115, 138–9, 185–204
Dembo, M.H., 113, 187

Department of Education and Science
(DES), 3, 7, 67, 91, 117, 125, 127, 177,
207, 215, 216, 217, 225
departments and faculties
accessibility of heads, 34–6
alternatives to, 206–14
evaluation, 42, 157–82, 221–2, 229
leadership styles, 32, 50, 51, 53, 62–3
role of heads, 3–8, 32–6, 40–2
support given to heads of department,
in-school support, 97–101
LEA support, 78–9, 95–6, 227–8
working day of heads, 19–31
Diaz-Ortiz, E.M., 132
Diffey, K., 119, 122
discipline
staff, 71–3
Dixon, P., 116, 120
Dorset Education Management Project,
225
Dunham, J., 187, 222

Earley, P., 4, 51, 91, 97, 113, 129, 137,
184, 228
education and training, 224–5
course content, 93–5
INSET - external based, 91–3, 102
INSET - school-based, 89–90
Education Reform Act, 78, 154, 182, 213,
225
Edwards, R., 8, 33, 37, 43, 157, 173, 183, 222
effectiveness, 45–64, 73
Elliott, D.L., 184
ethos, 60–1
Etzioni, A., 184
Evans, T., 219–20
evaluation - *see* departments and faculties
- evaluation
and curriculum - evaluation
Everard, B., 2, 117, 135, 184
examinations, 48, 94–5, 192, 193
Exton, R., 108

faculties - *see* departments and faculties
Farrar, E., 230
Fellows, T.J., 36
Fidler, B., 117
Fiedler, F., 184
Fletcher-Campbell, F., 8, 32
Flisher, B., 26, 27
Freeman, A., 26
Fullan, M., 92, 105, 110, 145, 184
further education, 129–30

Gibson, S., 113, 187
Glatter, R., 2, 214, 231

Gordon, G.E., 137
Grant, M., 182
Greenfield, W.D., 9
Guidelines for Review and Internal
Department in Schools (GRIDS), 93, 123,
162, 164, 176–7, 199

Hall, J.C., 36, 93, 228
Hall, V., 8, 24
Handy, C.B., 51, 54, 110
Hargreaves, A., 192, 193
Hargreaves report, 36, 37
Her Majesty's Inspectorate (HMI), 3, 6,
50, 63, 159, 160, 206, 213, 215, 216
Her Majesty's Inspectorate in Wales, 3,
4, 33, 71, 158, 173, 174, 207, 209
Hewton, E., 117
Hill, S., 8
Hodson, D., 159, 173
Holt, M., 131, 147
Hord, S.M., 132
Houghton report, 6
Howson, J., 187
Hoy, W.K., 137
Hoyle, E., 104, 183, 186, 187, 190, 191
Hull, R., 131, 133, 139, 144, 158, 173,
184, 186

incentive allowances - *see* salary scales
Inner London Education Authority
(ILEA), 36, 160
INSET - *see* education and training
in-service education and training
(INSET)
- *see* education and training

job descriptions, 36–40, 43–4, 58, 72, 128,
222
Joyce, B., 146

Kerry, T., 58
King, C., 116
Knoop, R., 186
Kyriacou, C., 117, 122

Lacey, C., 5
Lambert, K., 32
Latcham, J., 2
Lawley, P., 129
LEAs, 9, 11, 12, 13, 46–7, 67, 68, 78–9,
91–3, 94, 160–3
Lewin, K., 184
Likert, R., 184
Little, J.W., 187
local education authorities (LEAs) *see* LEAs
Lower Attaining Pupils Programme
(LAPP), 67

McCormick, R., 173
McGregor, D., 184
McGregor Burns, J., 186
McMahon, A., 3, 36, 93, 123, 127, 173, 176, 225, 226
Maden, M., 114, 137, 147
Maher, P., 2, 111, 115, 145, 156, 212
Manasse, A.L., 53
Marland, M., 5, 8, 32, 51, 104, 109
Miller, J., 130
Mintzberg, H., 24
Montgomery, D., 124
Morris, G., 2, 184
Mouton, J., 184
multicultural education, 49, 95
Murphy, R., 132

National Assocation for the Teaching of English (NATE), 68
national curriculum - *see* curriculum
National Development Centre for School Management Training (NDC), 3, 183, 225, 227
National and Local Government Officers Association (NALGO)
new teachers - *see* staff - probationery
Nias, J. 184, 186–7
Nuttall, D.L., 173

Oldroyd, D., 13, 228
Open University, 8, 170–1
O'Reilly, R., 186
Oxford Certificate of Educational Achievement (OCEA), 25
Oxtoby, R., 131, 158

parents, 77–8
pastoral/academic divide - *see* academic/pastoral divide
pastoral care, 205–6
performance indicators, 182
personality, 50–1, 224
Peters, T., 219, 230
Pocklington, K., 93
Potter, H.L., 36
Preedy, M., 211
probationery staff - *see* staff - probationery
promotion, 136–7

record-keeping, 6, 79
research
    case studies, 19–23, 28–31, 148–53
    overview, 15–18
    rationale, 14–15
reports, annual, 171–2, 179–80
resources, 59, 74–5, 136, 208–9
review - *see* evaluation

Ribbins, P., 5, 8
Richardson, E., 90
role of department and faculty heads
    perceptions, 40–2, 130–2, 221–3
    personality, 51, 224
    preparation for, 73–4, 87–9, 101
Rosen, N., 137
Ruddock, J., 90, 92
Rutter, M., 53, 184

salary scales, 6–7, 125–6
Schmidt, W.H., 184
school management
    difficulties and constraints, 59–60, 65–71
    effective practice, 2–3
    organizational structure, 68–70
    skills required for, 2–3
    style, 77
    team building within, 50, 53, 55, 62, 190–5, 203–4
    time given to, 65–8, 216–21
schools
    accommodation, 54–5, 70, 78
    aims of, 167
    grammar, 5–6
    maintenance, 49
    management of - *see* school management
    split-site, 54–5, 60, 76, 195
Sergiovanni, T.J., 184
Showers, B., 146
Siddle, J., 6, 131
special educational needs, 150–1
staff
    ancillary, 55, 74–5, 101, 220
    consultation/communication between, 54–7
    headteachers, 24, 51, 53, 63, 69, 97, 99, 199, 208, 209
    part-time, 6, 27, 56, 70, 108
    probationery, 27, 56, 57–9, 72, 115
    senior, 36, 48–50, 69, 71, 78–9, 97–100, 102–3, 163–4, 166–72, 174, 180, 181, 199, 228–30
staff appraisal
    observation in, 120–8, 175–6, 221
staff development, 104–27, 146
Stillman, A., 182
Straker, N., 60, 121, 218, 220, 221
Styan, D., 184, 212
Sumner, R., 173
Sutton, J., 184

Tannenbaum, R., 184
Tansley, P., 212
Taylor, W., 111
Teachers' Pay and Conditions Act, 6
team-building, 50, 53, 55, 62, 190–5, 203–4

Technical and Vocational Education Initiative (TVEI), 25, 67, 76, 96
Thomas, J.B., 36
timetabling, 76–7, 182
Torrance, H., 173
Torrington, D., 33, 38, 117
training - *see* education and training
Trethowan, D., 117
Turner, G., 117, 226
Tyldesley, N., 36, 144, 212

United States of America, 132

Wakefield, B., 182

Wallace, M., 92, 106, 226
Waterman, R., 219, 230
Waters, D., 115
Watkins, P., 213
Watson, L., 140
Watts, M., 158, 191, 192, 231
Weightman, J., 27, 33, 38
Weindling, D., 4, 51, 93, 97, 129, 137, 214
West Sussex County Council, 32
Winrow, W.K., 111
Woolnough, B., 187
Wragg, E.C., 117, 119, 122

Yeomans, R., 190, 222

THE NFER RESEARCH LIBRARY

Titles available in the NFER Research Library

TITLE	HARDBACK ISBN	SOFTBACK ISBN
Joining Forces: a study of links between special and ordinary schools (Jowett, Hegarty, Moses)	0 7005 1179 2	0 7005 1162 8
Supporting Ordinary Schools: LEA initiatives (Moses, Hegarty, Jowett)	0 7005 1177 6	0 7005 1163 6
Developing Expertise: INSET for special educational needs (Moses and Hegarty (Eds))	0 7005 1178 4	0 7005 1164 4
Graduated Tests in Mathematics: a study of lower attaining pupils in secondary schools (Foxman, Ruddock, Thorpe)	0 7005 0867 8	0 7005 0868 6
Mathematics Coordination: a study of practice in primary and middle schools (Stow with Foxman)	0 7005 0873 2	0 7005 0874 0
A Sound Start: the schools' instrumental music service (Cleave and Dust)	0 7005 0871 6	0 7005 0872 4
Course Teams–the Way Forward in FE? (Tansley)	0 7005 0869 4	0 7005 0870 8
The LEA Adviser – a Changing Role (Stillman, Grant)	0 7005 0875 9	0 7005 0876 7
Languages for a Change: diversifying foreign language provision in schools (Rees)	0 7005 1202 0	0 7005 1203 9
The Time to Manage? department and faculty heads at work (Earley and Fletcher-Campbell)	0 7005 1233 0	0 7005 1234 9